C000130556

Kipling *the Poet*

By the same author

George Gissing: New Grub Street
The Working Classes in Victorian Fiction
The Haunted Study: A Social History of the English Novel 1875–1914

ANTHOLOGIES
Into Unknown England
Nineteenth-Century Short Stories
The Victorian Prophets
Working-Class Stories of the 1890s

EDITIONS
Matthew Arnold, *Selected Prose*
Elizabeth Gaskell, *Cranford* and *Cousin Phillis*
Arthur Morrison, *A Child of the Jago*
Rudyard Kipling, *Selected Poems*

Kipling *the Poet*

PETER KEATING

Secker & Warburg
London

First published in England 1994
by Martin Secker & Warburg Limited
Michelin House, 81 Fulham Road, London SW3 6RB

Reprinted 1994

A CIP catalogue record for this book
is available from the British Library

ISBN 0 436 23249 9

Set in 12 pt Baskerville
by CentraCet, Cambridge
Printed and bound in Great Britain by
Mackays of Chatham PLC, Chatham, Kent

Contents

List of Illustrations

Acknowledgements

I am very grateful to the Authors' Foundation, which is administered by the Society of Authors, for an award to help with the cost of travel and research incurred in the writing of this book. I would also like to thank the staff of the Manuscripts Section of the University of Sussex Library, especially Bet Inglis, for guiding me through the Kipling Papers; the National Trust for granting me permission to quote from unpublished Kipling letters; and Trixie Schreiber, Lisa Lewis, and Norman Entract of the Kipling Society for answering queries so willingly and arranging for me to do some of my work at the Kipling Society Library. Permission to reproduce the illustrations has been given by The Trustees of the National Library of Scotland and The British Library.

Peter Keating

Preface

Although there has been a steady growth of interest in Rudyard Kipling since his death in 1936, there is still no general agreement on the nature and quality of his artistic achievement. Throughout his lifetime any mention of his name was liable to provoke extreme, contradictory responses, and much the same is true today. If he is acknowledged at all as one of the most important English writers of the twentieth century, it is for a handful of short stories such as "Mrs Bathurst", "'They'", "The Gardener", and "Dayspring Mishandled". Most of these were written late in his career, and their technical complexity has enabled them to be assimilated, with relative ease, into the modernist concerns of professional literary criticism. Other prose works – *Kim*, the stories for children, the travel sketches – have continued to arouse critical admiration, though generally of a less focused kind than that accorded to the "late" stories. Most of all, there has been a continuous fascination with the details and events of Kipling's life, especially his connections with India and the ideological and literary implications of his imperialism. Yet, whether biographical or critical, what most studies of Kipling seem notably to share is the curious conviction that his poetry was somehow peripheral to his life and his art. It was, in fact, central to both.

There is no single or simple reason for the neglect of Kipling's poetry. In his lifetime it was as renowned as the prose, in certain respects even more so. Many of Kipling's commentators have noted, as an indication of how deeply he affected Britain's consciousness of itself, that he contributed far more expressions, sayings, and maxims to everyday language than any other contemporary writer. It is less frequently observed that most of these sayings come from the poetry, not the prose. Hardly a day passes without Kipling's poetry being quoted on the radio or television, or in a newspaper, though usually with little accompanying sense of where the quotations come from, or, indeed, of them ever having had any other form of existence. Kipling has become a poet of memorable fragments, known to everyone and, at the same time, virtually unknown. It is a very strange kind of literary fame to have attained, and the recognition that it rests on more substantial poetic skills than a bland gift for phrase-making is rarely allowed. That Kipling wrote many poems which rely too easily for their effect on his extraordinary facility with rhyme and rhythm is undoubtedly true, but it is also true that many of his poems are not in the least facile and that his poetic technique often *is* extraordinary. Even his pioneering attempts to expand the subject-matter and language of poetry have received meagre critical appreciation.

One common explanation for Kipling's poetry being so much ignored is that he has been a victim of left-wing political prejudice. This view deserves to be treated with more care than it tends to get. The haughty dismissal of Kipling by left-wing opponents certainly features prominently in the history of his literary reputation, but the prejudice involved was by no means one-sided. Where politics were concerned, Kipling himself was intensely, unrelentingly prejudiced. The hatred with which he was regarded by many Liberals and Socialists was no deeper than the loathing he expressed for them. Nor was he in any sense a passive victim. On the contrary, he was a conscious and often ruthless participant in the debate on how newly-democratic Britain should be governed that runs from the late nineteenth century down to the present day. Not only is it unreasonable to object that political criteria have been applied inappropriately to Kipling's poetry, it is likely that the poetry was more often motivated by political considerations than many of his left-wing critics ever realised. This was partly because of the artistic subtlety he brought increasingly to the communication of his beliefs, and partly because after a while his opponents gave up on Kipling altogether and stopped reading him. His devoted admirers, however, continued not only to read him but to understand him as well, which is why, especially in the later years, they liked to refer to Kipling as their "prophet" rather than simply as their "poet". Kipling himself was fond of drawing attention to political predictions in his poetry which he felt had turned out to be correct.

A related, though slightly different, criticism of the poetry is that it is too overwhelmingly "public" and allows insufficient expression to Kipling's inner or "private" life. Here again there is no difficulty in seeing what is meant by the point, but the distinction on which it is based is misleading. Quite apart from there being no good reason to suppose that private and public experiences can be distinguished so easily, there was in Kipling's case a very close correlation between them. As we can see from his letters, public issues – whether the condition of England, imperial expansion, the state of the British Army, corrupt politicians, or the urgent need for English children to understand their country's history – were nearly always forcefully present in his mind: for much of the time issues such as these *were* his innermost thoughts. At some early point in his career Kipling appears to have decided that poetry would be a more effective and influential medium than prose for the advancement of his social and political views. While this decision placed his poetry firmly in the public domain and led inevitably to the writing of some poems which are hectoring or blatantly didactic, it also resulted in a body of work that offers an insight into early modern Britain, unique in its social range, linguistically adventurous, emotionally powerful, and deeply personal. Kipling's poetry should not be regarded as simply an outward chronicle of public events: it is more a record of his personal responses to those events, and of his thoughts and feelings on a range of other matters, not least the art of poetry, for which there is available no other source of comparable value.

This is the main reason why the present book is in the form of a biography: it is not only a study of Kipling as a poet, but also a life of Kipling as revealed in the poetry. Of special importance in this process has been the unravelling of the poetry's complicated publishing history. Kipling's poems were published in a wide variety of different ways and places – in the leading newspapers of many different countries; in numerous obscure journals; as broadsheets, pamphlets, and music-hall songs; to accompany short stories and travel articles; and in various "collected" editions. At five distinct moments in his life Kipling selected a number of poems from those which had already been published in newspapers and periodicals, added further poems, carefully blended the new with the old to make a statement that was both personal and public, and published them in volume form. These five books – *Departmental Ditties and Other Verses* (1886), *Barrack-Room Ballads and Other Verses* (1892), *The Seven Seas* (1896), *The Five Nations* (1903), and *The Years Between* (1919) – lie at the heart of Kipling's career as a poet, and I have used them to chart his artistic and intellectual development.

There are many poems which were not included in these particular volumes, and although most of them have now been reprinted in one way or another, they are often available only in the formidable *Definitive Edition* of Kipling's poetry, which was first published in 1940, or in the expensive and limited

Sussex Edition, or in other scattered publications. Although political prejudice is usually, and no doubt rightly, given as the main cause of the widespread neglect of Kipling's poetry, another important factor is that so little of the poetry is obtainable in sensibly organised and annotated modern editions. For the most part, the poetry still has to be read as it was published originally in volume form or in unsatisfactory collections. Either way, the reader can expect virtually no guidance on where, when, or how the poems were originally published; whether they were changed or re-written – as they often were – for volume publication; or why certain poems were grouped together in this or that volume. Apart from these kinds of bibliographical problems, there are other difficulties which today's reader of Kipling has to confront. As Kipling was once a genuinely popular poet it is sometimes assumed that all of his work is "simple" or "straightforward", but that is another of the treasured myths about him that bears hardly a moment's serious consideration. Many of the poems are tantalisingly subtle; quite a number are allegorical; others are syntactically complex and disclose their full meanings through literary, Biblical, and topical allusions. It is a sure indication of just how neglected Kipling's poetry has become that the writer of such poems is now commonly regarded as the composer of a vast number of catchy phrases that were once popular and have somehow managed to linger on.

There are two groups of words used frequently by Kipling, and also, therefore, in the present book, which require some initial clarification. First, Kipling rarely described himself as a poet: he preferred to be called a writer of "verse". There were good reasons for this as far as his earliest published work was concerned: largely comic in tone and written for publication in Anglo-Indian newspapers, it could quite properly be classified as "occasional verse". His more serious-minded productions at this time he tended to regard with genuine humility, feeling it was presumptuous to associate them with the work of the "poets" he most admired – Browning, Swinburne, Burns. They were real poets, not versifiers. Back in England, with highly-acclaimed volumes of poetry to his name, he set himself rigidly against the current aesthetic trends in poetry. Now he had no wish to see his work connected with what was passing in Britain as poetry. If being a poet meant following the example of the Aesthetes, then he would happily stay a writer of verse: that, quite apart from other considerations – and his determination to direct his work outwards into a wider world rather than ever deeper into his own soul has already been mentioned – would make his disapproval clear. And so it did, inflicting in the process lasting damage on his literary reputation. When T. S. Eliot compiled *A Choice of Kipling's Verse* in 1941 he followed Kipling's own preference in this respect, as in many others, and added some further ingenious arguments of his own for referring to Kipling as a writer of verse, not poetry. Eliot was, of course, one of the poets in Britain who had been instrumental in transforming nineteenth-century Aestheticism into what was now called Modernism, and in writing about Kipling he was divided between an understandable need to defend his own position as a leading Modernist and a determination to express his deep admiration for work which was regarded everywhere as the antithesis of modern poetry. That Eliot had emerged at all as Kipling's advocate caused enough of a stir in literary circles. It would have been considered unacceptably outrageous if he had taken the next step and called Kipling a poet. He did, however, suggest, very hesitantly, that some of Kipling's "verses" were really "poems". It is surely time that this rather foolish distinction, with regard to Kipling at least, should be dropped.

The second point has to do with political rather than literary susceptibilities. Kipling was fully aware of the cultural and national meanings of the terms Britain and England, and

British and English. He refers frequently, and specifically, to the Scots, Welsh, English, Irish, and British, but he also uses England and the English to include everyone living in the British Isles, as for example in such poems as "The English Flag" and "A Song of the English" where there is clearly no intention to denigrate the parts played by the Scots, Irish, and Welsh in creating a world-wide "British" Empire. Kipling was not simply being careless. It seems likely that he saw Ireland, Scotland, and Wales as themselves members of the Empire in that they had been conquered, militarily and culturally, by England. Of course he also believed that out of those national conflicts there had emerged a relatively harmonious, unified Britain dominated by England, but his awareness of Britain as, in reality, a federation of different nations is strongly apparent in his work. This aspect of Kipling's language did not go unnoticed at the time. Appropriately enough it took a foreigner to draw attention to the confusion it could cause. In his essay on Kipling in *Three Studies in English Literature* (1923), the French scholar André Chevrillon observed: "At the time when on the other side of the Straits people were beginning to say, not *England* but *Britain*, and when the term *British* became the official designation of the Queen's subjects, Kipling never calls them anything but *the English*." Chevrillon goes on to explain: "But this is pre-eminently the political nation, the one that worked in the country as its organising force, the one that gave it its power of action and expansion." That seems to be a very fair summary of Kipling's views on the matter.

[1]
"Reading as if for life"

Old is the song that I sing –
Old as my unpaid bills –
Old as the chicken that khitmutgars *bring*
Men at dâk-bungalows – old as the Hills.

"Army Headquarters"
Departmental Ditties

Rudyard Kipling was born in Bombay on 30 December 1865. At the age of five, together with his three-year-old sister Trix, he was brought by his mother to England and left in the care of a Captain and Mrs Holloway who lived in Southsea on the coast of Hampshire: they had one son of their own, several years older than Kipling. The two Kipling children stayed with the Holloway family for nearly six years. In 1877 their mother came back from India and immediately removed them from Southsea.

In his autobiography *Something of Myself*, written shortly before his death and published posthumously, Kipling gave a central place to the Bombay and Southsea experiences, offering them as the two most important formative influences of his life. In Bombay he was looked after by devoted Indian servants, accepted Urdu or Hindi as "the vernacular idiom that one thought and dreamed in", and spoke English "haltingly" and only when prompted to do so: the "first impression" he could recall was of "daybreak, light and colour and golden and purple fruits at the level of my shoulder," which he later realised must have come from early-morning shopping trips with his *ayah* to the local fruit market.[1] From the brightly-coloured, loving warmth of India he was transferred, suddenly and without explanation to the repressive lower-caste violence of England. Kipling published several fictionalised accounts of his Southsea experiences in addition to that in his autobiography, and the general impression they give is consistent. Mrs Holloway and her son were sadistic religious bigots, while Captain Holloway, frail of health and aware that he could not live long, befriended the young boy, took him on walks around the Portsmouth dockyards, entertained him with naval ballads, and tried to protect him from the irrational hatred of the other members of the family. Captain Holloway died in 1874, leaving Kipling defenceless.

Whether or not events at Southsea really were as Kipling described them has been debated exhaustively by his biographers, though without any kind of conclusive agreement being reached. Throughout his life Kipling held to his version of what occurred, and in keeping with the highly selective method of his autobiography, Southsea is one of those experiences which he uses to tell the reader "something about himself". The presentation is obviously mythic rather than documentary, with the young innocent child being expelled from the paradise of Bombay and forced to undergo punishment in the Holloway household for some unexplained crime. In *Something of Myself* Kipling was not interested in supplying accurate details of what exactly happened in Southsea so many years before: nor was he seeking revenge on the Holloways. His overwhelming concern was to try to explain how he developed into the particular kind of artist he was, and in that process the Holloways are credited with a crucial role.

"My ignorance," Kipling explains, "was my salvation." Constantly tormented and contradicted, he was forced to tell lies and was thus initiated into "the foundation of literary effort". To survive in this fallen world "demanded constant wariness, the habit of observation and attendance on moods and tempers; the noting of discrepancies between speech and action" and other qualities which, he observed wryly, were "not unsuitable preparation for my future." In Bombay no attempt had been made to teach him to read. That task was reserved for Southsea, and so successfully and enjoyably was it achieved that "deprivation from reading was added to my punishments. I then read by stealth and the more earnestly." There was, however, a gain to be recognised even in this, for to Mrs Holloway's Evangelical mind certain kinds of reading could function as salutary punishment, and the Kipling who in Bombay "had never heard of Hell" now learned his Collects by heart and much of the Bible as well.[2] Reading comforted and entertained; it was also a secret form of striking back. Most of all, in a world from which spontaneous love and instinctive knowledge had been removed, reading provided the crucial key to understanding and a promise of future power. In the "Baa, Baa, Black Sheep" version of these events, the father's parting words to his son are: "Make haste to learn to write and – and – ."[3] Clearly, it is regular letters that he is hoping for from this basic learning, but Kipling quickly found additional meaning in his father's words. The first chapter of *Something of Myself* closes triumphantly. Rescued by his mother from the "House of Desolation", he was taken on holiday to recuperate:

> By the end of that long holiday I understood that my Mother had written verses, that my Father "wrote things" also; that books and pictures were among the most important affairs in the world; that I could read as much as I chose and ask the meaning of things from any one I met.[4]

Something of Myself is a cunningly-structured *apologia* which places itself within a well-established literary and artistic tradition. Kipling draws the reader's attention to Fra Lippo Lippi, the artist-monk of Robert Browning's poem, who secretly nurtures his realistic ambitions in opposition to the monastery's official dictate that he concentrate exclusively on the souls of men.[5] And there are other literary parallels and associations evoked by *Something of Myself.* The sensitive child finding in the sounds and texture of language "salvation" from religious oppression is irresistibly reminiscent of James Joyce's *A Portrait of the Artist as a Young Man*; the joyful intuitive activity of childhood destroyed almost beyond recall by the development of reason is Wordsworthian; and constantly present in Kipling's account of his time at Southsea is the remarkably similar experience of Dickens. Like Kipling, Dickens wrote factual and fictionalised versions of what he regarded as his heartless abandonment in childhood by parents he had hitherto thought of as loving, and he authorised his close friend and biographer, John Forster, to state that David Copperfield's story was also largely his own. Justification for the ill-treatment of the young David Copperfield is that "the gloomy theology of the Murdstones made all children out to be a swarm of little vipers," a view of life that would have made him "almost stupified but for one circumstance". That circumstance is the unexpected discovery of "a small collection of books" which becomes his "only" and his "constant comfort":

> When I think of it, the picture always rises in my mind, of a summer evening, the boys at play in the churchyard, and I sitting on my bed, reading as if for life.[6]

Kipling doesn't refer directly to *David Copperfield*, but on the joyful holiday with his mother that marked his release from the Holloways, whose theology was just as "gloomy" as that of the

Murdstones, he was taken on a visit to the Victoria and Albert Museum, where among other treasures, he was shown a manuscript of a Dickens novel: "That man seemed to me to have written very carelessly; leaving out lots which he had to squeeze in between the lines afterwards."[7] Perhaps that is how the young Kipling responded, but the joke it embodies and the allusiveness it releases with such apparent casualness are more characteristic of the kind of writer he was to grow into.

The changed circumstances of Kipling's life once he had left Southsea did not lessen his enthusiasm for books, and everything connected with them. Looking back on the moment when his mother returned once again to India, leaving him and Trix to stay with "three dear ladies" in Kensington, the first detail Kipling gives of the interior of their house is that it was "filled with books".[8] As a schoolboy at the United Services College, Westward Ho!, he was renowned for his bookishness, a characteristic transferred to the stories he later wrote about his schooldays, *Stalky & Co.* To the character based on himself in those stories Kipling gave the name Beetle, an allusion to his exceptionally bushy eye-brows, but his schoolfriends called him "Giggers", at first because of his heavy spectacles or "gig-lamps", and later to identify him with Gigadibs, "the literary man" in Browning's "Bishop Blougram's Apology". Although *Stalky & Co* seems most remembered nowadays for the roughness of the justice dispensed by the three boys on their foes – masters and fellow-schoolboys alike – the two most important events in the book for Beetle/Gigadibs/Kipling are literary, and both of them are extensions of the transforming power of reading he discovered at Southsea. Puzzled by the nickname Gigadibs, Beetle asks a master where it comes from. In reply he has a volume of Browning's poetry thrown at him and is told to find out for himself. Beetle "quietly annexes" the book, and removing himself from the world around him, he drifts "at large with wondrous Men and Women".[9] That introduction to the poet who was to influence his own work more than any other is expanded by the headmaster giving Beetle "the run of his brown-bound, tobacco-scented library":

> There were scores and scores of ancient dramatists: there were Hakluyt, his voyages; French translations of Muscovite authors called Pushkin and Lermontoff . . . there were hundreds of volumes of verse.

It is a treasure-trove of literature even greater than David Copperfield's, and displayed with kindness and encouragement by a man who had actually known the authors of some of the books: "Slow breathing, with half-shut eyes above his cigar, would he speak of great men living, and journals, long dead, founded in their riotous youth."[10] Kipling himself met those same authors through close family connections with Edward and Georgiana Burne-Jones, his uncle and aunt. Southsea was not forgotten, and never would be, but it was now fully transformed from an experience in which the reading of books was a secret, and guilty, pleasure, to one in which he was openly encouraged to be not only a reader of books, but a writer of them as well.

In one of his accounts of being allowed access to the headmaster's library, Kipling claimed that it "made him write verses of his own": in fact, the library was offered to him because he was already an acknowledged poet.[11] He was probably writing his own poetry regularly from about the age of twelve, shortly before he went to the United Services College in January 1878. Later that year he was contributing poems about school life to *The Scribbler*, a magazine produced at home by the Burne-Jones family: one of those poems he submitted, unsuccessfully, to a popular American children's periodical, the *St Nicholas Magazine*. The poetry he wrote during his four years at school fell into two broad categories. It was regarded as either intensely private, and shown to no one, except, perhaps,

Flo Garrard, the mysterious girl with whom the fourteen-year-old Kipling fell in love in the summer of 1880, and to whom he remained frustratedly devoted for some years; or, it was flamboyantly public, read by school-friends, masters, parents, and relatives, and sometimes published in the college *Chronicle*, which Kipling edited in his final year at the USC. In 1881, his parents in Lahore collected together some of his poems, and, without consulting him, had them privately printed as *Schoolboy Lyrics*. When Kipling joined his parents in Lahore in October 1882 to take up the post of assistant editor on the *Civil and Military Gazette*, he was, technically at least, a published poet, though it seems that he disapproved of the publication of *Schoolboy Lyrics*, and its contents were not reprinted for many years.

No doubt, and quite reasonably, Kipling felt that the poems written at school were apprentice-work: ambitious as he was, *Schoolboy Lyrics* did not represent the kind of poetic achievement he wanted to see placed before a public wider than family and friends. In India, although his circumstances were, ostensibly, very different from those at school, the dual attitude of his poetry continued much as before. There were still private poems, addressed to friends, family, and Flo Garrard, or written to express his own inner feelings; and public poems, printed in the *Civil and Military Gazette*, its sister paper the *Pioneer* at Allahabad, or other local papers. He spent seven years in India – "seven years' hard" he liked to call them – and, in terms of labour, hard they must have been.[12] The large number of poems and stories he published, were all written in time left over from his work as a reporter and editor, and he claimed to have "burned twice as many as were published".[13] There is no reason to doubt his own account that these poems, the public ones, "arrived merrily, being born out of the life about me . . . and the joy of doing them was payment a thousand times their worth."[14] He was fascinated by India; the means of publication were ready to hand; his audience was limited in number, but responsive to every local allusion or joke; and he himself had a quick mind and an exceptional facility with words, rhyme, and metre. There was a fairly substantial tradition of Anglo-Indian poetry – of both newspaper ephemera and the more ambitious volume varieties – which Kipling read and commented on.

In 1884 Kipling and his sister Trix collaborated on a volume of verse parodies which was published in Lahore as *Echoes* "by two writers": the following year, all four members of the Kipling family contributed items, in verse and prose, to a Christmas Annual called *Quartette*, also published in Lahore. In 1886, inspired by the publication of these two volumes, Kipling collected together some of his poems, most of which had already appeared in newspapers, negotiated a price for the services of the *Civil and Military Gazette* printing-press, and produced *Departmental Ditties and Other Verses*. A few years later, when invited by Jerome K. Jerome to contribute to a series of articles by famous authors on their first books, Kipling ignored *Schoolboy Lyrics*; referred briefly, and without naming them, to *Echoes* and *Quartette*; and nominated *Departmental Ditties* as his "first book", which, of course, in the full sense of the term, it was. It was also, he hoped, the book that would mark the end of his literary apprenticeship and enable him to break out of the confines of Anglo-Indian society: nobody who read it, he admitted in a rare moment of unguarded confession, could have realised "how its author lay awake of nights in India, plotting and scheming to write something that should 'take' with the English public."[15]

As Kipling would soon be world-renowned as a poet of action, and was to be regarded by his first English readers – who *were* quick to "take" to *Departmental Ditties* and other poems and stories – as a kind of modern noble savage, come from the exotic East bearing tales of strange peoples and experiences, the most remarkable thing about his poetic apprenticeship is how literary, how dominated by books, it was. Beetle's reading is described, in one of the later *Stalky* stories, as "vast and omnivorous", and so was the young Kipling's.[16] Looking back on his childhood, Kipling refers to specific authors and books with special affection, but it is bulk that predominates: book-lined libraries, houses "filled with books", lists of authors' names. The reading went straight into his poetry. As with most other authors, it took time for Kipling to find his own voice. There were sudden, overwhelming enthusiasms for writers which were just as suddenly discarded, and other influences which lingered or were absorbed. What is unusual in Kipling is the range of influences apparent in his work. There was no single poet who fascinated him above all others, and whose influence had to be assimilated or overcome before his own apprenticeship could be seen to have ended. Bulk, again, predominates.

Kipling's prose is quite a different matter: even the earliest stories and travel-sketches reveal a writer who is distinctively himself. The explanation for this apparent dichotomy lies not, as many critics have unfairly supposed, in any inherent inferiority of the poetry to the prose, but in the special nature of Kipling's development as a poet, and the different roles he gave to poetry and prose. It was as a poet that Kipling served his literary apprenticeship, and he did establish a highly personal poetic voice: few twentieth-century English poets are more distinctive. But he did not achieve this by obliterating the influence of other poets, and he would probably have thought it unnecessary even to try to do so. What he most distrusted about late nineteenth and early twentieth-century poets was the tendency to remove their work from the public domain by rendering it excessively introspective and self-consciously aesthetic. Long before W.B. Yeats described the young poets of the 1890s as determined to "purify poetry of all that is not poetry",

Kipling was well aware that that was what they were doing, and had set himself firmly against the trend.[17] In conscious opposition to the modern Aesthete, Kipling placed the ancient singer of tribal lays, the troubadour, minstrel, and scop. Poetry, for Kipling, was a public activity, a communal rite; and the Poet, a seer or *vates*, whose power with words should be directed outwards, and not simply back into the work itself.

Kipling's early writing was influenced most strongly by nineteenth-century British and American poetry. Among British poets, Browning and Swinburne were the favourites, with Tennyson a little way behind them. Kipling also had varying degrees of acquaintance with the work of Arnold, Morris, Elizabeth Barrett Browning, Dante Gabriel Rossetti, Christina Rossetti, Kingsley, James Thomson, Macaulay, Wordsworth, Scott, and probably a little later, Burns, a poet with whom he was to feel a close affinity. With some of these poets it is possible to identify, or guess at, very specific lasting influences on Kipling's poetry. From Browning he acquired the method of allowing often obscure and hitherto unregarded *personae* to "speak" for themselves, to describe their own experiences in their own ways. G.K. Chesterton said of Browning's poetry that it was truly democratic because it represented the belief "that no man ever lived upon this earth without possessing a point of view."[18] Much the same can be said of Kipling, and he was drawn to the dramatic monologue for similar reasons, though he was more didactic than Browning, more eager to speak out in his own voice, and consequently less interested in trying to emulate the extraordinary psychological complexity of the older poet. It was no doubt also the example of Browning that encouraged Kipling to reject traditional Romantic theories of poetic diction, and employ in his own poetry an exceptionally large and adventurous vocabulary. The influence of Swinburne was less fruitfully assimilated. Kipling's taste for fluid, swinging rhythms was more responsible than any other single characteristic of his poetry for the reputation he developed among many literary critics as a facile versifier rather than a genuine poet. There was some justice, and some injustice, in the charge, and Kipling's early passion for Swinburne was largely to blame. It is significant that Swinburne's own reputation began to decline at about the same time that a critical reaction against Kipling's poetry set strongly in. From Swinburne particularly – and bolstered by the similar interests of a number of other nineteenth-century poets – Kipling adopted the long flowing poetic line of fourteen or sixteen syllables that was always to be a favourite with him, and was to sound almost wilfully old-fashioned as modernist concerns with imagistic compression developed. Two related characteristic techniques of Kipling's poetry – his insistent use of alliteration and snappy internal rhymes – are also traceable to the same source, or sources.

Kipling's youthful interest in American poetry of the same period was not quite as unusual as some commentators on his work have supposed. Throughout much of the nineteenth century American poetry was regarded as a natural offspring of its British parents: it was deeply influenced by European Romanticism and Victorianism, and was widely read and admired in Britain. Unusual or not, the young Kipling's enthusiasm was certainly strong. Emerson was a professed favourite, and perhaps Kipling's own frequent references to him have exaggerated his possible influence: as Ann M. Weygandt pointed out long ago, Emerson does not appear to have "aided in shaping Kipling's style outside of his deliberate attempts to recapture it."[19] On the occasions when there is more to it than simply that, Emerson was a restraining influence, making his presence felt in some of the more contemplative and tightly-organised of Kipling's poems. Whittier was another American favourite, and Kipling's interest in Whitman was long-standing, but it was Longfellow, Poe, and Bret Harte who most appealed to him. Like Swinburne, they provided him with rhythmic models and poetic techniques which were put to regular, and sometimes mechanical, uses. The rhythms of Longfellow's "Song of Hiawatha", and of Poe's "Annabel Lee", "The Bells", "To Helen", and "The Raven", haunted him for years, while the impact of Bret Harte was so powerful that stanza forms, narrative devices, and virtually complete lines from the American poet found their way not only into the immature work of the young Kipling, but into some of his most celebrated poems. Harte's "Her Letter" is a likely model for Kipling's "My Rival", and Harte's "What the Engines Said" probably suggested to Kipling the device of having the winds of the world glorify England's imperial greatness in "The English Flag". Sometimes, Kipling's indebtedness to Harte's poetry, though no doubt unconscious, is unmistakably present:

> Looking seaward, o'er the sand hills, stands the fortress, old and quaint
> ("Concepcion de Arguello")

became:

> By the old Moulmein Pagoda, lookin' eastward to the sea
> ("Mandalay")

And,

> Cicely says you're a poet; maybe; I ain't much on rhyme
> ("Cicely")

was transformed into:

> I've paid for your sickest fancies; I've humoured your crackedest whim
> ("The 'Mary Gloster'")

In the case of "Cicely", Harte's influence is felt not simply in the movement of the opening line, but also in the speaker's contemptuous rejection of poetry because of its apparent inability to portray the infinitely more "poetic" real world, a theme that Kipling was often to explore, in "The 'Mary Gloster'" and elsewhere:

> Poetry! – just look around you, – alkali, rock, and sage;
> Sage-brush, rock and alkali: ain't it a pretty page!
>
> ("Cicely")[20]

This side of Harte – typified by "Cicely" and his most popular poem "Plain Language from Truthful James" – was more self-consciously "American" than the poetry of Emerson, Poe, or even much of Longfellow. It was often given the generic title "Yankee dialect" literature, and is remembered today largely because of Mark Twain's connections with it. Kipling's admiration for Twain was deep and long-lasting, and he was also drawn to other members of the American dialect school. For a while Stalky & Co. were "severely infected" with the "songs and sayings" of Joel Chandler Harris's Uncle Remus; Kipling admitted to modelling one of his youthful poems on Joaquin Miller who was best known for his "Songs of the Sierras"; he would certainly have been familiar with the broad vernacular satire of James Russell Lowell's *The Biglow Papers*; and he was particularly fond of Charles G. Leland's *The Breitmann Ballads* which are written in mock German-American phonetics.[21] Kipling's response to this kind of dialect poetry was not simply a passing adolescent mania: it was part of a liking for broad humour and satire that surfaced at various points in his career, notably in some of the farcical short stories and knockabout political poems. It is observable in the anecdotes and quotations he sometimes uses in his travel sketches, the slanginess he often adopts in letters, and, more positively, in his own extensive use of dialect in stories and ballads. Uncle Remus, Mr Hosea Biglow, and even Hans Breitmann, may well have contributed to the eventual creation of Mulvaney, Ortheris, and the *Barrack-Room Ballads*.

The young Kipling tended to display rather than conceal these multifarious British and American enthusiasms. From the beginning he seems to have been conscious of different styles and periods of poetry, and wrote skilful imitations of many of them. One of the earliest of his extant poems, "The Pillow-Fight", written when he was fourteen, is an exercise in blank-verse mock-heroics: in his copy of the textbook used at the USC for English classes, he made brief entries in the styles of the poets the class was reading – Pope, Shelley, Keats. At roughly the same time, he wrote, among many such poems, "Told in the Dormitory", a superbly confident parody of "The Epic", Tennyson's introduction to "Morte d'Arthur"; and an equally accomplished free translation into Devonshire dialect of one of Horace's odes.[22] He was to write imitations, parodies, and pastiches of other poets throughout his life, from "Nursery Rhymes for Little Anglo-Indians" in *Echoes* (1884), through to *The Muse Among the Motors*, a series of poetic responses to motoring from the "early Chinese" to Robert Louis Stevenson, which he published periodically in the *Daily Mail*. His imitative skills were also employed to dramatic effect in stories such as "The Finest Story in the World" – in which the collapse of Charlie Mears's Keats-haunted imagination is demonstrated by a passage from one of Kipling's own schoolboy poems – and "Dayspring Mishandled", with its intimate knowledge of how to fake a fragment of Chaucer.[23]

While the poems written by Kipling at school give clear indications of some of the ways he would develop as a poet, they also reveal sides of his poetic sensibility that were later outgrown or suppressed. The personal, introspective poems were still based on Victorian models, but in contrast to the parodic exercises and lively evocations of schoolboy pranks, they display a melancholy preoccupation with the inner life that was to disappear from his poetry for many years:

Make we a fire in the dark
  Numb flesh to warm,
A little flame, a spark
  How shall it harm?

There is light on your face and mine –
  The shades retire –
Our arms meet and entwine
  Around the fire,
    Our flickering wind blown fire.[24]

If he had continued to write this kind of poetry he might have developed along similar lines to some of his close contemporaries, Yeats perhaps, or Ernest Dowson: there is no way of knowing. Certainly, his school-friends regarded him primarily as an aesthete, a romantic, a follower of the Pre-Raphaelites, and they were surprised when in March 1882 he responded to an assassination attempt on Queen Victoria by publishing in the college *Chronicle* an intensely patriotic poem "Ave Imperatrix!"[25] It was probably influenced by an Oscar Wilde poem with the same title. As has often been pointed out, "Ave Imperatrix!" was uncharacteristic of Kipling's poetry at this time, though it is very characteristic of much of his future work, uncannily so in certain respects:

And some of us have fought for you
  Already in the Afghan pass –
Or where the scarce-seen smoke-puffs flew
  From Boer marksmen in the grass.

The army careers that many of the boys at the United Services College were being prepared for would have made it difficult for even an aesthetically-inclined Beetle to be ignorant of some of the details of imperial warfare, but Kipling's careful references to Afghanistan and South Africa suggest that he had been paying close attention to recent events in distant parts of the Empire. The British defeat at Maiwand; the dramatic march of the British Army, led by General Roberts, from Kabul to Kandahar; and the humiliating reversals by the Boers at Majuba Hill and Laing's Neck, are not only alluded to here by the young Kipling, but were also to feature prominently, in one way or other, in his future career. Viewed retrospectively, the public theme and tone of "Ave Imperatrix!" do carry an air of inner recognition, an acknowledgement of a subject discovered, at least as genuine as the melancholy poems of adolescent love. Nor was it quite the only USC poem to express an active interest in imperialism. Shortly before he left school, he won a prize for a poem on the set subject of "The Battle of Assaye".[26]

Kipling's move to India did not lead immediately to further patriotic, imperial poems. As a full-time journalist, prose was now, for the first time, his main literary concern, and, in his own words, "all my verses were digressions from office work."[27] Even if he had wanted to write more poems along the lines of "Ave Imperatrix!", it is unlikely that they would have been welcomed by the average reader of the *Civil and Military Gazette*. Kipling was about to learn one of the key lessons of his career – that the attitudes to Empire held by people living in Britain were often totally different from those of their fellow-countrymen who were actively engaged on imperial business. What his new audience of Anglo-Indian readers wanted most from him was to be entertained by reading about themselves. This service Kipling supplied with instant success. Books had proved his "salvation" at Southsea, and given him personal status at school: they now did the same for him in Lahore. His poetry still had its private, experimental side, and he continued to write love-poems addressed to Flo Garrard, but in India it was his talent for comedy that predominated, from the broadly humorous, through the bitter-sweet, to the knowing-insider revelations of *vers de société*. Once again he drew for help on his "vast and omnivorous" reading.

To the various influences already mentioned, there must be added another list of models and inspirers, this time from the rich field of nineteenth-century British light verse. W.S. Gilbert's "Bab Ballads" were clearly well known to Kipling, while the Gilbert and Sullivan operas, being produced in London at this time, were as popular in India as everywhere else, and provided him with easily-recognised tunes and lyrics to imitate. The "Bon Gaultier Ballads" by W.E. Aytoun and Theodore Martin, were favourites with Kipling, and so were the limericks of Edward Lear. Other authors he turned to included R.H. Barham, Winthrop Mackworth Praed, Lewis Carroll, Frederick Locker-Lampson, and C.S. Calverley. Although Kipling plundered this literature ruthlessly for the poems he contributed regularly to the *Civil and Military Gazette* and other papers, no conscious deceit or plagiarism was involved. He was simply participating enthusiastically in a local, shared culture that was treasured partly for its entertainment value, and, even more, because it linked the imperial exiles firmly, and sentimentally, with home. Anglo-Indian readers would often have recognised and applauded Kipling's literary models, and if they weren't familiar with the originals, they would have been well in touch with the tradition through *Punch*, drawing-room ballads, amateur theatricals, and music-hall songs. Recognition, of various kinds, was all part of the fun.

The *Departmental Ditties and Other Verses* that Kipling printed on the *Civil and Military Gazette* press in 1886 was a very different book from the one known today: it was even different from the one that was so popular in the 1890s. The first edition was paper-covered, shaped like a government envelope, light brown in colour, loosely tied with a piece of red tape, and officially "sealed". The envelope was addressed to: "All Heads of Departments and all Anglo-Indians" from "Rudyard Kipling, Assistant, Department of Public Journalism, Lahore District." There was a contents list, but no title page – the cover serving this purpose – and the poems were printed on one side of the paper only. It contained eleven "departmental ditties" and fifteen "other verses". The success of the first edition encouraged an established Calcutta publisher of Anglo-Indian books, Thacker, Spink & Co., to take it up. They published a second edition in 1886, a third in 1888, and a fourth in 1890, gradually transforming *Departmental Ditties* into a handsome red hardback, with a gold blocked engraving of the first edition on its cover. For each of these editions Kipling slightly changed the contents, adding and deleting various poems. It was the fourth edition of 1890 that was published in London, and eventually reprinted by Methuen when they became the regular English publishers of Kipling's individual volumes of poetry.

As the book's title indicates, the departmental ditties deal with government employees – clerks, engineers, soldiers, administrators – and their wives and fiancées. All of them are on the make. Ahasuerus Jenkins of the "Operatic Own" is not much of a cavalryman, but he rises in life by singing duets with Cornelia Agrippina whose "controlled" husband "controls" a goverment department. Sleary, whose "pay was very modest", becomes engaged to the eldest daughter of Judge Boffkin, is promoted, gets out of the engagement by feigning epileptic fits, and immediately marries his true love, "an attractive girl at Tunbridge whom he called 'my little Carrie'." General Bangs, that "most immoral man", preys on the wives of the soldiers under his command: Exeter Battleby Tring, knowledgeable on all matters relating to railways, gives up his post to someone who knows nothing about railways in return for a handsome pension arranged by the "Little Tin Gods". In "The Story of Uriah", a cleverly understated and up-dated version of the

Biblical tale of David and Bathsheba (II Samuel 11-12), Jack Barrett's wife arranges for him to be sent to Quetta at the hottest time of the year, and there, according to plan, he dies. She mourns him "five lively months at most", and then marries her lover. The poem closes with the pious, flippantly-expressed belief that Jack Barrett will get his revenge on the Day of Judgement, but that seems highly unlikely. In the world of *Departmental Ditties*, people get what they are ruthless enough to plan for, not what they deserve.

The grandiloquent names, catchy rhythms, and facetious rhymes of the "ditties", barely conceal the serious view of life that informs them. For the first edition, Kipling wrote an introductory poem that he called, pointedly, "General Summary":

> We are very slightly changed
> From the semi-apes who ranged
> India's prehistoric clay;
> He that drew the longest bow
> Ran his brother down, you know,
> As we run men down to-day.

There is no progress, no change of any significant moral or social value. Mankind has always been motivated by greed, selfishness, and self-seeking. Any individual revealing some special talent or ability has always placed himself at the mercy of other, less talented, but more powerful people who will thieve, murder, steal, or do anything else that is necessary to help them get on in life: "As it was in the beginning/Is to-day official sinning/And shall be for evermore." The trouble with this cheerless philosophy was that it couldn't just be accepted as part of the overall joke. The first readers of *Departmental Ditties* laughed at the poems, but there was an element of unease in their laughter. It was rumoured that there really was a Jack Barrett whose wife arranged for him to be sent to Quetta, and everybody was familiar with someone who resembled Ahasuerus Jenkins, General Bangs, or Sleary and Judge Boffkin's daughter. The ditties brought Kipling praise and admiration, but not, one suspects, many friends. The young poet-journalist who not only knew all the local gossip, but was capable of exposing the unpleasant motives that lay behind it in catchy poems that everyone wanted to read, was a man to be wary of.

The "Other Verses" of *Departmental Ditties* offer a representative sample of the different kinds of poetry Kipling was writing at the time. Browning's influence was still strongly present, most obviously, and with no attempt at concealment, in "One Viceroy Resigns" and "A Tale of Two Cities". Several of the poems (notably "La Nuit Blanche" and "Two Months") reveal that one side of Kipling was still tempted to follow the Pre-Raphaelite way to poetic fame, an ambition soon to disappear entirely; while "The Ballad of Fisher's Boarding-House", and "The Grave of the Hundred Head", an exceptionally nasty tale of a village massacre, pointed forward to the more successful, extended narrative poems that he would write after he had left India. But it is in some of the occasional poems, inspired by particular events or experiences within the Anglo-Indian community, that his increased confidence as a poet is most strikingly demonstrated. When a popular dance-hall was closed to make room for government offices in Simla, the fashionable hilltown that was the Viceroy's place of summer residence, Kipling wrote "The Plea of the Simla Dancers", an immensely accomplished mock-heroic lament for lost social pleasures. "The Overland Mail" celebrates the postal service to distant parts of India with a new poetic gusto. It is the kind of rhythmic exercise, an infectious blend of sound and sense, that Kipling was to excel at, and that W.H. Auden would employ many years later in his very similar, though better known, poem "Night Mail". The movements of the runner carrying the mail are recreated by the varying rhythms of the poem, from the questions posed by physical obstructions:

> Is the torrent in spate? He must ford it or swim.
> Has the rain wrecked the road? He must climb by the cliff.

through to the steady ascent into the hills:

> From rail to ravine – to the peak from the vale –
> Up, up through the night goes the Overland Mail.

"The Overland Mail" is not simply a celebration of the postal service: it is also one of Kipling's most unashamedly joyful endorsements of imperial endeavour, with the postal activity offered as a microcosm of the far-flung Empire:

> Let the robber retreat – let the tiger turn tail –
> In the Name of the Empress, the Overland Mail!

"The Overland Mail" is the only poem in the collection written in a mood of unqualified happiness. More characteristic is the nostalgia for England expressed in "Christmas in India" and the mournful, ghostly partings of "The Lovers' Litany". Everywhere, there is a sense of not belonging, of exile, which is heightened by the choral voices used in both of these poems. The thought of Christmas in distant England ("At Home they're making merry 'neath the white and scarlet berry") provokes the realisation that the religious festivities taking place near at hand are even more distant: the lovers who swear that "love like ours can never die" as the ships carry one or other of them back to England, know, immediately the words are uttered, that they cannot possibly be true. At the quayside, sadness contends in vain with the cheering crowds:

Eyes of grey – a sodden quay,
Driving rain and falling tears,
As the steamer puts to sea
In a parting storm of cheers.

The feelings of exile, lovelessness, and alienation, are all rooted in a constant awareness of the fragility of life in India. In "Arithmetic on the Frontier", the expensively-trained officer "drops" to a solitary shot from a "ten-rupee" Afghan rifle: "All flesh is grass." Making much the same point, though to a macabre trotting rhythm, "The Undertaker's Horse" becomes an obsessive focal point. When not needed for his formal duties, the horse is used by various members of the undertaker's family ("The eldest son bestrides him/ And the pretty daughter rides him"), but to the onlooker his message is always the same: "Mend your pace, my friend, I'm coming. Who's the next?"

The few glimpses of Indian life given to the reader portray a stolid, hardworking, and incurious people. Of particular interest here, because of the fame of "Recessional" ten years later, is the poem "What the People Said" which Kipling wrote in India to mark Queen Victoria's Golden Jubilee in June 1887. The "Great Queen's voice" calls on the people of India to rejoice and be merry because she has been "granted dominion and power" over them, but the Indian ploughman is not impressed, or even interested. He simply goes on trying to turn the dusty earth, for "the wheat and the cattle are all my care/And the rest is the will of God." Set in complete contrast to the ploughman who understands only too well what little difference British rule makes to him, is "Pagett, M.P." who knows all about India and the Empire before his ship docks. A Liberal and a theorist, pompous and uninquisitive, he is treated with a total lack of sympathy, and allowed to suffer fearfully from the summer heat of India that he had dismissed, before experiencing it, as "the Asian Solar Myth". Among all the hard, conniving, selfish characters in *Departmental Ditties and Other Verses*, no one is potentially a bigger threat to the British Empire than Pagett, the "fool", "travelled idiot", and Liberal M.P. He was to play a very large and important part in Kipling's life. In 1904 when Methuen brought out their first edition of *Departmental Ditties*, they applied to it the practice they had established with *Barrack-Room Ballads* (1892) and subsequent volumes of Kipling's poetry, of placing a line-drawing on the title page. These drawings were chosen, presumably by Kipling himself, with great care to indicate to the reader the principal concern or emphasis of each volume.[28] The drawing in *Departmental Ditties* portrays a corpulent, wild-eyed Pagett M.P. slumped in a wicker chair, mopping his neck with a handkerchief, experiencing the reality of "the Asian Solar Myth".[29]

That Kipling regarded the 1890 edition of *Departmental Ditties* as marking the close of a distinct phase of his life, if not the end of his literary apprenticeship, is made clear by the two valedictory poems he wrote especially for the volume. "The Galley-Slave", in the form of a boisterous ballad, is an extended pun on the word "galley", which is used here in both its naval and printing senses. It is the newspaper office, not a slave-ship, that Kipling is being freed from. He emphasises, at this moment of personal liberation, the hard working conditions he has endured, the casual deaths of people around him, the companionship and occasional revelry he has enjoyed, and the manliness of the whole enterprise: "God be thanked! Whate'er comes after, I have lived and toiled with Men!" He also ponders the unknown effects that his experiences as a galley-slave may have on "whate'er comes after":

> By the brand upon my shoulder, by the gall of clinging steel,
> By the welt the whips have left me, by the scars that never heal;
> By eyes grown old with staring through the sunwash on the brine,
> I am paid in full for service. Would that service still were mine!

The final words of that stanza are, of course, conventionally pious. He has no wish at all to go back and rejoin the slaves. But, though now a free man, he bears the scars of his "seven years' hard", the scars "that never heal".

The second of Kipling's valedictory poems, "I have eaten your bread and salt", was written as a "Prelude" to the 1890 edition of *Departmental Ditties*, where its retrospective mood gives a slightly misleading impression of its relationship to the succeeding poems. Kipling thanks the Anglo-Indians for their hospitality, and for allowing him to share their lives. In return, he has written of those shared experiences "for a sheltered people's mirth". He seems to have forgotten that the departmental ditties were written originally for the "mirth" of the Anglo-Indians themselves, and not for that of the readers in England to whom they were now presented.

India features less prominently in Kipling's poetry than in his prose. Even when his Indian experiences were crucial to the poetry, as in *Barrack-Room Ballads*, they required additional, outside influences, a wider perspective, before they could be turned effectively into poems. The sudden change of audience was an important factor in this, and so was Kipling's dramatic attainment of independence. Kipling's career as a poet was to be dominated by his close involvement with a series of different types of community: the pattern was already established with the United Services College and India. He would write, with intimate spontaneous knowledge, as an insider; and then, when the poems were collected, with the more structured, objective concerns of the artist. When he returned to England from India at the close of 1889, he was determined, above all else, that his hard-won independence must be maintained: never again would he be a galley-slave. It was, of course, impossible that India shouldn't be special to him. He had been born there; his parents were Anglo-Indians; his first job had been in India, and it was there that he had served his public apprenticeship as a writer.

The debt he owed to India was an amalgam of all of these experiences, and much more beside, as he explained later in "The Two-Sided Man":

> Much I owe to the Lands that grew –
> More to the Lives that fed –
> But most to Allah Who gave me two
> Separate sides to my head.[30]

[2]
Poetry and Prose

> There were . . . little tales of a heady and bewildering nature, interspersed with unusual songs – Peacock was that writer's name.
>
> *Stalky & Co.*

In his celebrated essay on Kipling, T. S. Eliot pointed out that while there are many authors who write both poetry and prose – and he instanced Meredith, Hardy, and Lawrence – they usually keep the two activities apart from each other, but in Kipling his "prose and verse" are inseparable: "We must finally judge him, not separately as a poet and as a writer of prose fiction, but as the inventor of a mixed form."[1]

Eliot was exaggerating slightly. Although the blending together of poetry and prose was a major interest of Kipling's throughout his career, much of his poetry has no connection at all with prose and can be judged quite adequately by itself. There are also many occasions when he adds poetry to a prose work for decorative rather than structural reasons. Nor is it strictly correct to describe him as the "inventor" of this "mixed form" of poetry and prose. The use of a few lines of poetry as epigraphs, or chapter-headings, was a common practice in eighteenth- and nineteenth-century fiction, and there were many novelists who moved beyond this simple device to introduce complete poems or songs into the body of their narratives. The young Kipling was familiar with, and is known to have admired, the work of several of these poet-novelists. When Beetle is allowed access to his headmaster's library, he finds, among many books that are new to him, the novels of Peacock, in which the prose is "interspersed with unusual songs".[2] In going out of his way to draw attention to this aspect of Peacock's work, Kipling was, perhaps, acknowledging a debt, though he might just as well have mentioned a number of other authors. Charles Carrington identifies Emerson as the author from whom "Kipling borrowed the device of heading every tale with a relevant scrap of original verse."[3] That also is possible, though surely too categorical. If Kipling was influenced in this respect by a specific writer, and it is not really necessary that he should have been, then Bunyan, Scott, and Kingsley, in addition to Peacock, seem the likeliest candidates. Whatever the source, it was a method that Kipling was to develop with such skill, and to make so distinctive a part of his work, that he appears, as Eliot said, to have invented it.

A more puzzling question than where the idea came from, is why Kipling was drawn to it in the first place. When he began experimenting with poetry and prose, as a young and very ambitious author in the late 1880s, the practice was already out of date, and by the end of the century it had become old-fashioned. None of his close contemporaries – James, Conrad, Gissing, Wells, or Bennett – was attracted to it: nor were the younger "modernists", Joyce, Woolf, and Lawrence. Indeed, both of these generations of writers would have been actively opposed to the practice, though for different reasons. The older writers among them were obsessed with French theories of organic form which demanded that every part of a novel or story should contribute to a dominant total effect. Anything that appeared to be extraneous to that effect was being pruned rigorously away: fancy epigraphs and interpolated poems would have been regarded as characteristics of a less demanding age of fiction, and obviously dispensable. Joyce, Woolf, and Lawrence – together with their predecessors in this respect, Meredith and the later James – were also interested in bringing poetry and prose closer together, and Joyce and Woolf especially often used songs and poems allusively in their work, though not in the Kipling manner: they were more concerned with incorporating the lyrical and emotive qualities traditionally associated with poetry into their prose styles. For them also, the printed page of a Kipling story looked as though it had closer affinities with earlier fiction than with their own work: the illustrations that frequently accompanied the periodical publication of Kipling's stories and poems would have increased this slightly outmoded image. On these, as on most other artistic matters, Kipling simply took his own way, with a quick glance back at earlier writers he admired, but with surprisingly little interest in what his near-contemporaries were doing.

The traditional role of the epigraph was to illustrate, justify, authorise, summarise, or, in one way or another, comment on the material it introduced. Within the text, poetry was often quoted directly by an author for similar purposes: the principal alternative device was to allow a character to sing a song or recite a ballad. Sometimes the performance functions as an entertaining digression, but, more adventurously, it may voice a central theme of the narrative or comment allusively on the behaviour and attitudes of other characters. The poetry itself was sometimes written especially for its appearance at that particular point in the narrative, or it might be taken from the work of another poet: often, in Scott, Peacock, Kingsley, and Kipling, the poem on such occasions is in the form of an anonymous ballad or folk song.

These were the literary conventions Kipling followed when he began writing short stories in India. He also now developed a method of dealing with this aspect of his work that he was to follow for the rest of his life. Usually, the stories were first published in newspapers or magazines without the epigraphs with which they would later be closely associated: these were added when the stories were collected for publication in volume form. Sometimes they were extracted from already completed poems, sometimes they were written especially for volume publication. Either way, it is quite common for there to be a gap in time between the composition of an epigraph and that of a story. This was also to be the case later in Kipling's career when he used full poems to frame a story. A few of the epigraphs were revised by Kipling and included in his major volumes of poetry, but the great majority were kept separate from his other poetry and published together in *Songs from Books* (1913). Here again, some of the epigraphs were expanded into full-length poems, while others were left as first published and called "chapter-headings". In a brief preface to *Songs from Books*, Kipling gave the following account of his method:

> I have collected in this volume practically all the verses and chapter-headings scattered through my books. In several cases where only a few lines of verse were originally used, I have given in full the song, etc., from which they were taken.

The implication is that epigraphs were extracted from completed poems and then reassembled for *Songs from Books*, and this would have been the case for some items. But the statement gives a misleading impression of the methods employed by Kipling when linking poetry to prose, not only by ignoring the varied and complex relationships created by these "verses and chapter-headings" – Kipling could not be expected to point *that* out for himself – but by making appear mechanical a process that was continuously experimental. Its starting point can be clarified by looking at *Plain Tales from the Hills* (1888) and the other early stories.

When Kipling collected these stories for publication in volume form he added epigraphs to most of them. Some were quotations from favourite poets – Browning, Jean Ingelow, James Thomson, Hans Breitmann; some were given generic labels, such as "Hindu Proverb", "Ballad", or "Barrack-Room Ballad"; while others were either unattributed or given titles but no authors. Kipling never abandoned entirely the practice of using quotations from other authors, but he was already more interested in composing his own epigraphs. Most of the early unattributed epigraphs, and some of the generic ones as well, were written by Kipling, though for many years it was not obvious that they were his. In *Plain Tales*, for example, only the lines from "Diana of Ephesus" that introduce the story "Venus Annodomini" would have been readily identifiable as by Kipling, the whole poem having been included in the third edition of *Departmental Ditties* which was published in the same year as *Plain Tales*. He was not yet associated with the writing of barrack-room ballads, and it would have been reasonable to assume that the epigraphs given this general title were taken from traditional army songs, but not all of them were. The unattributed epigraphs, actually written by Kipling, carried titles, most of which were dropped or changed when the "verses and chapter-headings" were reprinted many years later in *Songs from Books*. No doubt some of the titles were of poems in draft from which Kipling extracted a few lines for use in *Plain Tales*, while others were invented on the spot to go with the fragments of poetry composed specifically as epigraphs.

It would be wrong to read too much conscious authorial manipulation into any of this, though it is also wrong to assume, as many of Kipling's critics have done, that a complex narrative interplay between poetry and prose is characteristic only of his later work. During his first few years in India, Kipling was a notoriously prolific writer, and much of his poetry – and, indeed, the fiction and journalism as well – reveals two conflicting impulses. There was the constant need to meet deadlines, to produce copy in a hurry, which resulted in a good deal of writing that was careless and facile, though often superficially attractive. Simultaneously, there is apparent a more considered experimental tendency, in which the young poet can be observed developing themes which would receive more memorable treatment later, and also beginning to display the textual playfulness that was to become the hallmark of his highly distinctive blending of poetry and prose. Most of the early epigraphs, for example, were employed in a fairly traditional, illustrative manner, but some of them were put to more adventurous uses.

"Look, you have cast out Love!" was first published with the story "Lispeth" in *Plain Tales*. Lispeth is an Indian hill-girl who is brought up in the Christian faith by a missionary and his wife. When Lispeth feels she has been betrayed by her foster-parents, she rejects Christianity and reverts to her own religion. The epigraph, which in the original is called "The Convert", expresses Lispeth's judgement on Christianity:

> Look, you have cast out Love! What Gods are these
> You bid me please?
> The Three in One, the One in Three? Not so!
> To my own Gods I go.
> It may be they shall give me greater ease
> Than your cold Christ and tangled Trinities.

The thematic relationship between epigraph and story is direct, though the lines of poetry give a fuller and more considered statement of Lispeth's thoughts. Within the story her equivalent words are: "Then you have lied to me . . . you and he . . . You are all liars, you English."[4] Her reversion to being a "heathen" is reported indirectly. The epigraph functions effectively as a poem outside the story, with the simplicity and dignified sharpness of the language embodying an unanswerable personal statement. Kipling included it unchanged in *Songs from Books* where it was listed as a "chapter-heading".

There is, however, more than just this to the poem. Built into it is an allusion to Swinburne's notorious anti-Christian poem "Hymn to Proserpine":

> Thou has conquered, O pale Galilean: the world has grown grey from
> thy breath;
> We have drunken of things Lethean, and fed on the fulness of death.

Kipling frequently added his own words to rhythms borrowed from Swinburne, but here he reverses that process, putting Swinburne's views into a very different poetic form. It is not a borrowing from Swinburne, but an announcement of affiliation with him. Lispeth, it is reasonable to assume, has not read Swinburne, and the allusion cannot be hers. Like him, however, and Kipling, she believes that Christianity merely parades a justification based on a warm and universal love when in practice it is morbidly preoccupied with death and suffering. Lispeth is a "heathen"; Swinburne a "pagan"; and "one side" of Kipling's head was always to remain more in sympathy with their religious stances than with orthodox Christianity.

Whatever the larger personal significance of "Look, you have cast out Love!", it serves its primary role as an epigraph well, commenting on and enhancing the main themes of the story. Other epigraphs in *Plain Tales*, though, seem to have been attached to their stories with far less care. To the story "The Rout of the White Hussars" he added eight lines of poetry with the title "Beoni Bar":

> It was not in the open fight
> We threw away the sword,
> But in the lonely watching

In the darkness by the ford.
The waters lapped, the night-wind blew,
Full-armed the Fear was born and grew,
And we were flying ere we knew
  From panic in the night.

This poem was also reprinted in *Songs from Books* as a "chapter-heading" when the seventh line was dropped – perhaps simply in error, as it was restored in the *Definitive Edition.* As an epigraph to this particular story, "Beoni Bar" is curiously inappropriate. The story deals, suitably enough, with a cavalry panic, but in a humorous manner, while the poem is intensely serious. Later in his career Kipling was to use incongruity of tone between prose and poetry to powerful artistic effect: here, it comes over simply as carelessness. Yet "Beoni Bar" also provides evidence that Kipling was using these fragments of poetry to create quite different poems in his mind, for out of it there was to develop "Ford o' Kabul River", one of the finest of the *Barrack-Room Ballads.* The atmospheric details of the later poem are all present – the setting of the ford itself, the river water, darkness, night wind, the fear and panic as the cavalry horses and the heavily-armed men are swept to their deaths. Even the haunting ballad rhythm – "in the darkness by the ford" – is being rehearsed, though incongruously so when allied to the semi-farcical action of "The Rout of the White Hussars".

The most striking evidence that at this very early point in his career Kipling was already considering the structural possibilities of linking poetry and prose is provided by *The Story of the Gadsbys,* the novelette written entirely in dialogue that was published in the "Indian Railway Library" series in 1888. The dialogue-novel was an experimental form that attracted several late-Victorian writers, none of whom handled it with conspicuous success, Kipling included. *The Gadsbys* is subtitled "A Tale without a Plot", indicating that the "story" is offered as an unvarnished archetypal human experience: it is told in the worldly-wise tone for which the young Kipling was often criticised. Captain Gadsby, a dedicated professional soldier, falls in love, marries, becomes a father, and for the sake of his wife and son, surrenders his army career and takes them home to the safer climate of England. The main theme is presented in a snatch of song: "A young man married is a young man marred!" There are various other lines of verse and song, all of which comment, from different points of view, on the familiar conflict between marriage and career. The epigraph attached to the opening chapter is attributed to a "Gypsy Song":

> The wild hawk to the wind-swept sky,
> The deer to the wholesome wold,
> And the heart of a man to the heart of a maid,
> As it was in the days of old.

That expresses the romantic view – animals are free and at home in natural settings: human being are only fulfilled when united in domesticity – but *The Gadsbys* is far from being a story of domestic bliss. Captain Gadsby does what is considered the right thing, not what he actually wants. By marrying he has thrown away his chance of military glory and the male company he so much enjoys: he is a "man marred".[5] The story closes with a poem which Kipling called "L'Envoi", the message or moral, a device and a term which he frequently used. When collected in *Songs from Books* it was given a pointed title, "The Winners".

The "winners" are those who ignore conventional human behaviour, and the advice of the opening "Gypsy Song", to live lives of complete selfishness. The cynicism of the poem (or "heretical song" as Kipling calls it) goes far beyond anything presented in the story. Friends are to be valued only when their help is needed: once the help has been given they must be discarded. In this life there is no room for gratitude or affection. Nothing and no one can be allowed to obstruct the individual's desire for "Gold or Fame". There are several allusions to Browning's "Childe Roland to the Dark Tower Came" and "The Statue and the Bust", poems which deal, respectively, with an unspecified but dedicated quest, and a morally despicable, unconsummated love affair. The rhythm of "The Winners" – a breathless gallop, hindered by occasional stumbles, then recovery and onwards again – is at one with the moral of the poem and captured in its refrain, the earliest of Kipling's numerous lines of poetry to enter everyday speech: "He travels the fastest who travels alone". It is the second stanza of the poem that contains the most forceful comment on the story:

> White hands cling to the tightened rein,
>   Slipping the spur from the booted heel,
> Tenderest voices cry, "Turn again!",
>   Red lips tarnish the scabbarded steel,
> High hopes faint on a warm hearth-stone –
> He travels the fastest who travels alone.

These lines – the most erotic Kipling was ever to write – re-enact the central conflict of *The Story of the Gadsbys*, though with a directness and in a tone that are alien to the prose version. The tension between marriage and a military career, which in the story is conveyed by a cloying and reticent domesticity, now becomes a passionate sexuality expressed in terms of military imagery. Captain Gadsby's disillusionment with marriage lies in his realisation, as expressed in the poem, that men marry not because they long for a wife and child, but because they surrender to their own sexual needs. Instead of trusting the false romanticism of the "Gypsy Song", he should have heeded the "heretical" message of "The Winners" and used women ruthlessly: his "high hopes" would not then have fainted "on a warm hearth-stone". Unfortunately for him, as the placing of the two poems informs the reader, the advice of the "Gypsy Song" comes before the experience of marriage, and that of "The Winners" only when it is too late.

The Gadsbys was not followed immediately by similarly adventurous experiments in poetry and prose, but the lesson was learned, an artistic interest declared, and Kipling was to adhere to it for the rest of his life. It was not a consistent or obviously progressive development: rather, a series of disparate tests, some of which were carried further, while others were dropped temporarily and then taken up again or reworked much later. Even the technique of enhancing the unity of a volume of stories by attaching one or sometimes two poems to each story, which was to be so important in Kipling's later work, was slow to develop. As J.M.S. Tompkins noted in her influential study of Kipling's stories, it was in the *Jungle Books* (1894–5), written for children, "that the tales were first systematically provided with their songs," but it was not until *Traffics and Discoveries* (1904) that a comparable systematic approach was taken to an "adult collection".[6] In the decade separating those volumes, only *Just So Stories* (1902), significantly another children's book, reveals the same kind of concern with establishing a total, overall balance between poetry and prose: elsewhere, at the level of individual stories, the experiments continued as before.

In so far as it is possible to assess Kipling's own views on this idiosyncratic artistic relationship, the poetry appears to have been given priority over the prose, or at least carried some personal significance for Kipling that is now inscrutable. Although a good deal of his poetry leads a contendedly independent existence, there is comparatively little of the prose that he did not feel was incomplete without being given some connection with poetry. The strongest evidence for this is his habit of adding poems to stories after they had already appeared in print, and been read initially, solely as prose; but a related concern is apparent everywhere in his work. Of the four novels he published – *The Light that Failed* (1891), *The Naulahka* (1892), *Captains Courageous* (1897) and *Kim* (1901) – only *Captains Courageous* does not make extensive use of poetry, and even that contains several songs. In the other three novels, substantial chapter headings, ballads, songs, and quotations from and allusions to poetry, are all employed to create atmosphere or to comment, in various ways, on the prose narrative. Nonfictional prose was treated in the same manner. For his father's book *Beast and Man in India* (1891), Kipling selected suitable quotations from the work of other poets, and contributed several poems of his own. His travel sketches were frequently accompanied by original poems, as were many lectures and speeches when published in newspapers.

Most of these poems, and fragments of poems, were subsequently removed from their prose settings and reprinted in one or other of Kipling's volumes of poetry, the assumption being, presumably, that they could be read and appreciated by themselves: when this was felt not to be the case, they were revised or expanded or completed, to make them more accessible. That assumption, however, was not entirely justified. Although, as we have seen, the connections between poetry and prose are sometimes slight, sometimes profound, they are always there. When a poem is separated from its original prose setting, it may survive perfectly well on its own, but it usually does so by becoming a slightly different poem. Because of Kipling's preoccupation with linking poetry to prose, what a reader makes of an individual poem may depend crucially not only on the context in which it is read, but whether it is read before a piece of accompanying prose, or after, or by itself. Some of the poems, though relatively few, are indissolubly blended with the prose. An extreme example of this is "The Runes on Weland's Sword" which is virtually incomprehensible when read by itself, yet still in many respects an instantly attractive poem.

Kipling was possibly aware of the difficulties "The Runes" could cause when published separately, as it was the only poem in *Puck of Pook's Hill* (1906) not to be reprinted in *Songs from Books*. Even within *Puck* it is given an exceptionally complex structural role to play. The poem is placed at the close of the story "Old Men at Pevensey", roughly halfway through the book, but it does not refer only to that particular story. Each stanza represents just one phase of a theme that develops gradually through all of the stories, with the recurring, unexplained images in the poem representing the "runes" or inscriptions carved on the sword:

The Gold I gather
Comes into England
Out of deep Water.

Like a shining Fish
Then it descends
Into deep Water.

The brief, heavily-stressed, alliterated lines are modelled on Old English poetry, fitting the poetic style to the historical period of the early stories in *Puck*. In doing this, Kipling's concern is to create a style that is an approximation of Old English: he is not writing a pastiche, in the manner of his Chaucerian poems. Indeed, the clear, simple, evocative language of "The Runes" is used to create effects which are modern rather than archaic. It is the Japanese *haiku* that comes strongly to mind here, together with the closely related Anglo-American Imagist poetry that was still a few years off when "The Runes" was first published. The "runes" that Weland carves on the sword are a prophecy in the form of a riddle, and it is this riddling aspect of the poem that allows it to weave itself so effectively into the prose narrative, and also denies it an independent life apart from the prose.

There is no such problem with the well-known poem "A School Song" which was written as an introduction to *Stalky & Co.*, and continues to serve that purpose. It was originally untitled, and known by its opening line "Let us now praise famous men", a quotation from Ecclesiasticus 44 ("Let us now praise famous men and our fathers that begat us"): the title "A School Song" was given to the poem when it was collected in *Songs from Books*. Although the poem and the stories were written at roughly the same time, the retrospective mood of the poem and the immediacy of the stories creates a distance between them. It is a quite deliberate device on Kipling's part. The schoolboys, recreated imaginatively as they used to be twenty years earlier, are portrayed as rebellious, opposed to all forms of authority, subversive. "A School Song", chanted to a rhythm based on Longfellow's "Hiawatha" by a chorus of those same schoolboys, who are now "old boys", is a celebration of imperial authority and service; "Save he serve no man may rule." The teachers, once a prime object of the boys' derision and practical jokes, have become revered for having instilled into the boys – by "beating" them "with rods", among other methods – the true values necessary for successful imperial rule. Ecclesiasticus 44 distinguishes between different kinds of fame. Some people become famous while alive, and they include among their number "such as found out musical tunes, and recited verses in writing." Others lead obscure lives, but are no less important than their celebrated contemporaries, for "these were merciful men, whose righteousness hath not been forgotten. With their seed shall continually remain a good inheritance, and their children are within the covenant." The teachers are "famous men" in this second sense, and are now given public recognition by one of their "children", Kipling, who has achieved public fame through his ability in reciting "verses in writing". There are many other possible links between the poem and the stories. In one episode of *Stalky & Co.* the school is addressed by a patriotic M.P. The boys are disgusted by him, and Beetle/Kipling settles down to write "a simply lovely poem about the Jelly-bellied Flag-flapper", much as Kipling/Beetle now writes a flag-waving poem explaining why it was right and proper for his earlier incarnation to react to vulgar patriotism in the way that he did.[7] It is also worth recalling that the young Kipling surprised his school-friends by writing "Ave Imperatrix!", a poem far removed from Beetle's attack on the "Jelly-bellied Flag-flapper", and closer in spirit to "A School Song". How the reader responds to "A School Song" depends on the context in which it is read. Taken as originally presented, it is a puzzling introduction to the stories; if read after the stories, it becomes the distanced commentary that Kipling probably intended it to be; when separated entirely from the stories, it is a lofty, stern, hymn of praise to dedicated men busily training the servants of Empire.

As "The Runes on Weland's Sword" and "A School Song" were first published, and remain available, in works of fiction, the connections or disconnections between poetry and prose are at least present for the interested reader to explore, but this is not the case with a number of poems which Kipling used in several different settings, some of them long since forgotten. "When Earth's Last Picture is Painted" is representative. On 20 August 1892 *The Times* published an article by Kipling called "Half-a-Dozen Pictures": it was one of a series of travel articles called *From Tideway to Tideway*. The article describes a visit to an art gallery and Kipling's reflections on the failure of most painters to match the beauty and vitality of the world around them. He offers some attractive verbal sketches of his own, though it is not part of his purpose to contrast the approaches to nature of writers and painters. His main concern is to urge artists of all kinds to get out and see the world for themselves:

> Now, disregarding these things and others – wonders and miracles all – men are content to sit in studios and, by light that is not light, to fake subjects from pots and pans and rags and bricks that are called "pieces of colour". Their collection of rubbish costs in the end quite as much as a ticket, a first-class one, to new worlds where the "props" are given away with the sunshine.[8]

Eight days later, the same article was published in the New York *Sun*. This time it closed with the untitled poem "When Earth's last picture is painted" which changed the article's emphasis from an exhortation to artists to become travellers and pioneers, to what sounds very much like a manifesto for realism in art:

> And only Rembrandt shall teach us and only Van Dyck shall blame;
> And no one shall work for money, and no one shall work for fame,
> But each for the joy of working, and each, in his separate star,
> Shall draw the Thing as he sees It for the God of Things as They are![9]

Four years later, Kipling changed the first line of that stanza to "And only the Master shall praise us, and only the Master shall blame," and used the poem as "L'Envoi" to *The Seven Seas*. In this context, with the references to Rembrandt and Van Dyck removed, the poem becomes a romantic encapsulation of the views advanced throughout *The Seven Seas* – that true joy in life comes from dedication to whatever work is in hand, and that the task of the Artist is to convey to others the excitement and wonder of an expanding world. The introduction of "The Master" maintains, in one sense, the imagery of painting on which the poem is based, but it also gives a religious or spiritual dimension to work, another recurrent theme of *The Seven Seas*. All of these various themes are present in the poem from the beginning, though given different kinds of prominence according to the setting. When the article "Half-a-Dozen Pictures" was eventually collected in *Letters of Travel* (1920), the poem was not included: its prose connections had been cut completely loose.

Some of the ways in which Kipling employed poetry in his short stories can be illustrated by two specific, and very different, examples: "The Brushwood Boy", from the middle of his career, and "A Friend of the Family", written nearly thirty years later.

At the turn of the century, and for some years after, "The Brushwood Boy" was one of Kipling's most popular stories. It was first published in the *Century Magazine*, December 1895, and collected in *The Day's Work* (1898), a volume of stories which presents Kipling at the height of his commitment to the British Empire. Today, for perfectly understandable reasons, "The Brushwood Boy" is regarded by even Kipling's most ardent admirers as something of an embarrassment. George Cottar, the central character, is handsome, courageous, hard-working, a sporting hero at school, and a military hero in India. He is also a virgin. Although adored by countless women, he displays no interest in them: the charming innocence with which he deflects their sexual advances merely increases the adoration. His apparently perfect life is flawed only by a frightening, recurrent dream. This, like every other challenge or threat, he takes in his stride. At home on leave, he is introduced to Miriam Lacy who sings a song which reveals that she is afflicted by exactly the same dream. The Brushwood Boy is thus united with his Brushwood Girl.

There is evidence that Kipling took considerable care over "The Brushwood Boy". It is the only story in *The Day's Work* that makes extensive use of poetry, and Kipling chose it to close the volume. We also know that it was revised between magazine and book publication, mainly to ensure that references to Cottar's schooldays did not clash with similar passages in *Stalky & Co.* which was being written in 1898.[10] The poetry in the story is of a wide variety of different kinds. These include an epigraph; Biblical and classical allusions; the chorus from a music-hall song, which for many years was thought to have been written by Kipling; quotations from, and allusions to, Tennyson, and perhaps Malory; and "every syllable" of "Over the edge of the purple down", the song composed and sung by Miriam, and given the title "The City of Sleep" when it was reprinted in *Songs from Books*. There can be no doubt about the deliberation with which Kipling introduces the poetry into the prose, but it is very difficult to determine what the relationship between them is, or what exactly the poetry contributes to our interpretation of the story. In many respects the poetry is as mysterious as the dream that joins Cottar and Miriam together, and perhaps Kipling was concerned primarily with creating an appropriately strange atmosphere; but the allusiveness of the poetry suggest that more was being attempted than simply this.

The epigraph is a five-line extract from the nursery rhyme "Boys and girls come out to play", the traditional evening call to children in a house to join their friends in street-games. Kipling transposes the opening words to "Girls and boys", and, omitting two lines from the original, closes with "Up the ladder and down the wall." The rhyme urges children not to go to sleep while there is still time to play. Sleep, however, is precisely what Cottar and Miriam long for but are prevented from enjoying until, presumably, they find each other. Whether or not the ladder against the wall suggests some kind of romantic elopement or escape, the house itself is certainly not a haven of peace. The opening line of the story presents the three-year-old Cottar sitting in his crib screaming, "his eyes full of terror". In the total context of "The Brushwood Boy", the nursery rhyme takes on a Blakean quality of innocence already tainted by some unexplained, though potentially sinister, experience. Kipling's narrative insists that Cottar is a virtually perfect specimen of English manhood, and, apart from the dream, no contrary view of him is advanced, though Kipling is also careful to make clear that he is portraying an exceptional, not a representative, Englishman. Cottar's fellow-officers in India nickname him "Galahad", and after one particular courageous exploit, apply to him the opening lines of Tennyson's "Sir Galahad" in which sexual purity is identified as the source of his strength and bravery. Although these comments are admiring, not sarcastic, Cottar's Commanding Officer does qualify the idealism. He acknowledges that he has only ever known one other officer of Cottar's "muster", and then adds: "Didn't do him much good, though. Shot at Wesselstroom the week before Majuba."[11] In other words, Cottar is too good for this world. The soldiers in the regiment take a similarly lofty view of him. Marching back from a successful campaign, they sing "'E's goin' to do without 'em", a music-hall song with a Gilbert and Sullivan flavour to it. Who and what exactly "'e" and "'em" are, is not made clear, but if Cottar is being referred to then the soldiers are announcing that he's "goin' to be a martyr/On a 'ighly novel plan."

Miriam's song is intense, dramatic, a mixture of child-like images and an adult consciousness of suffering. Together with her companion, at this point the unidentified Brushwood Boy, she takes "the road to Merciful Town" that is "hard by the Sea of Dreams", but is stopped by "Policeman Day" and sent "back from the City of Sleep". It is possible that the refrain of the song ("Back from the City of Sleep!"), and perhaps other aspects of "The Brushwood Boy", contain an allusion to Robert Louis Stevenson's poem "Young Night Thought", from *A Child's Garden of Verses* (1885). This poem opens with the child being put to bed by his mother. He lies comfortably, creating romantic images in his head, marching along with "armies and emperors and kings" until "we reach the town of Sleep." The child's daytime experiences are not mentioned: he relishes the opportunity bedtime offers to live in the world of his imagination, and then sleeps soundly. "The Brushwood Boy" reverses this pattern. The details of Miriam's song replicate those already given of Cottar's dream. Both of them lead waking lives of apparent fullness and achievement, and nights of terror. Miriam begs for "pity". Everyone it seems – the sick, the poor, the famous and the obscure – is allowed to enter the City of Sleep, except her and Cottar: they are stopped by Policeman Day. In this dream-allegory, Day is not simply the policeman who appears to be accusing them of an unspecified crime: he is the punishment as well. Miriam and Cottar must "go back" with him, to live constantly in daytime. If Miriam's song is a true representation of Cottar's inner thoughts and feelings – and he is rapturously sure that it is – then the daily experiences of this ideal Englishman, Galahad and martyr, have been a constant torment to him. The precise nature of that torment – sexual frustration, perhaps, or a denial of the imagination, or the psychological strain of living an ideal life – is not revealed by the story, but whatever it is, Miriam releases Cottar from it. The past, the dream-world, can now be left behind, and a new kind of daytime experienced. The final words of the story are full of hidden meanings. As Miriam and Cottar part to dress for dinner, he seeks assurance that she won't hide away in her room and "leave me all the evening". Her reply is carefully considered: "Yes, I'll come down to dinner; but – what shall I do when I see you in the light!"

Miriam's song is presented within the prose narrative: it comments on the story of which it is physically a part. Although its contribution to how we interpret "The Brushwood Boy" is more substantial than that of the references to Tennyson, it acts in much the same way. In his later work, Kipling tended to give less prominence to poetic allusiveness within a story – often allowing the prose itself to serve this function – and instead, framed the story with complete poems. The stories were still usually published first without the poems in magazines, and the poetic frame constructed for book publication. The relevance of the poetry to the prose also continued to vary considerably, but the reader of one of these collected, framed stories is obviously being invited by Kipling to experience, in the order they are printed, a poem, followed by a prose narrative, followed by another poem. The poems and the stories can be read, and enjoyed, separately, together, or out of sequence: they are interlocking units, the parts of which can be regarded as complete in themselves, but when placed together make up a richer, more expansive pattern.

"A Friend of the Family" was first published in 1924, and collected in *Debits and Credits* (1926), when the two poems which frame it, "A Legend of Truth" and "We and They" were added. The story is one of Kipling's many variations on the themes of revenge and retribution. The main character is called Hickmot or Hickmer – the uncertainty about what his name actually is reflects the mysteriousness of his personality. He is an Australian who has been brought up by Aborigines, "the black fellers, as they call 'em", and has known no other life until he joins the army and is posted to France. He rarely speaks to anybody, and has the ability to blend into the environment: his "*un*noticeability" is his most distinctive quality. In the army he becomes close friends with another soldier called Vigors who, in civilian life, had been a market-gardener, a reserved wartime occupation, but was conscripted through the connivances of a rival market-gardener. Vigors dies in France, and Hickmot is invalided out of the army. On leave in England, Hickmot visits the dead friend's village, skilfully fakes a bombing-raid, and totally destroys the rival market-gardener's home and business. In his customary manner, Hickmot fades into the village environment, and only the narrator of the story suspects the truth. Hickmot returns to Australia having proved himself a true "friend of the family".

The story combines a number of themes which recur in Kipling's later work. Hickmot's revenge is carried out successfully because he is able to draw on "primitive" skills absorbed from the Aborigines, and also on "modern" techniques of war learned in the trenches. Both are alien to the normal life of an English village, though no longer is it possible for civilians to feel themselves safe from the violence of war. The villagers are willing to accept that the bombs must have come from a German plane; as yet, they are incapable of understanding that the violent skills being taught to their sons will later be carried back into civilian life, something that Kipling himself was very quick to realise. He advanced the theme most explicitly in his poem "The Expert" which he attached to another story of revenge, "Beauty Spots" in *Limits and Renewals* (1932). However involved and concerned non-combatants may be, they are still unable to comprehend the horrific events and incidents experienced daily by soldiers at the Front. Even the soldier himself would often be aware only of what was taking place in his own small area of the war: anything could have been happening somewhere else. This was brought home to Kipling when he was sifting through a mass of personal documents in order to write his history of the Irish Guards: "The only wonder to the compiler of these records has been that any sure fact whatever should be retrieved out of the whirlpools of war . . . From first to last, the Irish Guards, like the rest of our Armies, knew little of what was going on round them."[12] The difficulty of writing about a war from which it seemed impossible to retrieve "any sure fact whatever" haunted Kipling's imagination. In "The Fabulists", one of the finest of his wartime poems, he explored the related issue of his own attempts to tell people the "Truth" that they did not want to hear, and suggested an alternative approach:

When all the world would keep a matter hid,
   Since Truth is seldom friend to any crowd,
Men write in fable, as old Aesop did,

Jesting at that which none will name aloud.
And this they needs must do, or it will fall
Unless they please they are not heard at all.[13]

Kipling always had been interested in communicating by means of fable and allegory: now, in the special conditions created by war, it had become an unavoidable necessity.

"A Legend of Truth" which introduces "A Friend of the Family" takes its starting point from two philosophical positions which had long been considered unshakeable pillars of Western culture. First, Christ's statement, "To this end have I been born, and to this end am I come into the world, that I should bear witness unto the truth." To which Pilate answers, "What is truth?" (John, 18: 37–8). And secondly, Aristotle's claim in the *Poetics* that imaginative literature is more philosophical than history because it deals with universal rather than particular truths. "A Legend of Truth" is an allegory in which the two sisters Truth and Fiction compete to see which of them can more truly represent wartime experiences. The first section of the poem is set before the war. Truth is so shocked by the world's dishonesty that she shuts herself away. Like Christ, she will not even attempt to answer Pilate's question. Why should she? She *is* Truth: that is enough. Fiction therefore takes over Truth's work. She thrives on it and "no one noticed Truth was otherwhere." During the war a distressed Fiction realises that she can no longer handle reality and begs her sister to take the job back:

And Truth assumed the record of the War . . .
She saw, she heard, she read, she tried to tell
Facts beyond precedent and parallel –
Unfit to hint or breathe, much less to write,
But happening every minute, day and night.

When she queries the accuracy of the reports that are sent to her, she is informed coldly: "This is not really half of what occurred." She immediately telegraphs to Fiction: "Facts out of hand. Unable overtake/Without your aid. Come back for Truth's own sake!" Truth concludes: "*They need us both, but you far more than me!*"

"A Legend of Truth" presents to the reader some of the philosophical and artistic issues to be raised by "The Friend of the Family", the story that now, in the context of *Debits and Credits*, follows the poem: it also provides a running commentary on the story as it is being read. If Hickmot's elaborate revenge appears far-fetched, well, "this is not really half of what occurred." Anyway, a realistic story of war is no longer possible: Fiction has given up on the attempt, and so has Truth. The facts are so hideous, so strange, that even if they could be put down on paper, they wouldn't be believed: they would be regarded as "fiction" and dismissed as "untrue". In such circumstances, there is no reason to believe that truth has any absolute reality. Perhaps the reason why Christ wouldn't answer Pilate's question was that he didn't know the answer. Aristotle's confidence that fiction is capable of expressing a higher truth than historical facts, was also beginning to look misplaced. The conclusion to "A Legend of Truth" does, however, go part of the way to accommodating Aristotle's position, for although, in the aftermath of war, both Truth and Fiction are required, Fiction is needed "far more than" Truth. But, from now on, fiction can no longer claim to be realistic in any straighforwardly mimetic sense. It must, like allegory and fable, approach life indirectly, obliquely. Otherwise, nobody will believe it.

After the philosophical speculations of "A Legend of Truth" and the bizarre violence of "A Friend of the Family", the closing poem "We and They" comes as a considerable surprise. It is a dramatic monologue; light, humorous, seemingly jokey, and, considered in relation to what has preceded it, incongruous:

Father, Mother, and Me,
 Sister and Auntie say
All the people like us are We,
 And every one else is They.

The speaker is a child, though whether a boy or girl is never disclosed. Nor is his, or her, age given. From the poem it is possible to deduce that he is about twelve or thirteen, still young enough to mouth all the prejudices of his parents and relatives, and, perhaps, just old enough to start thinking for himself. His family is comfortably off, and middle-class; rural rather than urban; inhabitants, perhaps the reader is intended to think, of the village in "A Friend of the Family" that Hickmot has just visited with such devastating results. Certainly the joke which starts the child off on his monologue – that the world is really divided into We (the English) and They (everyone else), but, ridiculous as it seems, there actually are foreigners who think of the English as "They" – refers back to "A Friend of the Family". At the close of the story, the narrator, tired of trying to make sense of Hickmot, gives up the attempt with a cliché: "It takes all sorts to make a world." That represents a degree of wisdom that the child of "We and They" might reach one day, if he is allowed to. Meanwhile, with little shrieks of amused horror ("Isn't it scandalous?", "Impudent heathen!"), and jokes about naked natives and cannibals, but totally unconscious of what he is doing, he reveals his parents to be smug, intolerant, unthinking bigots. There can be no doubt what they would have thought about Hickmot, the Australian, brought up by "the black fellers" and skilled in ways that are incomprehensible to the English. In the final stanza of "We and They" there is a change of emphasis to include "all" people in the joke, not just the English. Whether the child has giggled himself into genuine insight, or whether it is Kipling intervening to draw the moral, is not indicated:

But if you cross over the sea,
   Instead of over the way,
You may end by (think of it!) looking on We
   As only a sort of They!

[3]
"Soldier, Soldier"

O, why the deuce should I repine,
And be an ill foreboder?
I'm twenty-three and five feet nine,
I'll go and be a sodger.

Robert Burns, "I'll go and be a Sodger".

Kipling's barrack-room ballads are his most original contribution to English poetry. Beginning with "Danny Deever" on 22 February 1890, fifteen of the ballads were first published in the *Scots Observer*, an Edinburgh-based weekly review edited by W.E. Henley. Shortly after Kipling's connection with the paper began, its head office was transferred to London and its name changed to the *National Observer*. At the close of 1890 most of the ballads were collected with some of Kipling's earlier poems and published in New York as *Departmental Ditties, Barrack-Room Ballads and Other Verses*. This miscellany was quickly superseded by the standard English edition *Barrack-Room Ballads and Other Verses*, first published in March 1892. The same edition was published in America, though its title was changed, confusingly, to *Ballads and Barrack-Room Ballads*. To this 1892 volume Kipling added five ballads which had not appeared originally in the *Scots* or *National Observer* and a dedicatory poem "To T.A." The initials stand for Thomas Atkins, the type or specimen name for a private soldier that had been used in army documentation since the early nineteenth century and was now adopted by Kipling for much the same purpose: Thomas or Tommy Atkins, and then plain Tommy, is Kipling's representative British private soldier. Although the name had been around and had carried that meaning for many years, it was only now that it became part of everyday speech.

The twenty-one soldier poems in *Barrack-Room Ballads* were balanced with exactly the same number of "Other Verses", many of which were also reprinted from the *Scots Observer*. This symmetrical plan for the volume was slightly thrown out by personal circumstances. In December 1891 Kipling's close friend Wolcott Balestier died suddenly while Kipling was on a visit to India. Kipling returned to England immediately he heard the news and the following month he married Balestier's sister Caroline. As a tribute to his dead friend, Kipling prefaced *Barrack-Room Ballads* with a highly emotional, at times barely coherent, elegy ("Beyond the path of the outmost sun through utter darkness hurled") and dedicated the volume to Balestier's memory. Kipling was in such a rush to associate Balestier with *Barrack-Room Ballads* in this way that he did not even compose a new elegy but instead adapted a poem that had been published in the *National Observer* more than a year earlier.[1] Understandably, these events have become a focal point for conjecture by Kipling's biographers about the precise nature of his relationships with both Wolcott and Caroline Balestier. As far as his development as a poet is concerned, the most interesting thing about "Beyond the path of the outmost sun" is that it is an early wording of a philosophical position that would eventually find its most successful expression in "The Sons of Martha": one line of the Balestier elegy in particular ("It is their will to serve or be still as fitteth Our Father's praise") could be transferred to the later poem almost without notice. But in the context of *Barrack-Room Ballads*, the elegy struck an odd, slightly discordant note.

The nature of the barrack-room ballads' originality was defined with great clarity by Lionel Johnson in a review written for the *Academy*. Johnson was a leading aesthete and, as he himself admitted good-humouredly, the kind of bookish reclusive Englishman frequently mocked by Kipling. Of the ballads, he says:

> They are written in the dialect of "the common soldier", of "Tommy Atkins"; they are composed in his spirit also. It is a curious reflection that the British Army at large, and the British soldier in particular, have received so little attention in literature of any excellence. We have plenty of heroic poems . . . plenty of verse alive with the martial spirit, with the "pomp and circumstance of glorious war" . . . But of the British Army, as a way of daily life, as composed of individual men, as full of marked personal characteristics and peculiarities, our poets great and small have had little conception.[2]

The crucial distinction made by Johnson is between the plentiful poetry of "the martial spirit" – usually eulogising famous military leaders (Henry V, Wellington, Sir John Moore) or celebrating major battles (Maldon, Blenheim, Waterloo) – and the virtually non-existent poetry of the British army "as a way of daily life".

It was this imbalance that the barrack-room ballads corrected, and there really were no significant precedents for them: not within the formal canon of English poetry; and not even in folk songs or street and ballad literature. Kipling was familiar with much of this earlier poetry. The titles of two of his books – *Soldiers Three* and *Captains Courageous* – were taken from celebrated anonymous ballads; the question-and-answer technique that he uses so skilfully was traditional; and in his stories there are frequent allusions to, and quotations from, ballads and folk songs. His use of the term "ballad" indicates in itself the value he attached to these poems being accepted as modern contributions to an ancient tradition. But, at the same time, he had no intention of writing pastiche street or border ballads: when he does occasionally do this – as in "The Last Rhyme of True Thomas" or "The English Way" – the artifice is openly displayed. In matters of form, Kipling tended to follow the example of the literary ballads that were popular throughout the Victorian period, the poems he had admired since childhood by Tennyson, Browning, Kingsley, Macaulay, Longfellow, and many others. When late-Victorian critics found the barrack-room ballads startlingly different from anything that had preceded them, they were right enough, though they were usually referring to content rather than form. And where there were traditions on which Kipling was drawing they remained unrecognised because they were usually beyond the experience of literary critics and reviewers. Even specialists were dazzled. As one well-informed authority on military poetry observed: "Mr Kipling easily won the laureateship of the army. He brushed aside old conventions and introduced a new order of martial verse."[3] That is pardonable exaggeration. Kipling's veneration for the past was too great for him to "brush aside old conventions", especially as far as the army was concerned, but he certainly made something new of the material he found to hand. Some conventions he did "brush aside"; some he adapted; others he transformed beyond recognition.

One of the most important influences he absorbed was musical rather than literary. Before the mass commercialisation of popular culture really took hold at the close of the century, a soldier's knowledge of music came largely from military bands. This was particularly so for soldiers serving overseas, cut off as they were from the early development of the mass market in Britain. Kipling's career was affected in a variety of ways by modern mass communications, but even he, an alert and perceptive journalist in India for much of the 1880s, seems not to have been aware of the extent of these developments until his return to Britain at the end of the decade. In the still unreformed British Army that Kipling knew in India, the military band was a focal point of both discipline and entertainment, playing regimental marches, hymns, and adaptations of folk songs and popular tunes of the day; setting the appropriate mood, whether cheery or sombre, for all ceremonial occasions; and taking responsibility for the bugle-calls or drumbeats that announced the routine of a soldier's day, from Reveille to Lights Out. All of this music, and the words that went with much of it, was known to the soldiers in two contrasting forms. The official versions were stirring, up-lifting, or regulatory: the unofficial versions were parodic, obscene, or nonsensical. Individual soldiers would also have carried with them from home local songs and ballads, as Kipling's Irishman, Scotsman, and Cockney do in his soldier stories.

The influence of military music on Kipling is apparent everywhere in the barrack-room ballads. It is a standard point of reference for Tommy Atkins; bugle-calls are used to set the dominant mood in several of the ballads; while in "Danny Deever" a military band is actually present, to call the troops to Parade, play the Dead March as Danny Deever is taken to the scaffold, and finally to try to bring the "shakin'" troops back to normality by playing a stirring "quickstep" once the execution is over. Rhythms taken from military music are also employed, most directly in the marching or trooping songs, but also to give a dramatic change of tempo to the refrains of poems which are not in other respects marches. The contribution made by military music to the ballads was clearly significant, but it remains only one of many possible influences, and attempts to pin Kipling down to particular sources or models are notoriously prone to disappointment, as Lewis Winstock has demonstrated. When Winstock's book *Songs and Music of the Redcoats* was published in 1970, he was criticised for not making more use of Kipling's work as possible source material. His response was to examine all references to soldier songs and marches in Kipling's Indian stories. He succeeded in identifying some of them, but concluded that all he could say for sure was that "one way or another Kipling knew folk songs, music-hall songs, drawing-room songs and soldiers' songs" as well as marches and ballads, but how he came to know them, and whether they were authentic or invented, it was often impossible to decide.[4] Much the same has to be said of the barrack-room ballads which owe their distinctive character not to single identifiable models or events, but to Kipling's openness to a great variety of different experiences, literary and non-literary.

Among established poets, the closest in spirit to Kipling was probably Robert Burns:

> I am a son of Mars, who have been in many wars,
> And show my cuts and scars wherever I come:
> This here was for a wench, and that other in a trench,
> When welcoming the French at the sound of the drum.
> Lal de daudle, *etc.*
>
> My prenticeship I past, where my leader breath'd his last,
> When the bloody die was cast on the heights of Abram;
> And I servèd out my trade when the gallant game was play'd,
> And the Moro low was laid at the sound of the drum.[5]

That carries the authentic voice of the soldier in a drinking, boastful mood. He is a veteran of the storming of Quebec where Highland troops scaled the "Heights of Abraham" and where General Wolfe met a legendary death at the moment of military victory. Burns's soldier is himself a local hero, and making the most of it. His "song" is in the appropriate form of a stamping march rhythm, with the refrain "at the sound of the drum" recreating the drumbeat and allowing a break before the next verse starts. Like Kipling, Burns uses the military march rhythm to give authenticity to the speaker, and the antithesis in line three of the first stanza of Burns's poem was a technique that Kipling also frequently used. Yet in spite of these affinities, Burns's soldier remains type-cast as a "son of Mars", his language a mixture of simple colloquialisms ("This here", "cuts and scars") and theatrical hyperbole ("when the bloody die was cast").

In ballad and street literature, soldiers were also usually presented as clearly-defined types. The Recruiting-Sergeant trying to persuade young men of the glamorous and healthy life that lay before them if they would only "take the Queen's shilling", and often plying them with drink at the same time, was a familiar figure in broadside ballads, sufficiently so even to inspire anti-military parodies of his role:

Come and be a soldier, lads, come, lads, come!
Hark, don't you hear the fife and the drum?
Come to the battlefield, march, march away:
Come and lose your eyes and limbs for thirteen pence a day.[6]

Offering support to that jaundiced view of military glory was the wounded soldier who has served his country well but is now reduced to begging on the streets:

Good, your worship, cast your eyes
Upon a Souldier's miseries;
Let not my leane cheekes, I pray,
Your bounty from a Souldier stay.[7]

Most commonly the soldier was presented as newly recruited into the army or on the point of going overseas. In either case, the main emphasis of the poem is on the wife or girlfriend he is leaving behind rather than the soldier himself. Some of these are traditional bawdy ballads in which the soldier is portrayed as a roguish seducer, no different essentially from other men with itinerant occupations, such as tinkers, sailors, and actors. In a more lyrical mode, the woman fears for the safety of her man who is fighting in a distant war. Sometimes the soldier returns unexpectedly and the lovers are reunited: occasionally he finds that while he has been away she has married someone else. In "The Silver Tassie" Burns varies these conventions by giving the farewell words to the departing soldier:

> Go, fetch to me a pint o' wine,
>   And fill it in a silver tassie,
> That I may drink before I go
>   A service to my bonie lassie!
> The boat rocks at the pier o' Leith,
>   Fu' loud the wind blaws frae the Ferry,
> The ship rides by the Berwick-Law,
>   And I maun leave my bonie Mary.[8]

Along with many other poets who wrote what Lewis Winstock calls "loth-to-departs", Burns was no doubt influenced by a famous eighteenth-century march called "The Girl I Left Behind Me".[9] The mood of its lyric was originally bitter-sweet, but over the years other versions, many of them bawdy or ironic, accumulated: in one form or another it remained popular with soldiers themselves through to the Second World War. Kipling wrote several variants of it, one of which, "Rimini", he even attributed to a "Roman Legion of the Later Empire", so archetypal of the soldier's life were the sentiments it expressed.[10]

When earlier poets and balladeers portrayed the soldier as an itinerant, unfamiliar figure – someone not to be trusted with the local girls; on the point of leaving to fight in foreign wars; a multilated beggar on the streets; or, at best, a good drinking-companion with exotic tales to tell – they were usually writing from the only experiences of army life they had. The social status of the soldier was degradingly low, and that of the women who followed him (another favourite topic in ballads) even lower. The real problem lay less with the behaviour of individual soldiers than with the public image of the army. As Kipling was to insist repeatedly, it was despicable hypocrisy to make "mock o' uniforms that guard you while you sleep", but his argument was never accepted in any whole-hearted way.[11] Land battles were fought abroad, often in distant and unknown countries. They were necessary and applauded when a Napolean needed to be defeated, but even that acknowledgement rested primarily on the fear of Britain being invaded. Britain was an island and guarded by the Navy, not the Army, a view that was widely held even after the First World War had begun, and one that had an impact on literature as on every other aspect of the national life. The ordinary sailor's conditions of service and social status were, in reality, little better than those of the soldier, though he carried the aura of a national hero. His uniform and fighting prowess were not only not mocked: they had been celebrated for centuries, in ballads and songs, novels, poems, and theatrical spectaculars.

While the neglect of the soldier by other English poets left the way clear for Kipling to cause a sensation with his barrack-room ballads in the early 1890s, in many other respects the ground had been thoroughly prepared for their enthusiastic reception. The Crimean War (1854–6) and the Indian Mutiny (1857–8) had given the Army a public prominence it had not enjoyed since the close of the Napoleonic Wars. The scandalous condition of British soldiers in the Crimea, Florence Nightingale's intervention, and her transformation into a national heroine, played a part in changing attitudes; so did Tennyson's "The Charge of the Light Brigade" which attained the kind of mass emotional popularity that many of Kipling's poems were later to enjoy. When the country was obsessed with the plight of British women and children besieged by Indian "rebels", it was the British Army that relieved Delhi and Lucknow and avenged the much-publicised horrors of Cawnpore. As the rate of imperial expansion steadily increased in the second half of the nineteenth century, the names of Army Generals (Nicholson, Havelock, Roberts, Kitchener) and of battles (Laing's Neck, Maiwand, Tel-el-Kebir, Rorke's Drift), became not only widely known, but often took on symbolic or talismanic significance for supporters of the British Empire.

All of this was made possible by a burgeoning communications industry. The daily life of the British soldier may still have remained largely unknown to the British public, but the part he was playing in major and minor imperial wars became increasingly familiar from boys' adventure books, music-hall songs; from Royal Academy paintings, magazines and periodicals illustrated with vividly heroic engravings; and, perhaps most influential of all, from the newspaper reports of the war and "special" correspondents who were themselves often projected as modern heroic figures. Kipling was always intensely proud of his close connections with war correspondents and artists, and he portrayed them, with great bravado, in *The Light that Failed.* Clearly, late Victorian readers were well prepared for something like *Barrack-Room Ballads*, but they were still surprised by what they were actually offered.

Kipling's account in *Something of Myself* of how the barrack-room ballads came to be written is clear and concise. When he returned to England from India in October 1889 he settled in London, taking rooms in Villiers Street, by the side of Charing Cross Station, opposite Gatti's Music Hall. The area was, and still is, tiny, fairly self-contained, and shabby. Wherever Kipling lived he had the ability to immerse himself in the local atmosphere. From that immersion he would cull material for his stories and poems. In this respect, Villiers Street was no different from Westward Ho!, Lahore, Simla, or Sussex. He ate in a "Sausage and Mash" shop situated beneath his rooms, drank in a nearby pub (where he befriended and obtained local information from the barmaid), and visited Gatti's (where he enjoyed "the smoke, the roar, and the good-fellowship of relaxed humanity"). At Gatti's he was also delighted to meet the "English brother" of the private soldiers he had known in India who "sat and sang at my elbow any night I chose."[12] Out of these circumstances, and in this tiny pocket of working-class London, he wrote the first of the barrack-room ballads.

Although Kipling's account of the composition of the barrack-room ballads is no doubt substantially correct, their genesis cannot be attributed so totally to the Villiers Street period. We know that Kipling was writing at least snatches of what he called "barrack-room ballads" two years before he returned to England, and using them, as though they were taken from traditional songs and marches, as epigraphs for some of the Indian stories. The eight-line epigraph to "The Big Drunk Draf'", *Soldiers Three* (1888), which begins "We're goin' 'ome, we're goin' 'ome," was transferred unchanged to serve as the chorus of "Troopin'" in *Barrack-Room Ballads*. Other early verses were not re-used in this direct way, but they might well have been, as in tone and spirit they are little different from the later ballads, merely undeveloped fragments: it is also worth emphasising that there is a close relationship between the soldier stories and the barrack-room ballads, with phrases and attitudes being carried over from the one to the other.

Something of Kipling's working methods at this time can be deduced from "Private Ortheris's Song", the barrack-room ballad that did *not* become one of the *Barrack-Room Ballads*, and "The Ladies", which might have been included in the 1892 volume but was held over for a later series. Both poems are connected with the story "The Courting of Dinah Shadd". It was one of the soldier stories which Kipling published on his return to London, building on the reputation for such work that had preceded him. It was first published in *Macmillan's Magazine*, March 1890, and collected in *Life's Handicap* (1891). The story centres on Mulvaney's troubled courtship of Dinah Shadd and his fear that she will reject his proposal, or, his own term for this, "give me the go". The story closes with Mulvaney's friend Ortheris singing an appropriate song "My girl she give me the go onest". The complete song is given as part of the story, and it appeared in both *Macmillian's Magazine* and *Life's Handicap*. For the *Life's Handicap* version of the story, Kipling added an epigraph which he simply attributed, in the manner of the earlier epigraphs, to a "Barrack-Room Ballad", though by this time he was already renowned as the author of the barrack-room ballads which had appeared in the *Scots Observer*. This particular epigraph is of interest because it typified what was often seen as Kipling's cynical attitude to women.[13] It claims that however different from each other women may seem in terms of class or social status, when a man is involved they are all the same:

For the Colonel's Lady an' Judy O'Grady
  Are sisters under their skins.

The sentiments expressed here are immediately relevant to "The Courting of Dinah Shadd", though the lines are now remembered as the conclusion to "The Ladies" which was first published in its complete form in the "Barrack-Room Ballads" section of *The Seven Seas* (1896).

"Private Ortheris's Song" raises slightly different issues. Charles Carrington claims it as "the earliest of the ballads", whereas precedence is usually given to "Danny Deever". The evidence he advances to support his claim is misleading, though his instinct may well be correct.[14] Although Ortheris picks up the phrase "give me the go" as the starting point of his song, what he sings about has little direct relevance to Mulvaney's courtship dilemma, but is a re-working of the traditional material of older ballads:

My girl she give me the go onest,
  When I was a London lad,
An' I went on the drink for a fortnight,
  An' then I went to the bad.

Thrown over by his girl, the soldier gets drunk, is tempted by a Recruiting Sergeant offering him the Queen's shilling, and is sent to India where he has plenty of time to bemoan his foolishness. He is wounded in the Afghanistan and Burma campaigns; throws away his chance of promotion when he goes "on the bend with an intimate friend", and ends up "Confined to Barracks". It is left to him to draw the moral from his experiences – avoid "women and drink" and don't blame others for your misfortunes:

My very worst friend from beginning to end
  By the blood of a mouse was myself!

Vivacious and catchy though it is, "Private Ortheris's song" does not quite belong with *Barrack-Room Ballads*. The experiences it describes are generalised. They lack the small personal details that are used with such telling effect in a roughly comparable ballad like "Cells"; and the moral is too glibly accepted, and applied, by Ortheris. It is better classified as the last of Kipling's early experiments in this kind of poetry, rather than the first of the new.

To say that the conception of *Barrack-Room Ballads* was not as immediate as Kipling makes it sound in his autobiography does not lessen the important part played in the process by Villiers Street. It was here that contact with London working-class life persuaded him to write the ballads primarily in Cockney. Hitherto, Ortheris's Cockney and Learoyd's Yorkshire accents had been dominated by Mulvaney's rather stagey Irish, but now Kipling placed the main emphasis on the London accent and used it with a linguistic inventiveness that had been absent in literature since the death of Dickens twenty years earlier. Villiers Street also provided him with the crucial experience of music hall. The evidence of some of Kipling's early poems, written while he was still at school, indicates a familiarity with music-hall songs long before he visited Gatti's, and while in India he would have heard the more popular songs at entertainments organised by the Anglo-Indian community. Even so, Gatti's was a revelation to him. Separated from his family and the India that had been his home for the previous seven years, and already appalled by the cliquishness of literary London, he found in music hall an alternative community that was warm, happy, and, above all, united by an intimate relationship between performer and audience. Kipling recorded his exhilarating discovery in a sketch called "My Great and Only" in which the narrator's one and only song ("made up of four elementary truths, some humour, and, though I say it who should leave it to the press, pathos deep and genuine") is performed in a music hall to a rapturous reception.[15] The title of the song is "That's What the Girl told the Soldier", and Ortheris is given a chorus of it to sing at the close of "'Love-o'-Women'", a short story also written around this time.[16] Jacqueline Bratton has argued that this song of Kipling's was probably an adaptation of a James Fawn music-hall favourite of 1889 "The Soldier" and that many of the details in "My Great and Only" were taken directly from events at Gatti's while Kipling was living in Villiers Street.[17] Perhaps the whole of the sketch is autobiographical and Kipling really did write a song for someone at Gatti's and sat in the audience, enthralled and unacknowledged, while it was performed. In the future, a great many of his poems, though not written with this audience specifically in mind, were to be sung and recited in the halls.

The reason why the narrator in "My Great and Only" decides that he will not even try to follow up his thrilling debut as a music-hall composer is certainly relevant to Kipling himself. Excited as he is by the experience, he recognises that he is an outsider. If the truth is ever to be told about working-class life then it has to be by someone "speaking the people's tongue, steeped in their lives and telling them in swinging, urging, clinging verse what it is their inarticulate lips would express."[18] His conviction that some day just such a poet would emerge was widely shared in late-Victorian Britain: it was prompted by the spread of compulsory elementary education and the concern of many authors and literary critics that large areas of working-class life were completely absent from both poetry and fiction. "The current literature of the next generation will, I am quite certain, be written by the Board School Boy," announces a character in Walter Besant's *All in a Garden Fair* (1883), a novel, and an author, much admired by Kipling.[19] One of the aspects of music-hall songs that attracted Kipling was their direct involvement in both the lives of the audience and in public events: it was a fascination with ordinariness that he, virtually alone among contemporary poets, was capable of appreciating and building on. His personal connection with music hall was brief, but to the end of his life he retained an interest in it that was essentially historical, regarding the music-hall songs of the second half of the nineteenth century as an irreplaceable source of information about "the national life".[20]

He did not, however, make the mistake of believing that what he experienced at Gatti's was a genuine working-class culture. There were elements of that in it, and, as his call for a people's poet indicates, he felt that music hall could in many respects provide a necessary forum for working-class expression that might be developed in the future. But it was also clear to him that what he was witnessing was a skilfully-managed commercial operation. This was music for the people, and largely about those same people, but it was only incidentally by them. He was quick to recognise the emotional manipulation in a growing number of music-hall songs, and with it a loss of content, a decline in the range of working-class experience contained in the songs, that he was later to deplore.[21] Almost certainly he sensed something of this even while he was most excited by the halls. Like the narrator of "My Great and Only", Kipling took to heart the lessons that music hall had to offer him, and then distanced himself from it. In the dramatised performances of music-hall songs, often based on national or class stereotypes, he had discovered a form of the dramatic monologue that was not unrelated to the Browning model but one that communicated more immediately, more directly. He had also found that his own interest in the poetic possibilities of the language and rhythms of everyday speech was shared by composers of music-hall songs, though not by most respected poets of the day. Above all he had discovered a new kind of audience – large, emotional, good-hearted, and eager to be entertained – with whom he was instantly at ease. Kipling had nothing against entertainment, and he did not share the contempt for popular or mass culture expressed by many other writers of the time. As with Dickens, there was a side of Kipling that revelled in the alternating extremes of raucousness and sentimentality that typified both Victorian theatre and popular literature. He also held in common with Dickens the conviction that the serious writer had social as well as artistic responsibilities to his readers, that art should entertain and instruct. To many late Victorians such a view was laughably outmoded. The growing tendency was to regard the work of art as self-contained, above and beyond the vulgarity of the world; it was its own justification; it embodied its own morality; and once it was created the respectable artist disappeared, leaving the reader to make what he would of the autonomous creation.

In Villiers Street Kipling contemplated the early development of these aesthetic theories and compared them with Gatti's. There was no doubt which he preferred, but he belonged fully to neither side. On the crucial issue of the total freedom and independence of the artist he was as firm as, say, Henry James or Oscar Wilde; but he would not believe that the modern artist was incapable of making contact with a large audience, and talk of the exclusivity of art he found repellent. In India he had coveted the literary fame that he felt only London could supply. Once in London he realised that the kind of literary fame being promoted was a denial of virtually everything he believed and valued. In deciding to go his own way Kipling was not, however, only asserting his artistic independence. He was also challenging, quite consciously, the most influential centres of literary London; reaching beyond them to appeal directly to his individual readers, many of whom were distinctly unliterary; and, in the process, initiating the series of aggressively-fought battles with the literary Establishment that would ultimately affect every aspect of his reputation as a writer. For this reason alone, the short time he spent in Villiers Street was one of the most formative periods of his life.

The twenty-one soldier poems that make up *Barrack-Room Ballads* were framed with Kipling's customary care. The introductory dedication "To T.A." states his double purpose in writing the ballads. First, to "make a song" for and about Tommy Atkins, the truth of which only Tommy himself will be able to confirm; and secondly, to persuade civilians that the soldier deserves better treatment than he usually receives:

O there'll surely come a day
When they'll give you all your pay,
And treat you as a Christian ought to do.

The ballads open with "Danny Deever" in which the whole regiment is called on parade to witness a military execution, and they close with "Shillin' a Day", a lament by an ex-Troop-Sergeant-Major who is now discharged from the army and dependent for a living on an inadequate army pension and whatever tips he can pick up "commissairin'". The movement of the ballads is therefore from the complete military unit at a moment of tight discipline, to the solitary ex-soldier confronting the neglect he can expect in civilian life. In closing with an ironic toast, "GAWD SAVE THE QUEEN!", Kipling returns to the hope expressed in the introductory dedication to Tommy Atkins that the day will come when his true worth is acknowledged. The charge of civilian hypocrisy towards the soldier, which it is one of the main purposes of *Barrack-Room Ballads* to reveal and to counter, is put with legendary directness in "Tommy":

> Oh, it's Tommy this, an' Tommy that, an' "Tommy, go away";
> But it's "Thank you, Mister Atkins," when the band begins to play' –

The commissionaire's sadness comes from the contrast between his present humbled circumstances and the days of excitement when he "Went slap for the Ghazi, my sword at my side". Tommy is more astute. His sarcasm is provoked by a civilian double standard that he experiences whenever he moves outside the army confines, for "Tommy ain't a bloomin' fool – you bet that Tommy sees!" It is, however, Kipling who finally takes over from the commissionaire and urges the reader to "think":

> Think what 'e's been,
> Think what 'e's seen,
> Think of his pension an' –

This interplay of voices, expressing different moods, experiences, and levels of understanding, is characteristic of the techniques employed in *Barrack-Room Ballads*. It is used most obviously to convey different facets of Tommy Atkins's life in the army. In between the extremes of execution and civilian neglect, the soldier is portrayed fighting in imperial campaigns (successful and unsuccessful ones); fighting other soldiers; praising the courage of Sudanese troops and Indian ancillaries; languishing in the guard-room; dreaming about beautiful Burmese girls; drunk; nostalgic; beating "niggers"; mourning dead comrades; yearning for home, and for the East; looting; and confessing his bewilderment at the meaning of the imperial mission he is so actively engaged in carrying out. The individual voices, attitudes, and ballads, are fragments of a composite portrait, and are never applicable to all of the speakers. The soldier in "Cells", temporarily repentant for the drunkenness that has put him in the guard-house, but acknowledging that "as soon as I'm in with a mate and gin, I know I'll do it again!", is clearly not the same man in "Soldier, Soldier" who on his return from overseas service seeks out a dead comrade's girlfriend to tell her as gently as he can that her "true love" has met a violent death. Even the twist at the end of this ballad, when the speaker offers to take his friend's place is handled with great delicacy:

> An' I tell you truth again – when you've lost the feel o' pain
> You'd best take me for your new love.

The difference between speakers is not simply a matter of the particular experiences they represent, or the attitudes they adopt, though both of these are usually important: they are also distinguished from each other by subtle modifications in their Cockney accents and by their diction. For instance, the speaker in "The Young British Soldier" is a training sergeant preparing new recruits who are soon to go overseas. He must inculcate certain basic lessons, impress the recruits, even frighten them slightly, and impose his authority. His harsh accent is perfectly suited to the slow enunciation of most of his lines, while his use of pompous phrases, vivid metaphors, and poeticisms, are all part of the rhetoric necessary to the successful performance of his military role:

When the 'arf-made recruity goes out to the East
'E acts like a babe an' 'e drinks like a beast,
An' 'e wonders because 'e is frequent deceased,
Ere 'e's fit for to serve as a soldier.

He uses a well-rehearsed joke to attract the recruits' attention. "You shut up your rag-box an' 'ark to my lay," he tells them, with the pun on rag-box indicating that they should stop cleaning their rifles, and at the same time shut their mouths, and listen to what he has to say. The drink that he warns them not to buy from native grog-sellers is "Fixed Bay'nets that rots out your guts", and similar jokey and vivid metaphors are used to guard them against other dangers. He has a "poetic" side to him as well. Enemy guns wheeling into line are described as "shakin' their bustles like ladies so fine"; but his most powerful rhetoric is kept for the close of his lecture:

When you're wounded and left on Afghanistan's plains,
And the women come out to cut up what remains,
Jest roll to your rifle and blow out your brains
An' go to your Gawd like a soldier.

The horror of the first two lines is subdued by the resonant rhythms and by the elimination of the Cockney accent, which is immediately brought back to emphasise harsh reality.[22] The training sergeant varies his accent and his language for rhetorical effect, and "Gawd", which is not normally characteristic of his pronunciation, is employed as a deliberate final emphatic, as Kipling himself uses it at the end of "Shillin' a Day".

In "Screw-Guns", Tommy's contentment is expressed by a simple drawl: "Smokin' my pipe on the mountings, sniffin' the mornin' cool"; while the soldier whose life is so famously saved by the "regimental *bhisti*", Gunga Din, also speaks in a slightly modified Standard English which thickens at moments of strong emotion or tension and, more strikingly, is distinguished by the speaker's linguistic inventiveness. The opening of "Gunga Din", staled by countless mechanical recitations, is one of the finest moments in *Barrack-Room Ballads*:

> You may talk o' gin and beer
> When you're quartered safe out 'ere,
> An' you're sent to penny-fights an' Aldershot it;
> But when it comes to slaughter
> You will do your work on water,
> An' you'll lick the bloomin' boots of 'im that's got it.

The mood is quiet and thoughtful, with the opening line made up entirely of monosyllabic words, and the speaker remains calm as he tries to find the right terms to express his scorn for those of his listeners who have never experienced the ultimate test. As the terms are not ready to hand, he makes some up: "penny-fights" for small frontier wars, and, with true poetic flair, he turns Aldershot, the name of the army training camp in Hampshire, into a verb. With his audience fixed as people who are used to having an easy time of it, he tells them (with the help of a heavy rhyme and an emphatic long line) that moral values are determined by necessity, and, until they realise that, they might as well sit safely in quarters drinking their "gin and beer". The hero of the ballad is, of course, not the speaker, but Gunga Din, who proves himself to be brave, loyal, intelligent, and even courteous under fire: he is "white, clear white inside". As the narrative progresses the speaker gets carried away with his praise of the native water-carrier, but he means it when he proclaims "You're a better man than I am, Gunga Din."

"Gunga Din" has become something of a by-word for racial condescension, and it is easy enough to see why, but if the speaker comes over as condescending it is because of his determination to assert his own inferiority. The same cannot be said of the speakers of "Fuzzy-Wuzzy" and "Loot", the two barrack-room ballads that were to bring repeated charges against Kipling of glorifying violence and of revelling in the baser sides of human nature. Kipling was not alone in this. Similar accusations were flung at any writer of the time who could be regarded as helping to import the decadent practice of French realism into Britain, and at this stage of his career Kipling was widely regarded as a realist: it was the exotic nature of his material, rather than his treatment of it, that led other critics to label him a romantic. "Fuzzy-Wuzzy" and "Loot" are distasteful, and not very successful poems, but it is foolish to contend that Kipling is approving the attitudes they dramatise. They are exercises in realism, revealing the harder and darker aspects of army life, just as "Mandalay" conveys nostalgia for the East and "Ford o' Kabul River" deep affection or love between soldiers. The ugliness of the incidents described in "Fuzzy-Wuzzy" and "Loot" is matched by the ugliness of the speakers' Cockney accents. The tribute to the fighting qualities of Sudanese soldiers is paid by someone whose powers of expression are crude and limited: "'E 'asn't got no papers of 'is own/ 'E 'asn't got no medals nor rewards." In place of the imaginative language used in most of the other ballads to demonstrate Tommy Atkins's attempt to communicate his experiences, the speaker in "Fuzzy-Wuzzy" constantly retreats into sheer nonsense ("Then 'ere's *to* you, Fuzzy-Wuzzy, an' the missis and the kid"); and his descriptions of hand-to-hand fighting, though appropriately violent, are made to sound ridiculous rather than courageous:

> 'E rushes at the smoke when we let drive,
>   An', before we know, 'e's 'ackin' at our 'ead;

The sentimentality in this poem is employed to reinforce the speaker's inherent, and gratingly-expressed, sense of superiority.

The speaker in "Loot" has much greater verbal dexterity, and he uses it to turn his opinions on the subject into catchy jingles: this ballad is one of the closest to a music-hall song, with a flowing rhythm helped along by internal rhymes; interjections from a cornet; and a chanted chorus that plays mindlessly on the poem's title. As has often been said it is a glorification of looting, but it is less often remarked that it is also a defiant justification of looting. The singing shouting looter who enjoys treating "a nigger to a dose o' cleanin'-rod" and offers the advice that while looting isn't exactly encouraged, "You can mostly square a Sergint an' a Quartermaster too", is completely out of control. He was a familiar military figure of the 1880s, and well beyond, and one that Kipling felt could only be swept away by a well-paid decently-treated army.

Two of the ballads – "The Widow at Windsor" and "The Widow's Party" – show soldiers being so critical of British imperialism that they inspired the widely-believed rumour that Queen Victoria was personally annoyed by them, though there seems to be no evidence that she was. The two poems are quite different from each other in both form and attitude. In "The Widow's Party" it is incomprehension that is explored. Ordered by "The Widow" to take part in a frontier campaign or "party", the narrator answers questions put to him about the operation at first simply, and then in swinging slangy triplets:

> "What did you do for knives and forks,
>   Johnnie, Johnnie?"
> We carries 'em with us wherever we walks,
>   Johnnie, my Johnnie, aha!
> And some was sliced and some was halved,
> And some was crimped and some was carved,
> And some was gutted and some was starved,
> When the Widow give the party.

The final question, "What was the end of all the show?" is answered with a careless shrug, "Ask my Colonel, for I don't know."

The speaker in "The Widow at Windsor" fully understands what is going on, and he is given a more complex verse form in which to voice his opinions. The tone of the ballad is one of a boastfulness at the extent and power of the British Empire that is constantly undercut by a melancholy refrain recalling the human price demanded by imperialism. The final stanza extends this echoing discontent to open criticism:

> Take 'old o' the Wings o' the Mornin',
>   An' flop round the earth till you're dead;
> But you won't get away from the tune that they play
>   To the bloomin' old rag over'ead.
>   (Poor beggars! – it's 'ot over'ead!)

The opening line is an allusion to Psalms 139:9 ("If I take the wings of the morning/And dwell in the uttermost parts of the sea"). But the biblical meaning, that even here the Lord's hand will be a guiding influence, is overturned and the soldier transformed into some kind of grotesque wounded bird of prey, "flopping" directionless around the globe. His guiding light should be the Union Jack, but this becomes merely "a bloomin' old rag", that, like the Indian sun, is out of reach and impervious to the suffering it causes. It is hardly surprising that readers pondered the effect this particular poem might have on Queen Victoria, and, taking into account the range of attitudes and points of view presented in *Barrack-Room Ballads*, debated among themselves whether the young author from India was a flag-waving imperialist or a dangerous radical.

For about three years after *Barrack-Room Ballads* the soldier theme dropped out of Kipling's poetry. Then, while living in America and engaged on writing of a very different kind, he produced a new series of barrack-room ballads which were published at irregular intervals in various periodicals and collected in *The Seven Seas* where they appeared as a distinct group, separate from the other poems in the volume. They were presented with characteristic care. To introduce them Kipling used "When 'Omer smote 'is blooming lyre", a poem which has a wider relevance to Kipling's poetry, but here serves to acknowledge that the ballads, if not quite "stolen" from other writers, are at least drawn from established types of poetry, his own among them. The first poem of the group is "Back to the Army Again", in which a reservist, disillusioned with civilian life, pretends he hasn't been in the army before and re-enlists: by writing more barrack-room ballads, Kipling, like the reservist, is going "back to the army again". The final poem, "For to Admire", completes a circle. The speaker is a "time-expired soldier man" returning home after years of service abroad. He has lost touch with everyone he once knew in England and his civilian future is uncertain, but he finds consolation in thoughts of the wanderlust that army service has bred in him:

For to admire an' for to see
For to be'old this world so wide –
It never done no good to me,
But I can't drop it if I tried!

In style and subject the new barrack-room ballads were largely continuations of the old, and some of them rank with the very best of Kipling's soldier poems. Two of the eighteen new poems ("Bill 'Awkins" and "Mary, Pity Women") are music-hall songs with nothing to do with the army; and "The Mother-Lodge", though set in India and given army connections, is more a spirited personal tribute to the egalitarian atmosphere of freemasonry than a barrack-room ballad. Several of them ("That Day", "Soldier an' Sailor Too", "Sappers", "The Jacket") celebrate army traditions associated with particular regiments; "Follow Me 'Ome" takes up from "Ford o' Kabul River" the theme of a soldier's love for a dead comrade, though now with a strong flavour of music-hall sentimentality that was not allowed to intrude on the stark grief of the earlier poem. As before, individual ballads portray specific aspects of the soldier's life, from a rollicking embarkation song ("'Birds of Prey' March"), through training ("The Men that fought at Minden" and "The 'Eathen") to the dangers of everyday life in India ("Cholera Camp"). Two of the most successful, and morally adventurous, of the poems, "The Ladies" and "The Sergeant's Weddin'", are more properly recitations than songs or ballads, and once again probably reveal the continuing influence of music hall on Kipling.

The mixture is, therefore, much as before, though there are differences between the two collections. The new ballads are slightly more mannered and literary than the earlier ones: they are also more consciously manipulative of both the Cockney accent and the reader's emotions. These relatively minor flaws are more than balanced by Kipling's greater concern with the psychology of individual speakers. The reservist in "Back to the Army Again" places himself in a difficult position. Re-enlistment is illegal and he has to change his name and pretend he is signing up for the first time. During basic training where he is set to "learnin' the damned old goose-step along o' the new recruits!", there is no way his experience can be disguised, but, wanting him back in the army, the training staff connive at his deception. The language and rhythm of the poem shift constantly between innocence and experience, reflecting the reservist's personal dilemma. "The Men that Fought at Minden" is another ballad about basic training, or, as the subtitle indicates, "a song of instruction". At first sight it appears to be the same kind of poem as "The Young British Soldier" in *Barrack-Room Ballads* and "The 'Eathen" in *The Seven Seas*, with the training sergeant instilling much-needed discipline and manliness into the raw recruits. In this case, however, the Sergeant is full of bluster and boastfulness. The salutary examples he draws from military history become confused or absurd, and he seeks refuge in ribald jokes. He may promise the "rookies" that "we'll make you soldiers yet!" but meanwhile he is more interested in scrounging drinks from them.

The army Casanova-figure in "The Ladies" is a very different kind of narrator. He exudes confidence, except, of course, on the crucial issue of what "the ladies" are really like, because, "You never can say till you've tried 'em/ An' then you are like to be wrong." Meanwhile, each sexual relationship is carefully pondered, valued for the lessons it has or has not taught him, and narrated in poetic lines as regular and balanced as a military march demonstration. The practised balance is broken only by the refrain which in a recitation would receive a different stress after each stanza:

> Funny an' yellow an' faithful –
>   Doll in a teacup she were,
> But we lived on the square, like a true-married pair,
>   An' I learned about women from 'er!

What he finally professes to have learned is that when it comes to sexual involvement all women are the same, but whether that represents a state of final wisdom or simply bears out his earlier admission that he "aren't no 'and with the ladies" is left open to doubt. There is no room for doubt in the judgements reached by the chorus of narrators in "The Sergeant's Weddin'", though the reader is given few specific details of what exactly it is makes the Sergeant and his new wife so "rotten bad". As the sergeant in charge of the canteen, he has regularly robbed the soldiers, and she, well, "What's the use o' tellin'/ 'Arf the lot she's been?" Everything is implied, and expressed, by the soldiers' glee at the pretentious marriage of such a well-suited couple: "We know all about 'em/ They've got all to find!"

Although it was the subject-matter of the barrack-room ballads that attracted more critical attention, contemporary reviewers were also alert to Kipling's revolutionary assault on poetic diction. One anonymous reviewer wrote: "The material is of the vilest – is the very dregs of language, in fact."[23] It is not quite that, though Kipling certainly did more than any other poet of the time to break with the ultra-refined Romantic tradition that was still, in the 1880s and 1890s, deeply influenced by Tennyson and the Pre-Raphaelites. In this respect, as in so many others, Browning is a partial exception, but among younger poets it was Kipling who was "modern": in comparison, Yeats, Dowson, and Johnson were traditionalists. The linguistic world of Tommy Atkins is made up of slang, urban imagery, military terms, everyday working-class expressions, hackneyed proverbs, neologisms, and poeticisms which are usually mundane but sometimes startlingly original. If it is not, "in fact", the "very dregs of language", that is because he uses euphemisms instead of the swear-words, blasphemies, and obscenities, that would have been dominant features of Tommy Atkins's speech. Kipling does slip the occasional swear-word into the barrack-room ballads, but, even if he had wanted to move further in this direction, the rigid publishing conventions and restrictions of the day would have stopped him. Of course, everyone involved, including the soldiers themselves, understood that Kipling's barrack-room ballads, however truthfully they represented Tommy Atkins's experiences, were not actually the ballads that were sung in barrack-rooms, and there were many attempts to pass off bawdy poems as genuine Kipling items. Towards the end of his life Kipling received a query from a friend about one such poem called "On the Barrack Gate" which he had been assured was by Kipling. "It isn't mine," Kipling replied, "I ain't particular, but I have never written dirt – even for fun. It don't amuse me to write down the words."[24]

*

The "Other Verses" of *Barrack-Room Ballads and Other Verses* are a miscellaneous collection, most of which, like the barrack-room ballads themselves, had already appeared in newspapers and periodicals. The greater part of them are ballads of Indian life which were once popular for the local colour and spirit of imperial adventure the best of them evoke, but today there are probably few enthusiastic readers of poems like "The Last Suttee", "The Ballad of the King's Jest", "With Scindia to Delhi", or "The Ballad of Boh Da Thone". If they are remembered at all it is because one of them, "The Ballad of East and West", has provided hostile critics with an opportunity to discredit Kipling by partial quotation. The opening two lines of the ballad run:

> Oh, East is East, and West is West, and never the twain shall meet,
> Till Earth and Sky stand presently at God's great Judgment Seat;

Taken in isolation, we seem to have a statement that, in this world at least, there can be no worthwhile contact between different races, but when the quatrain is completed a very different point emerges:

> But there is neither East nor West, Border, nor Breed, nor Birth,
> When two strong men stand face to face, tho' they come from the ends of the earth!

The assertion really being made, as unequivocally as anyone could wish, is that issues of race, religion, birth or social status, are irrelevant when compared with the fundamental qualities of courage, honour, dignity, and truth to self, that actually unite mankind. The concept of "strong men" no doubt lays itself open to further objections, but racism is not one of them.

The ballads of adventurous life in India, like so much else in this phase of Kipling's rapidly changing career, consisted largely of material he had carried with him from the immediate past, and among the "Other Verses" of *Barrack-Room Ballads* they are placed alongside very different poems which reveal new interests and concerns. Although the army is the focus of attention in this volume, there are indications in "The Gift of the Sea" and the ballads of "The Bolivar" and "The Clampherdown", of an interest in the sea and naval life that is undeveloped here but was soon to become a preoccupation. Overnight fame in England had provided him with a market eager to print anything he cared to write, and he was already taking advantage of this opportunity to comment on political events that stirred him, make public his views on topical issues, and offer moral pronouncements which were calculated to influence public opinion and inspire others to action. When he felt he was being let down by fellow-writers on the question of American "piracy" he published "The Rhyme of the Three Captains"; a call from the German Emperor for an international conference to discuss industrial relations received a mocking reply from Kipling in the poem "An Imperial Rescript"; and when a Government Commission appointed to investigate Irish terrorist activities decided that there was no firm evidence to implicate Parnell and other Nationalist leaders, Kipling expressed his contempt for the decision in "Cleared!", revealing a taste for virulent political satire that was to resurface periodically throughout his life.[25]

He was also prompted, more fruitfully as far as the quality of his poetry was concerned, into defences of his own art. Defence for Kipling usually meant attack, and it was Aestheticism that he chose as his target. It was not completely inevitable that Kipling and the Aesthetes should have become outright enemies. For all his talk of strong men and military action, he shared the Aesthetes' desire to introduce new experiences and language into poetry, and much of the work that brought him fame explored the darker, dangerous sides of human life that fascinated them as well. They also admired, and were influenced by, many of the same poets – Poe, Rossetti, Swinburne, and Browning; and all that divided them on the obligatory issue of French Literature was Kipling's insistence that his knowledge of it was greater than theirs. They even shared a fascination with music hall. Much early criticism of Kipling's work came from writers who had no connection with Aestheticism, and the initial responses of the Aesthetes themselves were not notably hostile. Oscar Wilde's self-consciously smart comments about the journalistic vulgarity of *Plain Tales* would have irritated Kipling, and from 1892 onwards Max Beerbohm's determined use of cartoons to debunk and discredit Kipling at every possible opportunity was no doubt even more of an irritant.[26] But there was genuine recognition as well. The regular reviews that Lionel Johnson wrote of Kipling's work at this time were balanced and generally admiring: at the close of his review of *Barrack-Room Ballads* he "expressed his thanks" for the ballads, and repeated his praise of their "unforced vigour and unexaggerated truth".[27]

For his part, Kipling would have nothing to do with such overtures. As we have seen, his hostility to London literary circles and his horror at the ways in which young writers were talking about literature were apparent almost as soon as he arrived from India, and he took the offensive. In November 1889, hardly back in England, he sent a poem, "In Partibus", to the *Civil and Military Gazette* where it was printed with the wry editorial comment that Kipling "who was understood not to be always satisfied with life in India, is apparently at times dissatisfied with England."[28] The poem, clearly a product of homesickness, included the Aesthetes as one of the causes of his dissatisfaction:

> But I consort with long-haired things
> In velvet collar-rolls,

Who talk about the Aims of Art,
  And "theories" and "goals",
And moo and coo with womenfolk
  About their blessed souls.

The antidote to this aesthetic biliousness is the man of action:

It's Oh to meet an Army man,
  Set up, and trimmed and taut,
Who does not spout hashed libraries
  Or think the next man's thought,
And walks as though he owned himself,
  And hogs his bristles short.[29]

The contrast, however crudely drawn here, truly expresses Kipling's complete opposition to Aestheticism. The effete, epicene clothes and lifestyles affected by some of the Aesthetes, are symptomatic of their art which is over-refined, narrow, introverted, overly concerned with the minute exploration of their own feelings, and unconcerned with the wider world or any way of life outside themselves and their books. Two poems in the *Barrack-Room Ballads* volume pursue these issues: both are far removed from the crabbed verses of "In Partibus".

With "The Conundrum of the Workshops" Kipling developed a poetic style that was as original, in its very different way, as the barrack-room ballads. The opening stance is that of a story-teller setting the scene:

When the flush of a new-born sun fell first on Eden's green and gold,
Our father Adam sat under the Tree and scratched with a stick in the
  mould;

With the appearance of the Devil who asks of this first attempt at representation "It's pretty, but is it Art?" the main theme of the poem is established, and it is, we are told later, "as old as the Eden Tree – and new as the new-cut tooth." The eternal struggle to capture a lasting image of human life is conveyed by means of vividly sketched vignettes, ranging from the frenzied activity of the Tower of Babel to the luxurious calm of a West End club. As the poem develops, the simple narrative language of the opening begins to take on the inconsequentiality of a nursery rhyme or folk tale in which Biblical allusions, archaisms, and commonplace proverbs are metamorphosed into a series of bizarre, surrealistic images:

> We have learned to whittle the Eden Tree to the shape of the surplice-peg,
> We have learned to bottle our parents twain in the yelk of an addled egg,
> We know that the tail must wag the dog, for the horse is drawn by the cart;
> But the Devil whoops, as he whooped of old: "It's clever, but is it Art?"

The first and second lines point to the decline of church and parental authority; the third reinforces the point by inverting, and making nonsense of, two common sayings; the final line is the refrain, with the Devil (who always has the last word) now "whooping", as in earlier responses he has "bubbled", "chuckled", and "whispered". The verbs are all active, thus removing the possibility that these strange goings-on are imposed from outside. Responsibility is placed on the communal "we" who have "learned" to overthrow common sense in our use of Art to show off. That the poem has a criticism to make of contemporary artistic practice is of secondary importance to the insistence that these problems always have existed, and always will. There is no progress in Art, and no single right or wrong way for the Artist to set about his work. Whatever the Artist attempts to do, the Devil will always pop up to say, "It's pretty [or "clever" or "human"], but is it Art?" The techniques developed here and used so successfully by Kipling were to recur throughout his poetry, most notably in such poems as "In the Neolithic Age", "When Earth's last picture is painted", and

"The Gods of the Copybook Headings". They were also to have a strong influence on a number of later poets, prominent among them Auden and Brecht.[30]

Aestheticism takes its place in "The Conundrum of the Workshops" with all other artistic doctrines: in "Tomlinson" it is confronted directly and presented as a debilitating force in modern life. Once again Kipling uses an effective blend of Biblical allusions and colloquialisms, but now allied to Swinburnian rhythms and alliteration. Tomlinson gives "up the ghost in his house in Berkeley Square" and is carried far away, "Till he heard as the roar of a rain-fed ford the roar of the Milky Way." Both settings are appropriate: Berkeley Square because it is associated with the more luxurious manifestations of Aestheticism, and the Milky Way because Tomlinson is a "milk-sop". Called to justify the life he has lived on earth Tomlinson can only pretend to virtues and vices he has read about in books, and he is rejected in turn by St Peter and the Devil. Unable to point to anything he has ever done out of his own passion or desire, and pronounced as having "scarce the soul of a louse", he is returned to earth to carry to others the lesson: "that the sin they do by two and two they must pay for one by one".

Tomlinson is not advised on any particular course of action, but simply to act for himself, to live in life rather than in books, to view and delight in the world around him. Kipling's own position in the poem is once again close to that of Browning's Fra Lippo Lippi ("Why not do as well as say?"), while the tricky moral issue he places at the centre of "Tomlinson", that it is better to act in what is usually regarded as an immoral way than not to act at all, has affinities with another Browning poem, "The Statue and the Bust". Tomlinson's crime is that he is living vicariously, and the antidote to his lethargy is heralded throughout the *Barrack-Room Ballads* volume. The world is opening up, making it possible for people to see places and experience ways of life that earlier generations could only hear or read about, and the English have been given opportunities to participate in this world-wide movement that are denied to virtually all other nations. So favoured are the English that they should regard it as a duty, rather than simply a pleasure, to take an active part in this new era of adventure and expansion.

This was the message of "The English Flag" which had been published originally in the *St James's Gazette*, 4 April 1891. The poem's starting point was a newspaper report of the courthouse in Cork being set on fire and the Union Jack burned during a trial of five Irishmen who were charged with riot. The poem is not, however, concerned primarily with Ireland; it is, rather, a denunciation of all Little-Englanders, for "what should they know of England who only England know?" The opening two stanzas of the poem are aggressively satirical. Opponents of the British Empire are portrayed as "poor little street-bred people that vapour and fume and brag"; and as pet dogs, at one moment "whimpering to and fro", at another "lifting their heads in the stillness to yelp at the English Flag." The ironic possibilities of an alternative national flag are treated even more savagely:

> Must we borrow a clout from the Boer – to plaster anew with dirt?
> An Irish liar's bandage, or an English coward's shirt?

Or, in other words, is the Union Jack to be replaced by the white flag of surrender snatched from Boer or Irish rebels, or, worse still, cowardly Little-Englanders? With everyone who would define "England" as merely a small island scathingly dismissed, Kipling calls on the "Winds of the World" to "give answer", and effects a remarkable change in the poem's tone. Political invective now gives way to high romance. The "poor little street-bred people" at home may be unaware that the English Flag is being raised throughout the world, but the Four

Winds testify that that is precisely what is happening, and, furthermore, hail the courage and sacrifice involved:

> Never the lotos closes, never the wild-fowl wake,
> But a soul goes out on the East Wind that died for England's sake –

Each of the Winds in turn calls for more dedication and service from the English who, now that the evidence has been presented to them, have no excuse for not understanding what the Flag of England truly represents: "Ye have but my waves to conquer/ Go forth, for it is there!"

The spirit of adventurous travel in an expanding world is also invoked in the final poem of the volume, though it carries little of the linguistic excitement of "The English Flag" and the exhortation is personal rather than public. Called "L'Envoi" in *Barrack-Room Ballads*, and later given the title "The Long Trail", it has become a focal point for conjecture by Kipling's biographers because of what Carrington calls its "subjective undertone".[31] The most controversial lines are:

> Ha' done with the Tents of Shem, dear lass,
> We've seen the seasons through,
> And it's time to turn on the old trail, our own trail, the out trail,
> Pull out, pull out, on the Long Trail – the trail that is always new!

In an early draft of the poem it is a "dear lad", not a "dear lass", who is urged to "Ha' done with the Tents of Shem", and it is generally assumed that the lad was Wolcott Balestier and the lass his sister Caroline. That seems likely, but it has also led to some imaginative interpretations of "the Tents of Shem" which, within the context of *Barrack-Room Ballads*, have little relevance.[32] The Biblical reference is to Genesis 9:27, which closes the incident, in itself the subject of much critical discussion, when one of Noah's three sons sees his father drunk and naked and leaves him lying "uncovered": the two other sons refuse to look on their father's nakedness and cover him up. Shem is one of the sons rewarded for his piety, and the phrase "Tents of Shem" refers to the founding of his branch of the Noah dynasty. This, surely, is the primary allusion used by Kipling in "L'Envoi", and the addressee is clearly Caroline. As we have already seen, *Barrack-Room Ballads* opens with a hastily rewritten dedicatory poem to Wolcott, and it is characteristic of Kipling's obsession with framing his collections of poetry in significantly personal ways, that he should have closed it with another rewritten poem, this time dedicated to his wife: the volume was actually published while they were abroad on their honeymoon. It is certainly possible that the earlier draft of the poem carried coded messages that Wolcott alone would have understood, but the "envoi" or message of *Barrack-Room Ballads* urges Caroline to think of their marriage not as the beginning of settled domesticity but as an opportunity to strike out on an adventurous life together, on "our own trail", "the old trail . . . that is always new!"

[4] The Seven Seas

Still the world is wondrous large – seven seas from marge to marge –
And it holds a vast of various kinds of man;
And the wildest dreams of Kew are the facts of Khatmandu,
And the crimes of Clapham chaste in Martaban.

"In the Neolithic Age", *The Seven Seas*.

The title page of *Barrack-Room Ballads* carried a head-and-shoulders drawing of a helmeted bugler. *The Seven Seas* (1896) carried a similarly placed drawing, only this time of a bearded seaman in oils, at the wheel of a stormbound ship. The change of emblem marked a shift of emphasis, and of interest, between the two volumes. Although *The Seven Seas* contained a new batch of barrack-room ballads, these were placed in the second half of the book, set apart in exactly the same way as the "Other Verses" were in *Barrack-Room Ballads*. The soldier was not rejected or forgotten, any more than India had been in the earlier volume, but for the moment he was relegated. Now the seaman was the centre of attention, and his world was literally the whole world, wherever the four winds blow, wherever the seven seas reach, wherever the English Flag was flown.

Charles Carrington dates Kipling's "discovery of ships and harbours and seafaring men" from the time he left India in March 1889.[1] With his "seven years' hard" completed, Kipling decided not to return home directly, but to travel with friends via the Far East and America. They visited Burma, which Kipling was surprised to learn was a totally different country from the British India to which it had been united three years earlier; Hong Kong, where "a monument to certain dead Englishmen" provoked in him the observation that "they are but the seed of the great harvest whereof our children's children shall assuredly reap the fruits"; and Japan, where he was fascinated by the eagerness with which the Japanese were absorbing Western influences, and appalled by their determination to draw up a "Constitution of Japan . . . on entirely European lines".[2] Everywhere, he paid special attention to a country's political and military condition and to its Art, often linking these concerns together to make generalisations about the Britain he was yet to experience as an adult:

> Japan is a great people. Her masons play with stone, her carpenters with wood, her smiths with iron, and her artists with life, death, and all the eye can take in. Mercifully she has been denied the last touch of firmness in her character which would enable her to play with the whole round world. We possess that – We, the nation of the glass flower-shade, the pink worsted mat, the red and green china puppy dog, and the poisonous Brussels carpet.[3]

He stayed considerably longer in America than any other country. There were friends to visit, a pilgrimage to be made to Bret Harte country, the thrilling possibility of meeting Mark Twain, and, as in Japan, he wanted to observe for himself the country's military potential and political system. Neither impressed him. As his ship steamed into San Francisco harbour, he noted "with great joy" that "the block-house" which guarded it "could be silenced by two gunboats from Hong Kong with safety, comfort, and despatch."[4] America's much-vaunted democracy he found disgracefully corrupt. On a brief visit to Canada he was pleased to see "the old flag" flying on public buildings and "consoled" by the "sight afar off of three British men-of-war and a torpedo-boat".[5] At the close of the account of his visit to America, it is a surprise to find Kipling so approving of what he has seen. "Let there be no misunderstanding about the matter," he announces: "I love this People."[6] Given the harshness of Kipling's comments, misunderstanding was very possible, but he insists that his criticism is permissible because of his love. Despite everything that can be said against Americans, they are "the biggest, finest, and best people on the surface of the globe! Just you wait a hundred years and see how they'll behave when they've had the screw put on them."[7]

Kipling's leisurely return to England in 1889 influenced him in a number of important ways. Apart from laying the foundations for his future ambivalent relationship with America, it inspired his love of sea travel – there was to be hardly a year of his life when he did not take an extended sea voyage – and also his restless desire to visit, to observe for himself, as much of the world as possible. In the early 1890s alone he paid visits to America, Canada, Japan, and India; and he travelled for the first time to South Africa, Australia and New Zealand. From 1892 to 1896 he lived in America, and during that period made frequent visits to Britain. For those who could afford the leisure and luxury that the great liners offered, it was the heyday of sea travel. Kipling was never one to bother about luxury, and he disliked and avoided whenever he could the shipboard ritual of the Captain's Table. What he most enjoyed was the social life, apart from the Captain's Table, and the thrill of being part of an expanding, adventurous, swiftly changing technology. Unlike his close contemporary Conrad, who wrote primarily about the vanishing world of sailing-ships, Kipling's imagination was excited by steam, engine-power, speed, and the men who created and maintained such modern wonders. With the Scottish engineer in "McAndrew's Hymn" he prayed that the Lord would "send a man like Robbie Burns to sing the Song o'

Steam." Perhaps, for a while, he believed that he himself might fill that role, though with the genuine humility he always showed to this poet, he also described his attempts to capture the essence of the modern world as merely "roughing out the work" for a greater poet to come, "as Ferguson did for Burns."[8]

At the heart of Kipling's developing fascination with the sea lay a perception that his experiences in India had misled him about the true potential of the British Empire. As Carrington points out, India "was not the normal pattern of British expansion. The sailor and the merchant, not the soldier and the Indian civilian, were the common types of British overseas."[9] For centuries, seamen, buccaneers, and privateers, had developed British interests overseas, fighting off the same ambitions of rival nations, transporting settlers and troops, carrying food and raw materials back home, and leaving behind them British settlements scattered throughout the world. And none of this was ancient history: it was still in process, growing rather than declining; made more, not less possible, by modern naval technology. This view was reinforced by his own travels. Kipling's "discovery" of the sea represented far more than a new theme for him to explore in his work: it provided an historical structure and an ideology, linked the present with the past and foretold the future. It was out of these concerns that the irreverent satirist of Anglo-Indian society and the spokesman for the British Tommy was transformed into the prophet of Empire.

The transition is recorded in "The Exiles' Line", one of the poems that Kipling sent back from England for publication in the *Civil and Military Gazette*. It was published on 8 July 1892, though not collected until the *Inclusive Edition* of his poetry in 1919 where, confusingly, it was dated 1890. Perhaps that was when it was first written or drafted, or perhaps Kipling was placing the valedictory mood of the poem in his own career:

Now the New Year reviving old desires,
The restless soul to open sea aspires.

The P & O steamer moves slowly backwards and forwards between Britain and India, a steady monotonous task emphasised by the repetitions and slow rhythms of the verse, shipping the "exiles" out and bringing them home again. The ship is portrayed as a microcosm of Anglo-India, but there is no gaiety, no joy; the decks arrayed for games to pass the time are ghostly, the "sea-met loves" are transient. The passage is between two "homes", neither of which represents stability: the exile can never be ended, for these passengers are "the gipsies of the East", "Waifs of the land and wastrels of the sea", the servants of a great ideal that they pursue with melancholy dedication:

Bound in the wheel of Empire, one by one,
The chain-gangs of the East from sire to son,
  The Exiles' Line takes out the exiles' line
And ships them homeward when their work is done.

As we have seen, by the time "The Exiles' Line" was published, its mournful view of imperial service had already been supplanted by the exhilaration of "The English Flag" and "The Long Trail". The transformation of Kipling's reputation was under way, but there was much speculation on how his career would develop, and for a while in the early 1890s it was unclear which way he would turn. One view was that his spectacular early promise would simply fizzle out; another that he would pursue the romantic imperialism of "The English Flag"; yet another, that radical realism was his true strength as demonstrated by the more daring of the soldier stories and barrack-room ballads. Some critics begged him to return to India and bring back new literary treasures from that exotic land. His refusal to associate more than necessary with established literary circles added to the confusion. But Kipling's artistry was too individualistic and experimental ever to be slotted into any one literary category: sudden shifts and changes in his work were always to confound critical expectations, and this was especially the case in the 1890s.

What he did do shortly after the publication of *Barrack-Room Ballads* was move to America, a decision that was in certain respects more startling than if he had returned to India or announced himself a committed realist. In taking this step he appeared not only to be backing away from the great success he had achieved in London, but also to be moving against the contemporary phenomenon of large numbers of American writers leaving their own country to settle in Europe. They did so because, in Henry James's words, America was "the great country of the Philistines".[10] The issue aroused considerable national bitterness. On his first visit to America Kipling told a reporter that California was "hallowed ground" to him because of Bret Harte, and was told: "Bret Harte claims California, but California don't claim Bret Harte. He's been so long in England that he's quite English."[11] Now Kipling was reversing the trend. He lived in America from 1892 to 1896, and if personal circumstances had been different he might have settled there permanently. His American wife and his dedication to the memory of Wolcott Balestier helped him initially to adapt to Vermont society; on trips to England he astonished friends by speaking with a strong American accent, and he appears to have found what he considered an ideal setting in which to write.

It was an exceptionally productive period, yet little of what he wrote dealt directly with his new environment: his response to America was therefore very different from his response to Lahore or Villiers Street, and what it would later be to Sussex. His most substantial "American" work was *Captains Courageous*, the research for which broadened his present obsession with the sea to include deep-sea fishing, and there were occasional poems on American themes, notably the attractive and now largely forgotten "Pan in Vermont".[12] But he was concerned less with the details of everyday life in America than with the country's massive potential and future role in world affairs, the issues that had struck him on his first visit in 1889. Of central importance for Kipling were American relations with Britain and the Empire. If the achievements of the Empire were to be maintained, it was of vital importance that the American people should regard the imperial mission not only with sympathetic understanding but with sufficient enthusiasm to participate in its expansion. To Kipling's mind the imperial cause was no longer British: it was Anglo-Saxon. From now on he wrote with an American as well as a British audience in mind. It was not necessary to do this by handling specifically American themes. His work was already immensely popular in his adopted country, even though there was no obvious reason why American readers should be fascinated by tales and poems about British India and army barrack-rooms. Everything rested on the common heritage being strong enough for Americans to realise that British imperial values and aspirations should, if properly understood, unite rather than divide the two countries.

The signs that such a message would be welcomed in America were far from favourable. There clearly were Americans who shared Kipling's ideals, but more who were either indifferent or hostile, who were concerned with their own country's internal expansion and proud that they hadn't ended up as part of the British Empire. Kipling's awareness of this division is apparent in "An American", which was first published in 1894. It is in the densely-packed, oblique, reflective style, modelled perhaps on Emerson, that Kipling would frequently use for his overtly political poems. It was called originally "As it Strikes a Contemporary", not merely a casual allusion to Browning's similarly-titled poem, but also a sarcastic pun on a railway strike taking place in Chicago. Its later, more relevant title, portrays an American as made up of two conflicting personalities: there is the traditional, humane, wise, law-abiding "American Spirit", and his "avatar" the brash, loud-mouthed democrat whose "heart leaps, as a babe's, at little things". The poem's conclusion – that the true "American Spirit" will eventually triumph – is offered as a positive, but it has more the air of a faint, rather desperate hope. Closely related to the ideas being explored in "An American", and more generally to Kipling's developing concern with politics, are some of the poems in the two *Jungle Books*, written in America and published in 1894 and 1895. Mowgli, the white boy raised by wolves, survives in the jungle because he learns and follows "The Law". It is obviously important that he is human and white, but not totally so: after all, he is taught the Law by Baloo the bear and Bagheera the panther.

"The Law of the Jungle" is the first of Kipling's experiments in a type of poetry with which his name would become closely, and sometimes embarrassingly, associated. Its purpose was to inculcate fundamental values and beliefs by means of epigrammatic lines which would be easily memorised. Within the context of the *Jungle Books* Kipling's main concern was to compose moral precepts which had a suitably ancient or primitive feel to them. Baloo, we are told, "always recited them in a sort of sing-song."[13] If Kipling had an ancient model in mind, it may have been the Biblical Proverbs: nearer at hand there were such varied examples as Walt Whitman and Martin Tupper for him to draw on. In comparison with some of his later poems of this kind, the "laws" of the jungle are of limited or indirect relevance to human life: the original title of "The Law of the Jungle" was the more specific "The Law for the Wolves". However, two of what Kipling calls "rulings" are particularly important. First, the assertion that all communities are compact units, in which individualism must thrive but never be allowed to fragment the whole: "For the strength of the Pack is the Wolf, and the strength of the Wolf is the Pack." Secondly, the insistence that the well-being and safety of a community rest on all of its members accepting the primacy of "The Law" and "obeying" it. Those who are outside the law are portrayed as the "*Bandar-log*" or monkeys whose "Road - Song" is one of Kipling's more flamboyant rhythmic exercises. The rhythm of the lines follows the movements of the monkeys as they swing through the trees, reach for the moon, or drop to earth with their regular taunt thrown at anyone who is not with them: "*Brother, thy tail hangs down behind!*" So perfectly are sound and sense blended that even the curve of the monkey's tail, of which they are so proud, is reproduced in the movement of the lines. In the poem's final stanza, the monkeys continue to play, but the rhythm collapses into a clumsy prose which reflects the emptiness and vanity of their boasts:

Then join our leaping lines that scumfish through the pines,
That rocket by where, light and high, the wild-grape swings.
By the rubbish in our wake, and the noble noise we make,
Be sure – be sure, we're going to do some splendid things!

They may seem as light and graceful as flying-fish as they "scumfish" through the trees, but they are really the "scum" of society, feckless, irresponsible, lacking individuality, capable only of acting as a pack, dreamers who will never be doers. They are not only outside the Law: they are beyond it, and its enemies. In "An American", Kipling allows the *Bandar-log* element to be kept in check by a counteractive civilising tendency, the true "American Spirit": but in the *Jungle Books* the chattering *Bandar-log* are only silenced by Kaa the python's sinister hypnotic dance of death. For Kipling, as for Conrad, civilisation is a fragile crust which barely manages to keep suppressed the destructive powers of darkness, and, again like

Conrad, the only antidote is action, a constant effort to turn dreams into reality.

By early 1896 Kipling had to acknowledge that his own dream of addressing the Anglo-Saxon world from a sound American base was over. The reasons for him leaving America, or being driven away, were both personal and public. A long-standing quarrel with his brother-in-law had reached a point that made it impossible for Kipling to live in Vermont, and the need to move home was made more urgent when a dispute about the border between Venezuela and British Guiana provided President Cleveland with an opportunity to stir up the anti-British feeling that was never dormant for long in nineteenth-century America. Kipling was appalled by Cleveland's actions and deeply impressed by Britain's calm insistence that the matter should be settled by international arbitration, but like many people he felt that war between the two countries was a real possibility. In a despairing letter to C.E. Norton dated 8 January 1896, he explained that in the event of war breaking out he would have to play some part in it:

> You see it is obviously absurd for me to sit still and go on singing from a safe place while the men I know are on the crown of it; and it may be that when I am closer to the scene of action I may be able to help with a little song or two in the intervals of special correspondence.

Not that he any longer felt safe in America, which had become a "hostile country". The plan was that the whole family should get out, but in case that proved impossible and he should die in a war, he arranged his financial affairs "so that Carrie ought not to starve".[14] In the event, drastic action was not immediately necessary, though it was soon made so by further fierce quarrels with his brother-in-law. In September 1896 Kipling rented a house in Devon and took his family to England, a country that his two young daughters had never lived in. The following month *The Seven Seas* was published. Most of the poems it contained had been written in America, and many of them had already appeared in periodicals and newspapers. Outwardly, and with the obvious exception of "An American", there were few signs of Kipling's American experiences in *The Seven Seas*. He was now the spokesman for the British seaman and the celebrant of "English" national characteristics: nothing could have seemed to his readers more un-American, especially with the Venezuelan incident still current. Yet America was not simply the place where the poems were written: the new mood of prophetic confidence they displayed, the spirit of modern romance they invoked, and many of their underlying ideas, had all been formulated or brought to fruition in America. Kipling may have been driven out of that "hostile country", but he was more convinced than ever that the future of the British Empire, and therefore of civilisation itself, would depend on developments in America. He was still hoping that the true "American Spirit" would triumph over the *Bandar-log*.

Kipling prefaced *The Seven Seas* with a dedicatory poem to Bombay, the city of his birth and therefore the "Mother of Cities to me". The poem is a dedication in another sense as well. As he belongs to Bombay "neither by service nor fee" but by accident of birth, he still has a debt to pay to his mother-city. This he will meet by celebrating her place within the family of cities that now make up the Empire. She in turn, "after the use of kings", will "remit" Kipling's absence on "deep-sea plunderings/And purchase in all lands". In this manner Kipling presents his credentials and dedicates whatever talent he possesses to the Empire.

The solemn air of commitment to a great purpose is taken up immediately in "A Song of the English", the opening poem of the volume. It had been written three years earlier to mark the inauguration in London of the Imperial Institute, and first published in the *English Illustrated Magazine*, May 1893. Kipling made some revisions and additions to the text for *The Seven Seas*, though without altering the tone of the poem in any significant way. The importance he attached to this poem is apparent not only in the message it carries, but also in its ambitious structure which consists of seven interconnected "songs", several of them subdivided into separable units. Kipling's own description of the whole poem as "a song of broken interludes" captures exactly the effect achieved by his use of varied verse forms and different voices. In English versification it belongs with such works as Dryden's ode "Alexander's Feast" and Burns's cantata "Love and Liberty". "A Song of the English" is the overall title of the poem, though in some editions it has become misleadingly attached to the otherwise untitled prelude which begins "Fair is our lot – O goodly is our heritage!", an allusion to the *Book of Common Prayer* version of Psalms 16:7, a favourite text with Kipling.

The first response, in turning from *Barrack-Room Ballads* to "A Song of the English", is shock at Kipling's pomposity and loss of poetic inventiveness:

Fair is our lot – O goodly is our heritage!
(Humble ye, my people, and be fearful in your mirth!)
For the Lord our God Most High
He hath made the deep as dry,
He hath smote for us a pathway to the ends of all the Earth!

The initial mood of prayer, absurdly undercut by Kipling's own God-like interjections, portentous italics, exclamation marks, and religiosity, serves only to make the shameless boast that the English are God's chosen people, destined to rule the earth. It recalls the patriotism of Dickens's Mr Podsnap, though without the deflationary satire: "No Other Country is so Favoured as This Country . . . This Island was Blest, Sir, to the Direct

Exclusion of such Other Countries as – as there may happen to be."[15] The covenant between God and the English goes even further than anything Mr Podsnap could envisage. Although the people have "sinned", and their "rulers" have gone from "righteousness"; even though "Deep in all dishonour . . . we stained our garments' hem"; still, forgiveness will follow: "We were led by evil counsellors – the Lord shall deal with them!" The manner is that in which the God of the Old Testament comforted one of the leaders of His chosen people: "Fear not, Abram: I am thy shield, *and* thy exceeding great reward" (Genesis, 15:1). For Abraham the material, as well as the spiritual, reward was impressive –

> In that day the Lord made a covenant with Abram, saying,
> Unto thy seed have I given this land, from the river
> of Egypt unto the great river, the river Euphrates.
>
> (Genesis, 15:18)

– yet not quite as impressive as the reward promised to England: "He hath smote for us a pathway to the ends of all the Earth!"

The linguistic collapse that is so apparent in this opening poem of "A Song of the English" is barely redeemed by the "broken interludes" that follow. The rhetoric, often echoing phrases and rhythms carried over from "The English Flag", is noisy and hollow, with Kipling struggling in vain to invoke a spiritual justification and support for England's imperial success:

> Came the Whisper, came the Vision, came the Power with the Need,
> Till the Soul that is not man's soul was lent us to lead.

Even his celebration of the laying of the "Deep-Sea Cables", a remarkable technological achievement that linked Britain and America and might have been expected to stir Kipling to memorable pronouncement, produces only sub-Tennysonian bathos, with men talking "to-day o'er the waste of the ultimate slime", while "a Power troubles the Still that has neither voice nor feet." The most substantial poem of the series is "The Song of the Cities" which consists of fifteen brief tributes by the major cities of the Empire, an expanding "Exiles' Line" that now stretches across the world from Auckland to Victoria.

In "England's Answer", the mother-country's response to the cities' offerings, Kipling made the first of his several attempts to summarise the English character and to eulogise the distinctive qualities that link England with those overseas who "come of the Blood". The transmitted virtues are sturdy independence, an apparent slowness that deceptively conceals strength, a love that is deeper than speech (though with an ability to speak when necessary "in straight-flung words and few"), and most important of all, in this address by the mother-country, a belief in freedom and democracy that will allow the individual countries of the Empire to go their own ways while trusting that indissoluble links will remain "Because ye are the Sons of the Blood and call me Mother still." "England's Answer" is a bizarre mixture of mystical appeals ("the Blood"); negative as well as positive national stereotypes ("We do not fall on the neck nor kiss when we come together"); promises of future expansion based on ancient myths of motherhood ("I have borne many sons, but my dugs are not dry"); sharp insights into the problematic ways this family of nations might develop; and prophecies of a great war to come when the colonies and dominions will rally to the mother-country:

> In the day of Armageddon, at the last great fight of all,
> That Our House stand together and the pillars do not fall.

The poem closes with a declaration of faith in both humanism and manliness, for the English and the sons of the English "are neither children nor Gods, but men in a world of men!"

These various concerns – England's imperial destiny, the modern spirit of adventure, the romance of naval technology, and manliness – fascinated Kipling throughout the 1890s. The critics who marvelled at *Barrack-Room Ballads* and wondered which way the young poet would turn had received their answer. He now projected himself habitually as the moral conscience of the nation, promoting through his writing the qualities that he believed should be nurtured if Britain's leading position in the world was to be maintained. He was also a prophet, berating the government whenever he felt it was providing insufficiently dynamic leadership, and urging, like the young Carlyle whom he in some respects resembles, everyone to recognise the "signs of the times" and to act in accordance with them.[16] By the mid-1890s, still only thirty years old, he had become a self-appointed national institution, reviled by some readers, eulogised by others. The ultimate justification for his aggressive public role as a poet lay in his enormous popularity: without that he would have had no platform from which to pronounce on world affairs. Kipling, of course, understood this perfectly well, but it is unlikely that he would have allowed it to be considered as a factor influencing his opinions or his work. Of far more importance to him was his complete independence as a writer; a personal freedom from the restrictions imposed by government honours, party-political affiliation, popularity, even at times payment for his work, that allowed him to say whatever he believed needed to be said. This is the moral advanced in "The Last Rhyme of True Thomas" which was first published in 1894 and reprinted in *The Seven Seas*, some years before any of the official honours that Kipling might have had were actually offered to him. To this artistic independence was added an authority based entirely on his personal experience of the world. "What should they know of England who only England know?" he had asked in "The English Flag". His answer was not a contemptuous "Nothing!", but rather an injunction that they should be willing to find out: otherwise they were in danger of ending up like the pathetic Tomlinson. The prelude to "A Song of the English" closes with the lines:

> Through the naked words and mean
> May ye see the truth between
> As the singer knew and touched it in the ends of all the Earth!

Bolstered by his sea voyages "to the ends of all the Earth", Kipling, "the singer", announces his intention to use his skill with "naked words and mean" to inspire in others the romance of the sea and the excitement of modern technology.

Kipling's determination to jolt into life his readers' latent sense of romance pervades *The Seven Seas*. The appeal to racial superiority in "A Song of the English", was one attempt, and, considered in terms of the poem's great popularity, a success. But it was by no means the only possible way, as is made clear in "In the Neolithic Age":

> *There are nine-and-sixty ways of constructing tribal lays,*
> *And-every-single-one-of-them-is-right!*

In sharp contrast to the modernity of his message, Kipling's artistic figures are cavemen, troubadours, stone-age etchers, and, coming more up to date, banjo-players. In taking this line he was not simply thumbing his nose at the Aesthetes, though that was probably involved. Rather, he was celebrating the tribal nature of poetry, and proclaiming that the poet's role has remained unchanged, essentially, over the centuries: as the banjo announces proudly in his "song": "The grandam of my grandam was the Lyre." When the "maker of pictures" in "The Story of Ung" begins to despise the hunters as fools because they lack his vision, he is given a lecture on the economic basis of art by his father. He is told it is precisely because his way of viewing the world is so different from others that they admire his work and willingly allow him to live on their labour: "Son that can see so clearly, rejoice that thy Tribe is blind!" The banjo understands instinctively the lesson that Ung has to be taught. He is the late-Victorian explorer's companion and comforter, "the war drum of the White Man round the world!" When required he can "babble what the weakest won't confess" and stir hearts with "common tunes that make you choke and blow your nose". Though, like Kipling himself, he has more mysterious powers as well:

> I'm the Prophet of the Utterly Absurd,
> Of the Patently Impossible and Vain –
> And when the Thing that Couldn't has occurred,
> Give me time to change my leg and go again.

Not all of the poems in *The Seven Seas* share the banjo's optimistic view that the apparently "absurd" or "impossible" can be successfully communicated. In "To the True Romance", which was first published as an introductory poem to *Many Inventions* (1893), Kipling expresses the belief that "true" romance is unattainable on earth: it is something only "the careless angels know!" In poems like "The Miracles" and "The King", romance is portrayed as something that most people are incapable of recognising as existing in the present at all: it is always something that "was with us – yesterday!"

Kipling countered this backward-looking attitude with a series of poems about ships and seamen. *The Seven Seas* contained "Anchor Song", "The Derelict", "The Last Chantey", "The Liner She's a Lady", "McAndrew's Hymn" and "The 'Mary Gloster'". To these should be added other similar poems which were published slightly later – "Cruisers", "The Destroyers", "Poseidon's Law" and "The Wet Litany". In some of these poems, most powerfully "The Derelict", Kipling's approach is anthropomorphic, giving life and voice to the ships in order to heighten their majestic grandeur and national importance, but they are never allowed an autonomous existence. It is the relationship between man and machine that matters most, as the Derelict well understands:

> Man made me, and my will
> Is to my maker still.

The cruisers are portrayed as seaport prostitutes plying their ancient trade not for personal gain but to "accord and decoy to our masters' desires", and the destroyers and the Channel Fleet in "The Wet Litany" are similarly dedicated to the service and protection of Britain. When the different ships are presented as members of a family, as in "The Liner She's a Lady", they become a microcosm of British society.

For the seamen themselves, Kipling has nothing but praise. Like Tommy Atkins in India, the sailor is removed physically from the country it is his job to protect, and he also is part of a close-knit, isolated, and often misunderstood community. But in the poems about the modern navy we are never shown sailors drunk, swearing, fighting, or "goin' large a bit".[17] Tommy Atkins needed to be kept under tight control. Even in his army environment he was not quite to be trusted, for "single men in barricks don't grow into plaster saints."[18] But for Kipling's sailors discipline is a willingly-accepted rule of their job. Living under "Poseidon's Law", they must never "act or tell a falsehood" at his "shrine"; such behaviour is to be saved for when they are on shore mixing with civilians whose morality is markedly inferior to theirs.[19] In the historical poem sailors are allowed to act in a suitably rowdy manner, but for Kipling the modern naval man had become too indispensable in a dangerous world for him to be regarded with anything but intense seriousness: he is at one with the modern technology that will, if necessary, be Britain's salvation. It is for this reason that in many of these poems the ships, rather than the sailors, are the focal point of Kipling's attention. The Royal Navy responded enthusiastically to *The Seven Seas* and adopted Kipling as its unofficial representative in much the same way as the British Army had done four years earlier on the publication of *Barrack-Room Ballads*. In 1897 and again the following year he was invited to take part in naval manoeuvres with the Channel Fleet. He was deeply moved by both the ships and the men. "Cruisers are wondrous human," he announced in *A Fleet in Being* (1898), and of the Navy's modern weapon-systems:

> When you have been shown lovingly over a torpedo by an artificer skilled in the working of its tricky bowels, torpedoes have a meaning and a reality for you to the end of your days.[20]

Here was the perfect union of man and machine, the modern technological continuation of Britain's ancient dependence on the sea for protection from invasion and occupation, and, most impressively of all, the new men were up to the job as their forefathers had been. "We had a common tradition, one thousand years old, of the things one takes for granted," Kipling wrote after one of his visits to the Fleet. "And a foreigner would never have understood – will never understand!"[21]

Kipling's most memorable sea poems, however, have little direct connection with the Royal Navy, though everything to do with Britain's sea-going traditions. Taking Revelation 21:1 as his text ("and the sea is no more"), Kipling launches into "The Last Chantey" with an imaginative verve that places it high among the many rollicking celebratory ballads of life at sea. The first response of the "jolly mariners" when God seeks their advice on whether He should "gather up the sea" is to remember the hardships they have endured and say, yes "God may sink the sea!" But one by one the shades of the people through the centuries who have depended on the sea, call for it to be preserved: Judas, cooling on the ice floe granted to him once a year, St Paul undertaking his perilous journeys in order to spread the Gospel, slaves who were flung overboard, gentlemen-adventurers and whale-fishers – all urge the mariners to hold to the traditions of the sea. This the mariners do, rejecting the heavenly alternative offered by God:

> Must we sing for evermore
> On the windless, glassy floor?
> Take back your golden fiddles and we'll beat to open sea!

"McAndrew's Hymn" and "The 'Mary Gloster'" are also celebratory sea poems, though of a very different kind from "The Last Chantey". Both are dramatic monologues, and the closest Kipling came to following the model for such poems established by Robert Browning. They are quite distinct from the Browning parodies and pastiches he had previously written, and also unlike the music-hall types he was still using for some of the barrack-room ballads. Complex character analysis and psychological subtlety are not qualities usually associated with Kipling's poetry, and even here in "McAndrew's Hymn" and "The 'Mary Gloster'", both clearly poems of character, the experiences and opinions of the speakers are more obviously imbued with Kipling's own views than they would be in a comparable Browning monologue.

Both speakers are blunt, frank, down-to-earth. McAndrew is a ship's engineer, content with his job since a visionary experience at sea prompted him to shed his repressive Calvinist upbringing and adopt as his replacement "Institutio" a religion of the steam-engine. As published originally in *Scribner's Magazine*, December 1894, the monologue was introduced by a fictitious "extract from a private letter" which makes it clear that McAndrew is on deck reminiscing to a passenger: this setting is not apparent from the poem as printed in *The Seven Seas*. The passenger says that McAndrew admitted to being made "quite poetical at times" by the engines, something that is perfectly clear from the poem itself, but he also describes McAndrew as "a pious old bird". The poem leaves open just how "pious" McAndrew is: there are hints that he is priggish, given to the sin of pride, and not as free from Calvinist morality as he likes to claim. It is this note of ambiguity about how much reliability the reader can place on McAndrew's insight into himself that reveals the influence of Browning, and perhaps too that of Burns's "Holy Willie's Prayer".[22]

Gloster's character is more straightforwardly observed than McAndrew's. He is a successful ship-owner, a self-made man; wealthy, honoured, "not least of our merchant-princes". He is also coarse and mean-minded, whereas McAndrew is genuinely sensitive, if rather smug. Yet the social distance between the two men, and the contrasting moral qualities they possess, are nothing to what unites them. They are devoted to the sea and the hard life it demands from those who live by it; they are widowers and talk openly, though not boastfully, about other women they have had; both are given to grand romantic gestures; and both regard as unbearably effete any way of life other than their own. McAndrew is scathing about a visitor to the ship, "Wi' Russia-leather tennis-shoon an' spar-decked yachtin'-cap," who is unable to see that McAndrew, "manholin', on my back – the cranks three inches off my nose", represents the true romance of the sea. Gloster's verbal attack on his son makes a similar point, though, true to his harder character, it is more vicious and it also gives Kipling yet another chance to mock the Aesthetes:

> The things I knew was proper you wouldn't thank me to give,
> And the things I knew was rotten you said was the way to live.

For you muddled with books and pictures, an' china an' etchin's an' fans,
And your rooms at college was beastly – more like a whore's than a man's.

In Browning, these sentiments and the tone in which they are expressed would destroy any credibility claimed by the speaker whereas Kipling enlists them as allies in his campaign on behalf of manliness. Nor does McAndrew's greater sensitivity exclude him from being similarly placed. Like Sir Anthony Gloster, the most important thing about him is that he is a true man.

These two poems have always attracted admirers, among them T.S. Eliot, who was drawn to Kipling's experimental use of "the poetry of steam" in "McAndrew's Hymn".[23] An experiment it certainly is, but a very self-conscious one. McAndrew's references to "coupler-flanges", "spindle-guides", "furnace-bars", and "connectin'-rods", function within the poem more as appropriate atmosphere than realised images. The uninitiated reader may be convinced that a "spindle-guide" is important to McAndrew, but has no way of knowing why it is so significant – beyond its obvious general application to engineering – or indeed any way of understanding from the poem what exactly it is. Kipling's fascination with specialist terminology of many kinds makes this a recurrent difficulty in his poetry. He had already faced, and largely overcome, his readers' ignorance of the army slang of *Barrack-Room Ballads* by assimilating its meaning within convincingly-presented character sketches and dramatised situations. Naval terminology proved more intractable, not least because much of it was passing into history as Kipling was writing the poems.[24] There are no such problems with "Sestina of the Tramp-Royal", the poem with which Kipling closed the first half of *The Seven Seas*. Primarily an exercise in a notoriously difficult verse form, it is Kipling in his rambling, happy-go-lucky, "Gawd bless this world!" vein, and gives no

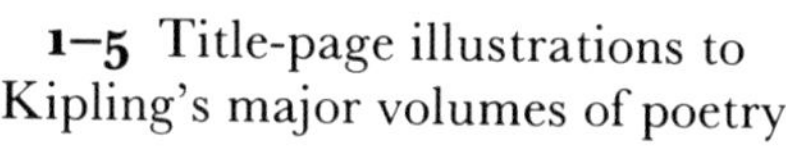

1–5 Title-page illustrations to Kipling's major volumes of poetry

Pagett, M P
(*Departmental Ditties*, see p. 23)
Bugler
(*Barrack-Room Ballads*, see p. 89)
Helmsman
(*The Seven Seas*, see p. 89)
Horseman
(*The Five Nations*, see p. 138)
Soldier
(*The Years Between*, see p. 192)

6 Recruiting Sergeants, from *Street Life in London* by J Thompson and A Smith, 1877 (see p. 58)

"And there was no more sea."

The Last Chanty.

THUS said the Lord in the Vault above the Cherubim,
Calling to the Angels and the Souls in their degree:—
"Lo! Earth has passed away
On the smoke of Judgment Day,
That Our Word may be established shall we gather up the Sea?"

Loud sang the souls of the jolly, jolly Mariners:—
"Plague upon the hurricanes that made us furl and flee!
But the war is done between us,
In the deep the Lord hath seen us—
Our bones we'll leave the barracout'; and God may sink the Sea!"

Then said the soul of Judas that betrayèd Him:—
"Lord, hast Thou forgotten Thy covenant with me?
How once a year I go
To cool me on the floe,
And Ye take my Day of Mercy if Ye take away the Sea!"

7 "The Last Chanty", from *Pall Mall Magazine*, 15 June 1893, illustrated by Laurence Housman (see p. 107)

SCRIBNER'S MAGAZINE

VOL. XVI DECEMBER 1894 No. 6

McANDREWS' HYMN

By Rudyard Kipling

ILLUSTRATIONS BY HOWARD PYLE

. . . and the night we got in, sat up from twelve to four with the Chief Engineer who could not get to sleep either. . . said that the engines made him feel quite poetical at times, and told me things about his past life He seems a pious old bird ; but I wish I had known him earlier in the voyage.

—Extract from private letter.

8 Title page to "McAndrew's Hymn" in *Scribner's Magazine* (see p. 108)

9 "The Editors at Work", frontispiece to Julian Ralph's *War's Brighter Side: left to right* H A Gwynne, Julian Ralph, Perceval Landon, Rudyard Kipling (see pp. 133–4)

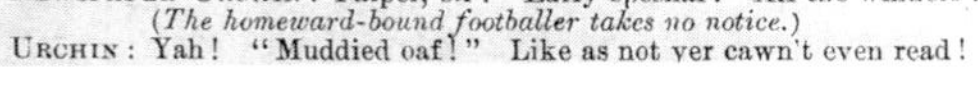

11 "A little Kipling is a dangerous thing": cartoon from *Windsor Magazine* April 1902 (see pp. 141–2)

10 "A gentleman in kharki", by R Caton Woodville, for "The Absent-Minded Beggar" (see p. 130)

The HOLY WAR by Rudyard Kipling

FOR here lay the excellent wisdom of him that built Mansoul, that the walls could never be broken down nor hurt by the most mighty adverse potentate unless the townsmen gave consent thereto.

BUNYAN'S *Holy War.*

A tinker out of Bedford,
A vagrant oft in quod,
A private under Fairfax,
A minister of God,
Two hundred years and thirty
Ere Armageddon came
His single hand portrayed it,
And Bunyan was his name!

He mapped, for those who follow,
The world in which we are—
"This famous town of Mansoul"
That takes the Holy War.
Her true and traitor people,
The gates along her wall,
From Eye Gate unto Feel Gate,
John Bunyan showed them all.

All enemy divisions,
Recruits of every class,
And highly-screened positions
For flame or poison-gas;
The craft that we call modern,
The crimes that we call new,
John Bunyan had 'em typed and filed
In Sixteen Eighty-two.

Likewise the Lords of Looseness
That hamper faith and works,
The Perseverance-Doubters,
The Present-Comfort Shirks,
And brittle intellectuals
Who crack beneath a strain—
John Bunyan met that helpful set
In Charles the Second's reign.

Emmanuel's vanguard dying
For right and not for rights,
My Lord Apollyon lying
To the Stall-fed Stockholmites,
The Pope, the swithering Neutrals,
The Kaiser and his Gott—
Their rôles, their goals, their naked souls—
He knew and drew the lot.

Now he hath left his quarters,
In Bunhill Fields to lie,
The wisdom that he taught us
Is proven prophecy:
One watch-word through our armies,
One answer from our lands:—
"No dealings with Diabolus
As long as Mansoul stands!"

A pedlar from a hovel,
The lowest of the low,
The father of the Novel,
Salvation's first Defoe,
Eight blinded generations
Ere Armageddon came,
He showed us how to meet it,
And Bunyan was his name!

12 "The Holy War", *Land & Water*, 6 December 1917 (see pp. 204–6)

GERMANY SAYS "YES"

OVERWHELMING VICTORY FOR HERR HITLER

QUEUES LINE UP TO VOTE IN BERLIN

PRESIDENT'S APPEAL FOR "PEACE, HONOUR AND EQUALITY"

Germany went to the polls yesterday on two issues. In the first place, a referendum was taken on the policy of the Nazi Government; and, in the second, a vote was taken on the election of the 685 Reichstag candidates, sponsored by Herr Hitler, *en masse*.

In the early hours of this morning it was obvious that Herr Hitler had obtained, as expected, an overwhelming victory. The final provisional figures were as follows, states Reuter.

REFERENDUM: Total votes, 43,464,420. For the Government, 40,618,147, or 93.4 per cent.

REICHSTAG ELECTION: Total votes, 43,007,577. For the Nazi candidates, 39,655,288, or 92 per cent.

In the elections for the Reichstag just dissolved the number of citizens entitled to vote was 44,685,764.

HERR HITLER speaking at Munich at the conclusion of his electioneering tour.

"Arrested" Trawler Vanishes

NAVAL OFFICER AND MEN ON BOARD

Lost in the Fog

GUNBOATS IN PURSUIT

A story of a trawler which is alleged to have made a dash for the open sea after having been ordered to port by a fishery cruiser was told at Fleetwood early this morning.

Two steam trawlers, one a Fleetwood vessel and the other a French boat, were fishing between the north-west coast of Scotland and Ireland, in what is stated to be prohibited waters.

One vessel was "arrested" by naval authorities, and the other, the Fleetwood boat, it is alleged, made full speed ahead in a bid to escape.

Chase was given by the fishery cruiser Doon, and both ships made off in the direction of Campbeltown, off the Argyllshire coast.

On the way the trawler was overtaken, and a Sub-Lieutenant and two Naval ratings from the Doon were put on board. Orders were given to the Fleetwood skipper to proceed to the nearest port.

It is alleged that instead of this the trawler made South, with the naval officer and ratings still on board. Hot pursuit was at once begun by the fishery cruiser, but fog enveloped the vessels, and they parted company. Another gunboat was summoned by wireless, and both scoured the seas without locating the trawler.

DETECTIVES AT GANGWAY

The Doon berthed at Fleetwood, but before she had been in port long she steamed off again and was lost to sight.

Her brief visit and hurried departure deepened the mystery. In the evening fishermen were surprised to see both the Doon and the Fleetwood trawler steam into port together.

Messages were sent to the relatives of the Fleetwood crew by friends, but when they arrived at the docks they found that both vessels had swung round and were berthed at the Isle of Man landing stage near the harbour entrance, about half a mile away.

When the relatives hurried to this point they were informed both vessels had gone to sea. Two Lancashire County police detectives were stationed at the gangway and no one was allowed on board, though it was seen that an armed naval guard was pacing the deck of the trawler.

After a brief wait telegrams were handed to the naval officer in charge, and on receipt of these orders were immediately given for the trawler to follow the gunboat, it being stated that the destination was Stornoway, a distance of over 200 miles from Fleetwood.

It was reported early this morning from Glasgow that the French trawler had arrived at Stornoway. Her papers had

Bonfires on the Ice

> "Gesture . . . outlook . . . vision . . . avenue . . . example . . . goodwill . . . achievement . . . appeasement . . . limit of risk." *Common Political Form.*

We know the Rocket's upward whizz;
  We know the Boom before the Bust.
We know the whistling Wail which is
  The Stick returning to the Dust.
  We know how much to take on trust
Of any promised Paradise.
  We know the Pie—likewise the Crust.
We know a Bonfire on the Ice.

We know the Mountain and the Mouse.
  We know Great Cry and Little Wool.
We know the purseless Ears of Sows.
  We know the Frog that aped the Bull.
  We know—whatever Trick we pull—
(Ourselves have gambled once or twice)
  A Bob-tail Flush is not a Full.
We know that Bonfire on the Ice.

We know that Ones and Ones make Twos
  (Till Demos votes 'em Three or Nought)
We know the Fenrys Wolf is loose.
  We know what Fight has not been fought.
  We know the Father to the Thought
Which argues Babe and Cockatrice
  Would play together, were they taught.
We know *that* Bonfire on the Ice.

We know that Thriving comes by Thrift.
  We know the Key must keep the Door.
We know his Boot-straps will not lift
  The frightened Waster off the Floor.
  We know these things, and we deplore
That not by any Artifice,
  Can they be altered . . . Furthermore,
We know the Bonfires on the Ice!

RUDYARD KIPLING

"Paul Pry" Joins the Liberal Party

Tetrazzini Sings Her Farewell

LAST ENCORE IN MIDST OF ADMIRERS

Platform Stormed

Madame Tetrazzini has been heard in public (in London, that is) for the last time.

This fact will seem incredible to those who are connoisseurs of the human voice. For them the name Tetrazzini has come to have something of the thrill that for their elders the names of Patti, Lind and Nilsson had, and they will be feeling greatly regretful at this moment of parting with a favourite.

But they at least are fortunate in having heard so rare a voice as this and they will be envied by those who come after to whom Tetrazzini must now perforce be not a reality but a legend.

The Albert Hall was well-filled yesterday for the prima donna's farewell. The programme also included violin solos by Lisa Minghetti, pianoforte solos by Mr. Niedzielski and songs by Mr. Joseph Hislop. The accompanist was Mr. Ivor Newton.

OPERA AND SONGS

It is as an operatic singer that Madame Tetrazzini has become famous, and in her singing of the Mad Scene from Thomas's "Hamlet," she showed once again with what remarkable assurance she uses her voice. The absolute truth of the intonation was not the least notable characteristic of her performance. Not one of all the extraordinary decorative effects with which this aria is so plentifully bedizened was dealt with in any but a masterly fashion.

In the group of songs which came later in the programme, the same astonishing power of vocalisation was present; although she undoubtedly has a technique that is more telling in an operatic aria.

Finally, Madame Tetrazzini sang the aria, "Ah, fors e lui," from "Traviata," the opera in which she made her first appearance at Covent Garden.

Enthusiasm had by now reached a climax. The audience invaded the platform, and Madame Tetrazzini's last encore was sung from among a compact mass of admirers. S. G.

Where the Money Goes

You are a ratepayer.

Even if you are not a property-owner, you may pay rates in addition to rent.

Even if you pay no rates, the fixing of your rent was probably affected by the local rate level.

Therefore you are a ratepayer.

STORM HAVOC IN S. AFRICA

Death-Roll Already Twenty

HAILSTONES LIKE ORANGES

Thousands of Sheep and Cattle Killed

From Our Own Correspondent

JOHANNESBURG, Nov. 12.

At least twenty deaths are recorded in violent storms sweeping the Union following the breaking of the unprecedented drought. In the Rustenburg district of the Transvaal a party of six natives were struck by lightning, and they were instantly killed. Charred bodies of other victims are being found on the veld.

Rivers which were hitherto a small series of pools are now coming down in full flood, trapping many whites and natives, and sweeping them to death. Hail has been particularly heavy, stones the size of small oranges being common. In many cases there has been an "aerial bombardment" of lumps of ice the size of a fist, smashing through corrugated iron, and battering every vestige of vegetable life to pulp.

One storm did damage to the extent of £40,000 to Johannesburg suburban fruit growers, and hailstones killing two natives instantly. In the Lichtenburg district huge jagged hailstones killed thousands of sheep, cattle, and donkeys. One farmer found 80 sheep dead in a huddled heap, and another lost 200 cows and donkeys. The veld was left barren of all life with buck, hares, and birds lying battered to death everywhere.

Natal has been under water for the past forty-eight hours, with the roads almost impassable, the bridges being swept away. Four inches of rain fell in Ladysmith and six inches in Port Shepstone.

HERRING BUYING TO STOP

YARMOUTH CURERS' DECISION

From Our Special Correspondent

GREAT YARMOUTH, Sunday.

The adjourned meeting of the fish curers of Lowestoft and Yarmouth held here last night decided definitely to

13 "Bonfires on the Ice", *Morning Post*, 13 November 1933 (see pp. 236–8)

hint whatsoever of the gravity with which he was now viewing world affairs or of his direct involvement in them.

The changing mood of Kipling's poetry in the second half of the 1890s is typified by two poems, "Hymn before Action" and "Et Dona Ferentes", which were both published in London newspapers in March 1896. He was still living in America, though preparing to return home, and the Venezuelan crisis that had turned America into a "hostile country" was an important factor in the prophetic tone and increasing pugnaciousness of his poetry. Kipling realised that if a war with America should break out then it would be fought primarily at sea and across the Canadian border. That would be bad enough, but America wasn't the principal danger. More worrying was Kipling's conviction that in any Anglo-American conflict Germany would side with America, certainly foment discontent in British colonies, and probably take the opportunity to wage war in Europe. Such fears were not peculiar to Kipling. In South Africa, at the close of the previous year, there had been a desperate attempt, led by Dr L.S. Jameson and backed by Cecil Rhodes, the premier of Cape Colony, to overthrow the Boer government of the Transvaal and reassert British influence. Although the "Jameson Raid" as it became known was a humiliating failure, the international repercussions it caused were potentially grave. Following Jameson's surrender, the German Emperor sent a telegram of congratulations to Paul Kruger, the President of the Transvaal, making it clear that Germany supported Boer independence against attacks by outside Powers, a move that was generally taken to indicate the open adoption by Germany of a more aggressive anti-British foreign policy. The hopes that Kipling had held only two years earlier of the American people growing to sympathise with, and even perhaps support, the British Empire, now seemed totally misguided. Canada and South Africa were under threat; an alliance between America and Germany was a possibility; and if that happened the British Empire could soon be at war in North America, South Africa, and Europe. It would be a repeat of the situation a century earlier when, following the loss of the American colonies, Britain had been committed to a world-wide imperial war with Napoleon's France.

The opening stanza of "Hymn before Action" is a clear expression of Kipling's mood early in 1896:

> The earth is full of anger,
> The seas are dark with wrath,
> The Nations in their harness
> Go up against our path:
> Ere yet we loose the legions –
> Ere yet we draw the blade,
> Jehovah of the Thunders,
> Lord God of Battles, aid!

It is Britain who is threatened, "our path" that is being hindered by other nations armed ready for battle, though if necessary Britain's "legions" can be "loosed", the "blade" drawn from the scabbard. The appeal to Jehovah – and, later in the poem, to the Madonna – is, however, not to aid in battle, but for intercession to avert a war. The part that British pride may have played in the crisis is acknowledged, and a special plea is made for the non-Christian peoples of the Empire:

> For those who kneel beside us
> At altars not Thine own,
> Who lack the lights that guide us,
> Lord, let their faith atone!

If Britain has been wrong to "call" these peoples, then Britain must take the blame.

The decision to write this poem in the form of a hymn was obviously made with care. It was based on a popular Church of

England hymn, "The Church's One Foundation", composed in 1866 to assert Anglican unity in the face of Bishop Colenso's controversial challenge to the historical authenticity of some parts of the Bible. "The Church's One Foundation" had a stirring tune, "Aurelia", and as recently as 1885 had been adapted to serve as a processional hymn in Salisbury Cathedral.[25] In making his appeal to the "Lord God of Battles" Kipling was therefore able to use rhythms that were already familiar to many of his readers and a tune that was associated with a call for Anglican unity to defeat debilitating schism. His original title for the poem was "A Little Sermon" and that too has a wider relevance, for Kipling's prophetic tone was becoming increasingly indistinguishable from that of a preacher. Kipling's religious views, expressed throughout his life, were exceptionally broad-minded and tolerant: freedom for all peoples to worship their own Gods was one of his inviolable beliefs.[26] He was no missionary, at least as far as religion was concerned. In the lines just quoted from "A Hymn before Action", non-Christian members of the Empire may "lack the lights that guide us", but a truly Christian God is expected to recognise that they possess their own valid faith. Yet in poems like this (and the earlier "Song of the English") Kipling's use of religious language seems to have little theological or doctrinal meaning: rather, it serves to establish an appropriately solemn tone and a set of values that is crucial to the maintenance of "the Law". When Kipling addresses the British people in this way, he is not calling on them to be more religious, but to be true civilising imperialists. That involves, centrally, the application of Christian principles and the exercise of religious tolerance. It also implies that if God is not quite an Englishman or an Anglican, he is at least on England's side, as long as the English follow *His* will: there is also more than a hint that, in this matter, Kipling is God's Prophet.

Although "Et Dona Ferentes" is a response to the same

international crisis as "Hymn before Action", there is nothing remotely hymnal about it. The title (which means literally "even bearing gifts") is an allusion to the wooden horse episode in Virgil's *Aeneid*. The Trojan leaders are so delighted to see the Greeks depart that they are eager to accept the wooden horse as a peace-offering, but Laöcoon warns them that the Greeks are always treacherous: "Trojans, never trust that horse. Whatever it proves to be, I still fear Greeks, even when they offer gifts."[27] In Kipling's poem, the English replace the Greeks: they are not exactly treacherous, but their outward appearance is deceptive, and, Kipling warns, foreigners who accept the English surface as the real thing are set for trouble. "Et Dona Ferentes" is Kipling's crudest contribution to the national stereotype of the Englishman as strong, silent, slow to act but deadly when forced to do so. He is languidly elegant and, for the purposes of this poem, polite: "but oh, beware my Country, when my Country grows polite." The central action of the poem which is intended to demonstrate the superiority of the English character over that of all foreigners – the whole "pentecostal crew" – is a brawl in a casino. The English calmly accept the insults thrown at them, responding with exaggerated politeness "till some idiot went too far": they then smash up the casino and the foreigners, as, presumably, the Greeks emerged from the silence of the wooden horse to massacre the Trojans. The message of the poem is, however, better summed up by the chorus of a music-hall song written by G. W. Hunt in 1877 to express Britain's willingness to go to war with Russia, which introduced the term "jingoism" into the language:

> We don't want to fight, but by Jingo if we do,
> We've got the ships, we've got the men, and got the money too.[28]

Kipling was now the unchallenged, and unofficial, Poet Laureate of the Empire, pronouncing on international affairs on behalf of the British people, if not the government. When a preferential tariff treaty was signed between Britain and Canada in 1897, he celebrated the event with a poem, "Our Lady of the Snows", in which he not only praised Canadians for going their own way "soberly under the White Man's law", but mocked the objections of other countries as "Gentiles' clamour". Four years later, when the six Australian colonies were united into one commonwealth, he wrote a similar celebratory poem "The Young Queen". A Kipling poem was expected on any important public occasion that involved the Empire or national prestige, and never more so than on the celebrations that marked Queen Victoria's Diamond Jubilee on 21 and 22 June 1897. He was urged by *The Times* to write a special Jubilee poem, and began to do so, but then put the uncompleted draft aside, and spent a fortnight on naval manoeuvres before finishing the poem. "Recessional" (originally called "After") was published in *The Times*, together with an approving editorial, on 17 July. To Kipling's admirers and detractors alike the poem was a surprise. It was not loftily condescending, in the manner of "Our Lady of the Snows", or pugnaciously vulgar, like "Et Dona Ferentes": instead, it took up the solemn strain of "Hymn before Action" and, dropping the veiled threat that that poem contained, called for national humility and responsibility to counterbalance the imperial pomp of the formal Jubilee celebrations. Why exactly Kipling was so long delayed in completing the poem is not known. Carrington points out that Kipling was unhappy with the early draft and also that he always resented any suggestion that his public poems were written to order.[29] Both factors are clearly pertinent. In addition, he may have been temporarily embarrassed by the jingoistic mood in Britain to which he himself in poems throughout the 1890s had substantially contributed. Many years later he described "Recessional" as being "in the nature of a *nuzzur-wattu* (an averter of the Evil Eye)".[30] This is neatly applicable to the poem's central message that if Britain becomes "drunk with sight of power" then the Empire will end up at "one with Nineveh and Tyre", but there is little reason to believe that Kipling himself was at this time the possessor of "an humble and a contrite heart". On 24 June he visited Spithead to see the Jubilee Naval Review and marvelled at the power it represented. "Yesterday I got a chance to see the fleet and went off at once," he wrote to a friend. "Never dreamed that there was anything like it under Heaven. It was beyond words – beyond any description!"[31]

"Recessional" is virtually a compilation of Biblical allusions, quotations, and echoes. Like "The Song of the English", it is based on the assumption that God has made a special covenant with England, but whereas the earlier poem had centred on the forging of the covenant, "Recessional" points to its possible collapse. The principal text, from which Kipling took the refrain of his poem ("Lest we forget – lest we forget!") is Deuteronomy, 6:12: "Then beware lest thou forget the Lord, which brought thee forth out of the land of Egypt." One of the biblical allusions in particular has been the subject of much controversy. Kipling warns of "Wild tongues that have not Thee in awe", a reference, presumably, to triumphalism within Britain, indulging in:

> Such boastings as the Gentiles use,
>   Or lesser breeds without the Law –

The relevant Biblical text is Romans, 2:12–15 where Paul warns: "For as many as have sinned without law shall also perish without law." The "Gentiles" and the "lesser breeds" are, in this context, those people who "have no law" and therefore become "a law unto themselves". Paul acknowledges that such people may have a natural inclination to the law, but God's judgement of them will depend on their actions, whether they "shew the work of the law written in their hearts". As we have just seen, Kipling had recently made a similar reference to "the Gentiles" in "Our Lady of the Snows". In both cases it is likely that he had the Germans primarily in mind, though in "Recessional" he is surely also referring to non-white races. Both are outside the Law, though in different ways. The Germans have turned their backs on it deliberately: the non-white races have still to be shown the benefits of living within the law.

The obliquity of this Biblical allusion and the general humility of "Recessional" are best seen as an indication at this particular moment of Kipling's uncertainty about who exactly could be regarded justifiably as "within" or "without" the law: the evidence of "Recessional" suggests that even England is in danger of losing God's favour. Kipling's concern about international relations and the possible isolation of the Empire reflects the wider frantic diplomatic activity and treaty realignments taking place at the close of the century between the major European countries and the emerging powers, especially America and Japan. The imperial poems published shortly after "Recessional" either celebrate, in a highly patronising manner, the work being done by the Empire in spreading the Law to non-white races ("Pharaoh and the Sergeant" and "Kitchener's School"), or they call for a more solid alliance between the white Dominions to prepare for possibile hostility from the rest of the world. Already in "Et Dona Ferentes" Kipling had presented his symbolic casino brawl as being between two halves of the world, with "the men of half Creation damning half Creation's eyes". Now in his little-known poem "The Houses", first published in the *Navy League Journal*, 28 July 1898, he repeated his conviction that the world was split into two halves, with Britain and the white Dominions defending civilisation against the barbaric threat of the rest:

> By my house and thy house hangs all the world's fate,
> On thy house and my house lies half the world's hate.

For my house and thy house no help shall we find
Save thy house and my house – kin cleaving to kind.

The mood of embattled isolation expressed in this poem, and in others of the time, did not, however, last long. For Kipling at least, it was dispelled in the most sudden, unexpected and spectacular way.

On 25 April 1898, after several months of naval skirmishes, a bloodthirsty press campaign and bitter internal debates between expansionists and non-expansionists, America declared war on Spain. Naval and military activity centred on the Spanish colonies. The war lasted until August and ended with America the decisive victors. Under the Treaty of Paris, drawn up in December, Cuba, Puerto Rico, Guam and the Philippines were ceded to America, and added to Hawaii which the Americans had already annexed. Virtually overnight, the country that had once been a British colony and had developed into one of the British Empire's harshest critics, the country that only a few years earlier was threatening war with Britain over an imperial boundary dispute, had itself become an imperial power, taking over colonies from another country, and committing itself to expansion in the Pacific. Kipling was thrilled. "Haven't your views on matters imperial changed in the last few months?" he asked an American correspondent. "I sit here and chuckle as I read the papers over the water. The land seems to be taking kindly to the White Man's Work."[32] He pursued the theme exultantly in letters to other American friends, calling upon them to support "the White Man's work, the business of introducing a sane and orderly administration to the dark places of the earth that lie to your hand."[33] To Theodore Roosevelt, who was soon to become President of the United States, he insisted that having "stuck a pickaxe into the foundations of a rotten house" American was "morally bound to build the house over again from the foundations."[34] While a divided America was examining its own conscience on these matters, in September 1898 an Anglo-Egyptian army under Kitchener's command crushed Khalifa Abdullah's dervishes at Omdurman, reoccupied the Sudan, and to public rejoicing in Britain, avenged the death of General Gordon thirteen years earlier. The following month Kipling published another of his oblique political ballads in *The Times*, "The Truce of the Bear", urging that friendly overtures by the Czar of Russia should be ignored, for there could be "no truce with Adam-zad, the Bear that looks like a Man!" Clearly "the white man" was in the ascendant, and it was by no means simply the non-whites who were being excluded. The Russians did not qualify for admission to the Anglo-American Club, nor did the Boers, Germans or Spanish. Most of the Irish were suspect, while the French – always deeply admired by Kipling – were allowed honorary membership, as long as they did not return to their ancient imperial rivalry with Britain. It was in this excited, civilising and missionary mood that on 4 February 1899 Kipling publishing in *The Times*, and on the following day in several American newspapers, what would come to be regarded as his most infamous poem which pulled together and advanced as a clear statement his thinking as it had developed over the whole decade.

"The White Man's Burden" was first subtitled "An Address to America", though this was later changed to the more descriptive "The United States and the Philippine Islands". In it the imperial process is advanced as a lofty, self-denying mission, a "burden". It demands of America "the best ye breed" who are to "bind" themselves "to exile" so that they can serve their "captives' needs". They must suppress feelings of "pride", develop "patience", and "veil the threat of terror" in order:

> To seek another's profit
> And work another's gain.

In return they can expect ingratitude, hatred, sloth, and "heathen Folly". Like Moses leading the Jews out of Egypt (Exodus 16: 2–3; stanza 5), they will be told that the slow path to "the light" is too arduous to bear, and that all the "hosts" they "humour" really desire is an easy return to their "loved Egyptian night". However discouraged, the Americans must persevere, not for their own glory, but for the good of the conquered peoples:

> Take up the White Man's burden –
> The savage wars of peace –
> Fill full the mouth of Famine
> And bid the sickness cease.

Whatever the avowed justification, there can be no doubt that the poem is profoundly racist in sentiment. The "white man" may be a civilising force rather than someone who is simply white, but the "captives" have no choice, no alternative way of life that is worth considering. They are "fluttered folk and wild", "sullen peoples", "half devil and half child". It is precisely the transformation of these qualities that constitutes the "burden" of the white man, and in coming to realise this America enters its period of destiny. *Their* "childish days" are now behind them; no longer can they stand aside from the rest of the world; their "manhood" is about to be tested; they must present themselves for the "judgement" of their "peers". The poem represents Kipling at his highest point of imperial faith and confidence. Immediately, however, it was not America, but Britain and Kipling that were to be tested, and the judgement of their peers was not to prove favourable.

[5]
A White Man's War

Towns without people, ten times took,
  An' ten times left an' burned at last;
An' starvin' dogs that come to look
  For owners when a column passed.

"The Return", *The Five Nations*

Kipling first visited South Africa in September 1891 en route to Australia and New Zealand. At Cape Town he was welcomed as a celebrity, and with his reputation as the chronicler of Anglo-India in mind, the *Cape Argus* expressed the hope that "at some future day we may have the pleasure of hearing what he thinks of the Karroo . . . Kimberley's big diamond-hole and the Rand."[1] He was impressed by the country, describing it as "a most fascinating place" with "unlimited future possibilities"; but, considering how large a part it was to play in his life, his initial response was surprisingly reserved.[2] In "The Song of the Cities" (1893) he acknowledged the strategic importance of Cape Town in the world-wide chain of imperial cities linked together by the Royal Navy, and, also, the "dream" it represented "of Empire to the northward", though the major harbours and staging-posts of India, Australia, Canada, and New Zealand, were all given more prominence. In the mid-1890s, the only poem in which South Africa featured centrally was

"Hymn before Action" which, as we have seen, was prompted in part by the Jameson Raid.

Even his second visit in January 1898 was not undertaken with any avowed purpose more immediate than a family holiday. "We are all off to South Africa," he told his American friend James Conland, "to play about in the sunshine of Cape Town until April . . . It will be a rest for the wife: and Cape Town is the paradise for children. Little Josephine faces the prospect with great calm and serenity. She tells me that the best way of studying geography is 'to go about in ships, Father, till you have seen them all' and frankly I am somewhat of her way of thinking."[3] By this time, however, he was a much bigger celebrity, renowned as the imperial prophet of *The Seven Seas*, and his acquaintances included two of the most important spokesmen for British expansion in South Africa – Sir Alfred Milner, the British High Commissioner and one of the main architects of the Boer War; and Cecil Rhodes, who had been forced to resign as Chairman of the British South Africa Company and as Prime Minister of Cape Colony because of his involvement in the Jameson Raid, and was now dedicated to the creation of the country to the north of South Africa that would bear his name. When Kipling wrote again to James Conland in April 1898, on the point of returning to England, he was still referring to the trip as a family holiday, but the "Royal Time – the best of good times" he described himself as having had, focused on visits to the Kimberley diamond mines, Matabeleland, and Bulawayo ("a town of 5,000 white men. They treated me like a prince"). In Johannesburg, the capital of the Transvaal, he noted proudly "they gave me a banquet," and added: "but the white man there is a slave to the Boer; and the state of things turned me sick. They are without votes: and forbidden to carry arms."[4]

The "white men" Kipling refers to were the "Uitlanders", immigrants mainly from Britain or the British South African colonies of Cape Colony and Natal, though including a substantial number of Americans as well, who had been drawn to the Transvaal by the discovery of gold. Although heavily taxed, they were allowed no political and few civic rights, and their persecution by the Boers was to be advanced as a major cause of the war between Britain and the Boer Republics that began in October 1899. The plight of the Uitlanders was in itself the kind of cause that Kipling might well have felt persuaded to take up, but he saw the resolution of this particular issue as part of a more comprehensive settlement. In "The Song of the Cities" the importance of Cape Town to the Empire had been recognised instinctively, almost off-handedly. Now, his larger experience of South Africa revealed to him how sure those early instincts had been. No longer was Cape Town just one among many imperial cities. Like Milner and Rhodes, he had come to regard it as a crucial point of connection between Britain's Indian Empire in the East and the white dominions in both the Northern and Southern hemispheres, while the inspirational example of Rhodes especially had given Kipling a greater awareness of the advantages to the Empire of further expansion into Africa. If the work, already well under way, of such commercial and territorial ventures as Rhodes's British South Africa Company and Sir William Mackinnon's British East Africa Company, was successful, then it was possible to foresee a time when Britain would control the entire eastern half of Africa, from the Cape to the Mediterranean. South Africa would be connected with "British" Sudan and Egypt, and the two major sea routes to India – via the Suez Canal and the Cape – firmly secured. Crucial to all such dreams – and through the creation of Rhodesia, Kenya, and Uganda, they did become something of a reality – was a stable South Africa, sharing British ideals and aspirations, and becoming eventually, together with Canada, Australia, and New Zealand, a self-governing white dominion, allied to Britain by family ties and a common political purpose. On these "five nations" rested the future of the British Empire, and, therefore, the greater part of the civilised world.

Kipling's interest in South Africa was not entirely political: personal factors were also involved. The romantic in him responded strongly to the physical beauty of the country, its topographical and climatic variety, colours, size, and its agricultural and mineral wealth. In many respects it supplanted India, a country he had not visited for almost a decade, in his imagination. Important as India was, Kipling realised that it could not be held for ever within the Empire. India was itself an empire, a complex ancient structure of competing religious and social values to which the British could contribute, and, to some extent administer, but never totally permeate or control. By contrast, South Africa was a new country, long though sparsely settled by Europeans, mainly the British, and the Dutch, who felt so much at home that they were known as "Afrikaners" (the people of Africa) or simply "Boers" (farmers). It was open country, settlers' country, fertile, healthy, with great opportunities for hardworking immigrants. As America was so much on Kipling's mind at this time, it is likely that he saw in South Africa a possible repetition of the loss of the American colonies more than a century earlier. Once again, Britain was not giving sufficient support to its own people and not taking advantage of the sacrifices it had already made to maintain the long-established British presence. Kipling always believed that the American colonies were lost because the rebels had waited to act until Britain had successfully seen off the rival colonising ambitions of France and Spain. That situation also looked as though it could be repeated in South Africa. The only serious military threat from the indigenous black population had been settled in the Zulu Wars of the late 1870s, but these campaigns failed to lead to a consolidation of Britain's position in South Africa; instead, it was the Boers who seized the advantage, inflicting defeats on the British Army at Laing's Neck in 1880 and Majuba Hill the following year, thus further increasing their independence from the British Crown. By early 1898 when Kipling was "turned sick" by the Boers' treatment of the Uitlanders in the Transvaal, it was clear to most insiders that another Boer War was virtually inevitable; that there were British representatives in South Africa (Milner and Rhodes among them) who were working actively for such a war; and, that unlike most colonial conflicts this would be, in the phrase commonly used at the time, a "white man's war", or, as Kipling reworked the phrase to serve as the title of one of the best of his South African stories, a "Sahibs' War".[5]

Shortly after his return to England in April 1898, Kipling was invited by Rider Haggard to address the Anglo-African Writers' Club of which Haggard was a founder-member. In an effusive introduction Haggard described Kipling as a "true watchman of our Empire", someone who, like Haggard himself, believed in the "divine right of a great civilising people", and he defined the role that writers of Kipling's quality could play in the process: "They it is who, having the golden gift of words, embody in fitting language the aspirations of thousands, and awake and encourage in them the love of country." In reply, Kipling spoke of his recent experiences in South Africa. He condemned the "unprogressive" Boers who were not concerned with spreading civilisation and improving the material conditions of the people, insisted that there was room for all in South Africa, and urged patience rather than an assertion of British "rights by force". Military action could only be justified if the Boers "rise up and give trouble".[6] It was a firm, calm, and conciliatory response, though not for the first time his admirers succeeded in making him seem more militaristic than he actually was. As Morton Cohen has pointed out, when Kipling's speech was reported in the *African Review*, it was accompanied by an anonymous, Kiplingesque poem called "A

Humble Tribute" which offered a different interpretation of his words:

> "Then I listened to yer speakin' (I was 'id behind the screen),
> An' I said, 'Well, this 'ere Kiplin', 'e's a *man*, an' no mistake';
> An' I said, 'Oh—this waitin', chuck it, let's go out an' fight,
> I should like to punch some fellow's 'ead for good old England's sake!' "[7]

Punching "some fellow's 'ead for good old England's sake" without genuine justification was hardly a policy that Kipling would have endorsed. The theoretical justification of the "White Man's Burden", with which he was currently preoccupied, was precisely that it should be taken up not for self-aggrandisement but for the sake of others. This was what rendered it morally acceptable. In *A Fleet in Being* (1898) Kipling marvelled at the potential destructive power of the Royal Navy and confessed himself astounded, and proud, that it was being employed with such moderation: "Any other breed with this engine at their disposal would have used it savagely long ago."[8]

In January 1899 Kipling, together with his wife and their three children, journeyed to New York. They had been planning to spend the winter months in South Africa, but finally decided instead to go to America to settle outstanding family and publishing business. Their arrival in New York coincided with the publication of "The White Man's Burden". At their hotel, Kipling and his daughter Josephine were taken ill with pneumonia. Kipling slowly recovered: Josephine died on 6 March. The family stayed in America until June when they returned to England. Three years earlier Kipling had felt himself driven out of America by anti-British sentiments. Now, just as it seemed that America might be becoming more sympathetic to his imperialist views, he was driven away again, and this time for good, by the painful associations the country would always have with the death of his daughter.

These harrowing personal events meant that Kipling was not involved in South African affairs as Britain and the Boer Republics manoeuvred themselves into irreconcilable positions in the first half of 1899. His campaign against the Boers did not open until 29 September when he published in *The Times* a poem called "The Old Issue". Its immediate context was the accelerating mobilisation of troops in South Africa and the decision by the British government to send reinforcements, though when the poem was later collected in *The Five Nations* Kipling added to its title the date 9 October 1899, making it refer to Kruger's final ultimatum to Britain: he also, at this point, substantially extended the poem, framing it with new opening and closing lines. "The Old Issue" is written in an elliptical, ponderous style, and Charles Carrington has described it as the type of Kipling poem that "to a modern reader, steeped in the propaganda of the anti-imperialists . . . has become almost unintelligible."[9] That is true enough, though there must have been quite a few of its original readers who would have been just as confused if *The Times* had not printed it alongside an editorial which pointed out that the Boers had "sought safety in the discredited devices of despotism, resisted and overthrown by our fathers at home centuries ago, as Mr Rudyard Kipling bids the world mark, in the spirited poem we publish this morning." The poem itself contains no direct references to the Boers or South Africa. As revised for *The Five Nations*, it is even more obscure. The trumpet fanfare that introduces the poem, and, allusively, two of England's ill-fated monarchs – King John and Charles I – suggests that a rather stagey pageant is to follow, with just one line ("Trumpets at the gang-plank where the brawling troop-decks fill!") invoking a contemporary atmosphere. It is only when the historical setting is established and the verse form changes to epigrammatic couplets that the meaning of the poem is allowed to emerge:

Over all things certain, this is sure indeed,
Suffer not the old King: for we know the breed.

The "old issue" is the monarchical tyranny that the English people once suffered from, struggled long against, and eventually overthrew, replacing it by freedom for the individual and allegiance to a new kind of monarch, who "is one with us, first among his peers". In this cryptic manner Kipling announced to the British people that the war about to be fought was in the cause of ancient English liberties and that the principal opponent was Paul Kruger, a false "King".[10]

While "The Old Issue" laid Kipling open to the justifiable charge of obscurantism, his next poetic contribution to the war effort was unashamedly to the point and comprehensible to anyone who cared to listen. Approached by the *Daily Mail* to support a fund to raise money for the dependants of soldiers serving in South Africa, he replied with "The Absent-Minded Beggar" which the *Mail* published on 31 October. It was the kind of occasion Kipling relished. He was speaking on behalf of ordinary soldiers – reservists and volunteers as much as regulars – who were being shipped overseas to fight for the honour of their country; and, just as importantly, he was addressing not the soldiers themselves, but the people who were *not* going to fight for their country. In these circumstances, he obviously decided that an appeal needed to be patriotic, assertive, populist, conscience-stirring, and, perhaps, just a little vulgar. Neither hymnal solemnity nor historical precedent would do the trick. The title of the poem alone shows how brilliantly successful he was. The soldiers were heroes, not "beggars": it was Kipling and the *Mail* who were doing the begging, and mainly on behalf of the wives, girlfriends and children (whether legitimate or illegitimate, as the poem makes clear) who would be deprived of financial support by the patriotism of their men. Beggar was also a widely familiar euphemism for "bugger", an affectionate term to describe someone who is lovable as well as a bit daft, irresponsible, or feckless. "Absent-minded", however, has other connotations here. At first glance it is a strikingly odd adjective to choose: beggars are not generally thought of as particularly absent-minded, and it is hardly a quality desirable in a soldier. It is used to characterise Kipling's soldiers because they have put their country before all else: as they are fighting for everyone, it becomes the responsibility of those who are not going to South Africa to look after the dependants who might otherwise suffer from the soldiers' absent-mindedness.

The refrain of the poem, in the form of a chant or a series of shouts, shifts the focus away from the plight of the dependants to assert the class unity of the compaign ("Cook's son – Duke's son – son of a belted Earl"), before returning, in the most unambiguous manner, to the need for money:

> Pass the hat for your credit's sake,
> and pay – pay – pay!

"The Absent-Minded Beggar" reworks the theme of civilian hypocrisy towards soldiers that he had already captured memorably in the *Barrack-Room Ballads* ("Oh, it's Tommy this, an' Tommy that, an' 'Tommy, go away';/ But it's 'Thank you, Mister Atkins,' when the band begins to play – "), though now advanced with a deeper concern for the possible long-term effects of the British public's temporary bursts of enthusiasm for the soldier:

> Let us manage so as, later, we can look him in the face,
> And tell him – what he'd very much prefer –
> That, while he saved the Empire, his employer saved his place,
> And his mates (that's you and me) looked out for *her*.

It was not the first time Kipling had argued that a properly trained and equipped army should occupy the Government's attention in peacetime, and not just during moments of national crisis. Nor was it a recent conviction that once the war was over the demobilised soldiers would be quickly forgotten. Both concerns, however, were to be reinforced by the Boer War. Both were to trouble him for the rest of his life.

The success of "The Absent-Minded Beggar" appeal has become legendary. Various newspapers and periodicals reprinted the poem from the *Mail*; Sir Arthur Sullivan set it to music; Lady Tree gave recitations at the Palace Theatre; Lillie Langtry introduced it into her current play at the Garrick Theatre; it was reproduced on scarves, handkerchiefs, matchboxes, caps, vases, and biscuit-barrels. Kipling waived copyright of the poem so that there could be no hindrance to its reproduction, and donated his fee to the Fund: other artists and performers followed his example. The most celebrated reproduction of the poem was on a piece of folded cardboard, with a portrait of Kipling on the cover, a facsimile of the poem in Kipling's handwriting, and, at the centre, a drawing by Richard Caton Woodville of a determined and rather raffish British soldier, his head bandaged, a bayoneted rifle held across his body ready for action. It carried the title "A gentleman in kharki": the feeble phonetic spelling of "khaki" was later dropped. During the period of the war, the "Absent-Minded Beggar" Fund raised more than three hundred thousand pounds.

In recognition of his fund-raising activities Kipling was offered a knighthood by the Prime Minister Lord Salisbury: it was politely declined. There were other, less flattering, responses to the poem's phenomenal success. To the Aesthetes, its jangling strident rhythms seemed the final proof that any poetic talent Kipling might once have possessed had now been sacrificed to the barrel-organ vulgarity of the masses. To the pro-Boers and anti-imperialists, who were to maintain a long and courageous opposition to the war, Kipling was confirmed as the arch-jingoist and militarist. Then, as now, "The Absent-Minded Beggar" was often regarded as a recruiting poem. In intention it was nothing of the sort, though the air of military enthusiasm and excitement it generated was no doubt an aid to recruitment. Even in the music hall, where it was generally welcomed as the most recent of a long line of patriotic songs, there were dissenting voices. Albert Chevalier, who shared something of Kipling's reputation for sentimental Cockney songs, had two complaints to make. Not all of the performers and composers, he felt, were responding in a suitably high-minded manner: instead they were cashing in on the "patriotic reciter" vogue that Kipling had inspired. More seriously, he claimed that much of the money going into the "Absent-Minded Beggar" fund was being diverted from other charitable causes which were just as deserving. In Chevalier's parody of the poem, the Fund is acknowledged as worthy, but as "Kip's looking after Tommy", Chevalier decides "to take out a poet's licence for some fighters left behind", and in doing so makes a powerful social point:

> Brave fight! vain fight! fight that the strong would shun!
> Fight without hope or glory – fight that is never won;
> Battle in filth and squalor – sordid, spiritless fray!
> Through the roll of the drums hear the cry from the slums, and pay!
> pay! pay![11]

When Kipling arrived in South Africa early in February 1900 the war was about to turn in Britian's favour, though immediate news was still of British reverses. Control of the Army in South Africa had recently been handed over to two soldiers with renowned imperial qualifications. The elderly Field Marshal

Lord Roberts of Kandahar (whose title derived from the Second Afghan War in 1880) was appointed Commander-in-Chief, and the much younger recent hero of Omdurman, Lord Kitchener of Khartoum, became Chief of Staff. Their task was to reorganise the Army and halt the humiliating progress of the Boers. That was to take a further eighteen months, but at least Roberts and Kitchener were soon able to send some good news back to Britain. In February the sieges of Kimberley (where Cecil Rhodes was trapped) and Ladysmith were lifted, and the following month Bloemfontein, the capital of Orange Free State, was captured. Kipling knew both the Army Commanders personally. Kitchener he admired, but was wary of. Roberts he regarded with admiration and affection, not least because of his reputation for looking after the welfare of the ordinary soldiers in his command. Several years earlier Kipling had written a jaunty poetic tribute to "Bobs" which emphasised this aspect of Roberts's career:

> This ain't no bloomin' ode,
> But you've 'elped the soldier's load,
> An' for benefits bestowed,
> Bless yer, Bobs!

The poem was only collected by Kipling after Roberts's death in 1914.[12] Apparently, Roberts was not impressed by the image of himself the poem projected: the diminutive imperial hero was not stuffy, but he might well have been shocked by Kipling's description of him as a "Pocket-Wellin'ton an' *arder*" (i.e. "and a half").

Nothing is more illustrative of the unique position as a poet that Kipling held at this time than the effortless manner in which he was instantly in touch with all the principal centres of power in South Africa. In addition to his contacts with the Army High Command, he was welcomed by the special correspondents covering the war, and with one of them, H. A. Gwynne, formed a close friendship that was to be very important to him in later years; he was now on intimate terms with Milner and Rhodes, both of whom would come to be seen as discredited by the parts they had played in the Boer War; and, most strikingly of all, he was greatly at ease with private soldiers. One of the war correspondents, who knew Kipling well at this time, said of him: "He was like a comrade when he talked to a private, and talk to them he did. Jack tar, Colonial, regular, and Pathan, he talked to all alike."[13] Whatever literary critics, Little-Englanders, and Aesthetes may have been saying about him back home, here, where the fighting was actually taking place, it was no disadvantage to be known as the author of *Barrack-Room Ballads* and "The Absent-Minded Beggar". Like "Bobs" he was often described as "the soldier's friend", and this reputation was enhanced by his activities in South Africa. He helped transport the wounded on hospital trains, wrote letters home for soldiers who were unable to do this for themselves, and was horrified when one of the letters was used to raise money for a war charity.[14] He personally drew money from the "Absent-Minded Beggar" Fund to make sure it purchased "comforts" the soldiers really wanted, notably tobacco; and, ignoring official regulations, he intervened at hospitals to obtain for them supplies of bandages and pyjamas that he had been told were not available.

In mid-March Roberts decided that Kipling's popularity and special talents could be usefully employed to help edit the *Friend*, a newspaper for the soldiers that a group of war correspondents, at Roberts's instigation, were setting up in Bloemfontein. The paper was to contain some entertaining items, but its main purpose was to be informative. It was typical of Roberts that he should think it necessary to keep the troops in touch with developments in the war, a sentiment that Kipling shared. He accepted the invitation to join the paper, and for his final two weeks in South Africa worked on it as a sub-editor. He was welcomed to the paper with a special editorial written by Gwynne in which Kipling was described as the writer who "has contributed more than anyone perhaps towards the consolidation of the British Empire" and who "alone can translate to the world the true inwardness of Tommy's character."[15] His visit to the paper, Gwynne announced, "will have in it something of the triumph of a conqueror." Kipling's own response seems to have been more down-to-earth. "Now, what shall I do?" he is reported as asking on his arrival at the office, "Write a poem, fill out cables, or correct proofs?"[16] He did all of these things, and more, clearly relishing his active return to a newspaper office after so many years. One task that fell to him was judging whether the genuine "Tommy poetry", much of it Kiplingesque in style, that was submitted for publication was worth printing. The editors tended to deride it as "outrageous twaddle", while Kipling "praised its quality".[17] He himself wrote a series of "Fables for the Staff", some "Kopje-Book Maxims", and an elegy on the death of General Joubert, a former Commandant-General of the Transvaal Army. Kipling's best-remembered contribution to the paper, however, is "A Song of the White Men" which had been written earlier but received its first publication in the *Friend*.

One non-poetic contribution made by Kipling to the paper deserves special emphasis. For the editorial of the *Friend* on 6 April 1900 one of the editors, Julian Ralph, drew up, with Kipling's assistance, a declaration of "British principles" addressed to the people of the Orange Free State. Ralph says that Kipling helped him phrase the principles "concisely and with force" and that the full draft was "'proved' while he was with us".[18] It was published shortly after Kipling left Bloemfontein, and its composition credited to "Messrs Kipling and Ralph". It is of interest because although Kipling frequently made political statements in his poetry, newspaper articles, and public speeches – sometimes explosively controversial statements – he rarely outlined in any detail the kind of society or political system of which he approved or to which he believed people should aspire. As we have seen, he tended to use vague terms like "The Law" or the civilisation of "the White Man" as a kind of shorthand, leaving his views open to widespread misinterpretation. The "British principles" he and Ralph compiled for the *Friend* are the fullest statement of political belief he was ever to make. It opens with the affirmation that "the basis of the British Government is that of an enlightened and progressive democracy," and then lists the following principles:

> The absolute independence of the individual, so long as he does not interfere with his neighbour's rights.
> Prompt and equal justice, before the Lord, to all men.
> A natural and rooted antipathy to anything savouring of military despotism, in any shape or form.
> Absolute religious toleration and freedom of belief for all peoples.
> Prompt and incorruptible justice to all men in every walk of life.
> The right of every man to make his home his castle.[19]

There is no reference to universal suffrage, which Kipling, like most other major British writers of the time, regarded with suspicion: nor does racial equality appear as a fundamental principle, though very few people, British or South African, would have thought that omission remarkable. It is, perhaps, more surprising that nowhere does the word "white" appear. In a policy statement signed by the editors of the *Friend* before Kipling was connected with it, the paper was dedicated to: "The maintenance of British Supremacy in South Africa and Equal Rights for all white men without respect of race or creed."[20] This was in accordance with the official view that the war was between white races – the British and Dutch – for the white control of South Africa. In fact, large numbers of black

South Africans took part in the war, mainly in supportive roles – it was conscious policy that the actual fighting should be between whites – and mainly on the British side. What political rights black South Africans would have if Britain won the war and set out to establish an "enlightened and progressive democracy" was always present as an issue to be settled, but it was constantly pushed aside as more urgent matters arose. Kipling's attitude was paternalistic. It was the white man's duty to serve black Africans, to instil into them, and to treat them in accordance with, principles of tolerance, justice, and equality, and only the British could be relied upon to do this. He despised the Boers' contemptuous treatment of "Kaffirs", regarding it as a clear demonstration that, whatever the colour of their skins, the Boers were not "white men" in the full meaning of the term: they were more truly allied with the "lesser breeds", a grouping that also included their supporters in the war, Germany. There was no doubt in Kipling's mind that a decisive British victory in South Africa was as important for the black as for the white inhabitants.

That even this early Kipling's thoughts were running on future as much as present problems is apparent from an article, "The Sin of Witchcraft", he sent to *The Times* for publication in March 1900, in which he denounced those settlers in South Africa who, while paying allegiance ostensibly to Britain, were collaborating with the Boers in order to preserve their own lives and property. When the war was over, he argued, these settlers should not be allowed to benefit from their treachery. The angry tone of the article was a portent of still more furious anger to come, but it does not fairly reflect Kipling's mood in the opening months of 1900. His visit to South Africa had been a personal triumph. He had done whatever he could to help, and in return had been fussed over and fêted. It was important to him that he should experience war conditions at first hand, and this he had done. There were lighter moments as well.

Banquets had been given in his honour, and fund-raising concerts, for one of which he re-wrote the words of "Auld Lang Syne" as another tribute to "Bobs" and saw it performed by a South African singer, Florence Fraser.[21] Contemporary descriptions of him working on the *Friend* or dispensing money from the "Absent-Minded Beggar" Fund, portray him as genuinely happy, even schoolboyish; very much, in fact, the author of *Stalky & Co.* which had just been published in England. Similar attitudes are observable in his letters. In July 1900, bringing a friend up to date with family news, he wrote chirpily: "As you know we went down to South Africa (Cape Town) for the winter and there happened to be a bit of a war on, and I had the time of my life."[22] When he returned to South Africa at the end of that year, the war, and his own feelings, had totally changed. A Boer defeat was now certain, but it was disturbingly unclear just what kind of British victory would emerge.

Roberts had been recalled to Britain, leaving Kitchener to inaugurate a final push against Boer guerillas. The plan was to deny them any local support by sweeping the country clear and interning women and children in "laagers" or "concentration camps" as they soon came to be called. In Britain, opposition to the war was already becoming more organised, and in the new year, as reports of the squalid conditions in the camps appeared in the press, there were increasingly vocal demands for a negotiated settlement with the Boers. On this second visit to South Africa there were no high-spirited adventures for Kipling, and his principal contacts were with Rhodes and Milner. From both he would have learned that the imperial ambitions for Africa that they all shared were under threat. Rhodes knew that he had only a short while left to live, and he discussed with Kipling his hopes for the future of Rhodesia and his plans to endow scholarships which would enable needy scholars from the new world to study at Oxford. Milner was also concerned with maintaining links between Britain and

South Africa, though in a more urgent manner than Rhodes. He would do everything in his power to ensure the Boers' total defeat, but felt that he could not rely on Kitchener's support or, for much longer, that of the British Government. A peace treaty was eventually signed at Vereeniging on 31 May 1901. Under its terms, the Boers pledged their allegiance to the British Crown. In return, self-government for the Transvaal and the Orange Free State was promised at some future date: the question of votes for non-white South Africans was postponed until after self-government had been agreed. The British Government also gave three million pounds in grants to help restore the devastated farmlands. Rhodes died in March 1902. Milner stayed on as British High Commissioner, hoping now to strengthen British influence in South Africa before the self-government clauses of the treaty were implemented.[23] Kipling shared that view. Their greatest fear was of a change of government in Britain that would bring back into power the hated Liberals.

The fourth of Kipling's five volumes of poetry, *The Five Nations*, was published in September 1903, fifteen months after the close of the Boer War. Like the earlier volumes, it carried a line drawing on the title page to indicate the poetry's dominant theme. Pagett M.P., the bugler, and the seaman, were now succeeded by an armed and bandoleered mounted infantryman riding across the South African veld. In *The Five Nations* Kipling gathered most of the poems he had written about South Africa over the previous four or five years. He also included a number of pre-Boer War poems – among them, "The White Man's Burden" and "Recessional" – which had been written after the publication of *The Seven Seas* and were now collected in volume form for the first time. Considered as a whole, these poems make up a record of Kipling's involvement in the Boer War, from the early celebrations and admonitions of Britain's imperial mission through to Vereeniging. As many of the poems were written in the period between the end of the war and the publication of *The Five Nations*, there is a summarising, even a valedictory, air to the book, and perhaps a touch of defiance as well. In collecting the South African poems in this way Kipling was acknowledging, but certainly not apologising for, his full involvement in the war.

The poems written towards the close of the war and in the months following Vereeniging can be divided into two distinct groups. On the one hand, poems addressed to the British public on the progress of the war; and on the other, poems which dealt largely with military events and which were first published in *The Five Nations* as "Service Songs". The first group consists of four poems which appeared originally in *The Times*: "The Lesson" (29 July 1901), "The Reformers" (12 October 1901), "The Islanders" (4 January 1902), and "The Settler" (27 February 1903). Although totally different from each other in form and mood, they were all attempts to influence public opinion in Britain, to deflect support away from the pro-Boer faction, and to focus attention on long-term developments in South Africa and elsewhere. The assumed relationship between the poet and his readers varies so dramatically in these poems that it is tempting to believe they represent mercurial shifts of mood on Kipling's part, with two of them being simply bad-tempered outbursts. But that explanation seems unlikely. The poems, though striving for different effects, are closely related in theme. Considered together, they demonstrate Kipling's increasing awareness of the need to appeal to his audience in a variety of ways if his message is to be understood and accepted. They also show Kipling beginning to line up his political supporters and opponents.

"The Lesson" is a jocular attempt, written as the war was moving into its final phase, to get the British people to face up to the mistakes made in South Africa:

> *Let us admit it fairly, as a business people should,*
> *We have had no end of a lesson: it will do us no end of good.*

Heavy, slightly discordant, comic rhymes ("from Pietersburg to Sutherland . . . with a fulness accorded no other land") reminiscent of W. S. Gilbert, are employed throughout the poem; while the refrain, "It was our fault, and our very great fault," echoes the Judge's Song in *Trial by Jury* (1875): "It was managed by a job – and a good job too!" In the gentle satirical style of Gilbert and Sullivan, Kipling attacks "all the obese, unchallenged old things that stifle and overlie us," and insists that if the lesson has been fully learned, "it may make us an Empire yet!" Just over two months later, this time in the dignified tones of "The Reformers", Kipling called on the British upper classes to sacrifice something of their love of "ensnaring ritual" in order to ensure the future security of the country. The young have shown the way in South Africa, now it is the turn of their fathers to look anew at:

> Ultimate issues, primal springs,
> Demands, abasements, penalties –
> The imperishable plinth of things
> Seen and unseen, that touch our peace.

The obscurity of the poem was clarified on its original publication in *The Times* by an introductory note, said to be an "extract from a private letter". It read: "The men who have been through this South African mill will no longer accept the old outworn explanations. They know too much, and it is to them we must look, when they come back, for the real reform in every direction." It was reform at the top that Kipling wanted, and he was not going to get it.[24]

Another two months on, and employing the jangling long poetic line that he so often favoured, Kipling switched from the ruminative obliquity of "The Reformers" to a full-frontal attack in "The Islanders". Once again his target was a ruling-class selfishness that was being passed unthinkingly from generation to generation, though now he concentrated more intensely on the specific issue of national service or conscription. Many people involved in the Boer War had come to believe that the inadequacies revealed in the preparedness of the British Army for a large-scale war should be corrected by all young men in Britain undergoing a short spell of military training. Neither of the two political parties was interested in the idea, bringing against it the customary argument that, unlike Continental countries, Britain's power rested on the Navy, not the Army. In 1901 a National Service League was founded to argue the case for conscription. Kipling supported the League, and enthusiastically organised a Rifle Club in Rottingdean to demonstrate what could be done on a voluntary basis until the government was persuaded to back formal conscription. The man most prominently associated in the public mind with the policy was Lord Roberts. At first he refused to join the League because of a disagreement whether conscripts should serve overseas, or, Roberts's own preference, would be used only for home defence. He did not become President of the League until 1905, but it was Roberts who, in December 1901, urged Kipling to write something on the subject, and therefore prompted the composition of "The Islanders".[25]

Although the poem is addressed initially to "The People", and is sometimes described as a criticism of the British as a whole, it is above all an attack on the land-owning class, as the many references to the trappings of wealth make perfectly clear. Indeed, one of the criticisms of the people being addressed is that during the war they protected themselves behind the "Sons of the sheltered city – unmade, unhandled, unmeet", pushed them "raw to the battle", and then returned to care for their "horses and dogs". The assault is virulent and comprehensive, with the ruling classes condemned not only for "grudging" their sons to service and refusing to allow their vast estates to be used as much-needed army training areas, but, more generally, for their stupidity, triviality, and lack of true patriotic feeling. It was, however, Kipling's jibe at the British obsession with sport that drew blood:

> Then ye returned to your trinkets; then ye contented your souls
> With the flannelled fools at the wicket or the muddied oafs at the
> goals.

That was clearly going too far. The publication of the poem followed closely on a Test match in Australia which England had won, and in the uproar over these lines it was Kipling who was made to seem unpatriotic. The long editorial that accompanied "The Islanders" in *The Times* took issue with Kipling over the need for compulsory national service, but expressed sympathy on the matter of sport which, it noted, led to streets being "filled with placards about these athletic contests as if issues depended upon them as vital to our race as those decided at Trafalgar or Waterloo." Kipling told Rider Haggard that he found it "delicious to see *The Times* backing and filling", and unrepentantly expressed his disgust at the "d – d hired pros" earning large fees playing cricket in Australia when they should have been supporting Britain in South Africa: "I ought to have written *hired* fools instead of flannelled fools. That might have made my meaning clearer. But as usual people have gone off on a side issue."[26] Any disagreement Kipling might have had with *The Times* about "The Islanders" was wiped out with the publication of "The Settler". Written to commemorate the end of the war, it is calm, balanced, humane, reconciliatory:

> Here, where my fresh-turned furrows run,
> And the deep soil glistens red,
> I will repair the wrong that was done
> To the living and the dead.

The calm, however, was slightly deceptive. When Kipling reprinted "The Settler" in *The Five Nations*, he placed it beside "South Africa", a similarly commemorative poem, though one that draws attention to the suffering endured to keep South Africa British, and closes possessively:

She is Our South Africa/ Is Our Own South Africa/ Africa all over!

The "Service Songs" section of *The Five Nations* opens with a brief dedicatory poem to the common soldier, just as, eleven years earlier, *Barrack-Room Ballads* had opened with a dedication to Tommy Atkins. In repeating this device, Kipling's purpose, however, was not to emphasise continuity, but rather to draw attention to the enormous changes that had taken place between the two books. "'Tommy' you was" when the war began, he tells the soldier, but now that it is over "You shall be called the Service Man/ 'Enceforward, evermore." The immediate reference is to a post-war army reform which introduced flexible "terms of service" to encourage recruitment, though more is involved than simply that. It was the first time Kipling had written a batch of soldier poems of this kind without calling them barrack-room ballads. Like Tommy Atkins, the barrack-room ballad had been rendered obsolete by the special nature of the war in South Africa: tents were more appropriate than barracks; "irregular" soldiers as prevalent as regulars; the "thin red line" still being honoured in *Barrack-Room Ballads* had been replaced by the new, and often hastily-trained, "Mounted Infantry". Even the assumption that there was a special category of "soldier songs" was in doubt. This was the first war in which many of the songs the troops sang had been composed for them by Tin Pan Alley. Everything was changing, and perhaps Kipling was making a wry comment on all of this when he adapted an obscure verse form for one of the "Service Songs" and called it "Half-Ballade of Waterval".

There were still marching songs, and "Boots" is one of the simplest and best of them, with the dogged mood of the troops captured perfectly by the heavy repetitive chant ("We're foot-slog-slog-slog-sloggin' over Africa"), and the sardonic refrain, "There's no discharge in the war!" There were also the by now familiar tributes to gallant foes, as in "Piet", and some overdone exercises in sentimentality, such as "The Married Man" and "The Instructor". Always the spokesman for the ordinary soldier forced to suffer from inefficient or incompetent military commanders, Kipling now produced one of his most memorable poems on this theme. Stellenbosch was the name of the main base-camp in Cape Colony to which officers who had proved incompetent in the field were posted: they were, in the phrase then current, "stellenbosched". In Kipling's "Stellenbosch" the General in charge of the troops is not so much incompetent as totally self-seeking: he is taking no risks, not really fighting a war at all, but simply "markin' time to earn a K.C.B." He gets "'is decorations thick . . . An the soldier – 'ad the work to do again!" For Kipling, Stellenbosch is a disgraceful façade, and the phrase he coined for an official cover-up is used to the present day: "And it all goes into the laundry/ But it never comes out in the wash."

More notable than this kind of satire, for which Kipling was already renowned, was a new mood of lyricism in his poetry. The subject of "Lichtenberg" is the perennial one of the soldier on active service yearning for home, and Kipling had handled it many times before, mainly by means of a character sketch. Here, for an Australian soldier on escort-duty, memory of home is suddenly and ovewhelmingly provoked by the scent of wattle. Confronted with that, all else is obliterated:

That must be why the big things pass
And the little things remain,

Like the smell of the wattle by Lichtenberg,
  Riding in, in the rain.

A similar lyrical power is apparent in two other poems about the Boer War which were included in *The Five Nations*, though not, surprisingly, in the "Service Songs" section: "Dirge of Dead Sisters" and "Bridge-Guard in the Karroo". Kipling's elegy to the nurses who died on voluntary service in South Africa is a perfectly modulated blend of landscape – against which the red capes of the nurses were always defiantly prominent – war, and the non-stop activity of the nurses, reflected in the restless movement of the long poetic line:

Who recalls the morning and the thunder through the foothills
  (Tufts of fleecy shrapnel strung along the empty plains)
And the sun-scarred Red-Cross coaches creeping guarded
  to the culvert,
  And the faces of the sisters looking gravely from the trains?

"Bridge-Guard in the Karroo" is another tribute to dedicated non-combatant service, this time to lonely pickets guarding the railways in isolated areas. As in "Lichtenberg", the dominant mood of the poem is encapsulated in the simple, evocative language of the refrain:

(Few, forgotten and lonely,
  Where the empty metals shine –
No, not combatants – only
  Details guarding the line.)

Despite this melancholy tone, the keynote of "Service Songs" is the spirit of irreversible change that was struck in the opening dedicatory poem "The Service Man". As Andrew Rutherford has said of these poems, they represent "lessons to be learned . . . and the overwhelming impression is of the steepness of the learning-curve for all those capable of learning."[27] The infantry-man in "M.I." who, quite unexpectedly, has to learn how to ride a horse, opens his monologue: "I wish my mother could see me now, with a fence-post under my arm." In "The Parting of the Columns", British soldiers ponder the friendships they have made with, and the things they have learned from, the Australian, Canadian and New Zealand soldiers who have come to support the mother-country. "Wilful-Missing" is a sympathetic study of what it feels like to be a deserter, and "Half-Ballade of Waterval" a related study of captivity. In "Chant-Pagan", a discharged irregular returns to his job in Britain, but after the openness and excitement of South Africa he is unable to accept the staid, class-ridden society he once accepted as home. In the roughly similar situation of "Shillin' a Day" in *Barrack-Room Ballads*, the discharged soldier was a figure of pathos, dependent on hand-outs. Now, in "Chant-Pagan" he looks with bewilderment at what he is expected to be in England ("Me!"), and emigrates. The need to face up to the enormous changes brought about by the war, while at the same time not being quite sure what those changes are, is epitomised by the speaker in "The Return":

> I did no more than others did,
>   I don't know where the change began.
> I started as an average kid,
>   I finished as a thinkin' man.

There can be no doubt that these poems, written after Vereeniging, reflect Kipling's own feelings of bewilderment at the outcome of the war. The lessons he had learned from it were various. He was now totally convinced that another war would follow shortly, almost certainly with Germany and in Europe; that, in the words of the General in one of Kipling's South African stories, the war had been "a first-class dress-parade for

Armageddon".[28] America had not come out in support of Britain in the Boer War, and probably could not be relied on in the future, but the Empire had fulfilled the prophecies he had made in "A Song of the English". More than eighty thousand troops from the colonies and dominions had fought for the British cause in South Africa, and in doing so had created closer ties with Britain than ever before. They could be relied on in any future conflict. For Britain itself, the main lesson to assimilate was that the nature of armed conflict had changed drastically: new technology was needed, new thinking at the top, and commitment to a programme of compulsory military service to build up an army equal to those of Germany and France. In South Africa, the most urgent need was to increase the number of British immigrants, and for the British government to postpone the granting of independence to the Boer republics until Britain's presence in South Africa was unchallengeable. Kipling continued to spend much of his time in South Africa where, he was later to claim, there was for a while "a joyful strong confidence after the war", though, he added grimly, it was soon "murdered".[29] If Kipling really did experience any post-war confidence in South Africa's future, it must have been very fleeting indeed.

From the moment the peace treaty was signed he would have known that for him personally the Boer War had been a disaster. In Britain his views were now liable to be treated with derision as the rantings of a war-mongering reactionary, or totally ignored. Many of his closest friends and allies were losing the influence they once had. The Conservative Government, Kipling's only hope that his views on South Africa might prevail, was openly split on the issue of tariff reform. In 1904 Lord Roberts was ousted from his post as Commander-in-Chief of the Army, and Milner was shortly to be driven back to Britain after becoming embroiled in a political scandal over the employment of Chinese labourers in South African mines.

Kipling's principal task in South Africa at this time was to help plan a memorial to Cecil Rhodes, something that could only have increased his melancholy. In January 1906 everything that remained fell apart when the Liberals were returned to power in Britain with a massive majority. During the war, Campbell-Bannerman, the new Prime Minister, and Lloyd George, President of the Board of Trade, had both been pro-Boers, and they were now determined that South Africa should be settled once and for all. Self-government for the Boer Republics was immediately granted. In 1909, now with Asquith as Prime Minister, the British colonies and the Boer Republics were brought together in an uneasy Union of South Africa. In spite of the objections of a small group of Labour Party members of Parliament, led by Keir Hardie, the Liberals refused to confront the issue of political rights for non-whites in South Africa and, in effect, left it to be settled by the Boers.[30] On 28 January 1909, in a letter to Rider Haggard, Kipling dismissed the Liberals as "all such a set of flagrant and persistent liars that I *can't* believe in their rectitude over anything."[31] The winter months of 1907 he had spent once again in South Africa. After that it became, along with India and America, one of the countries which had played a major role in his life but which he would never again visit.

[6]
The Garden of England

> "No roads, no nothing!" said Sophie, her short skirt hooked by briers. "I thought all England was a garden."
>
> "An Habitation Enforced", *Actions and Reactions*.

Although *The Five Nations* was concerned primarily with the Boer War, it also contained a number of poems which had, apparently, nothing at all to do with the war or South Africa. Most of them were new: like "Service Songs" they were appearing here for the first time. They are personal, largely prophetic in tone, and often allegorical in form. Apart from "Sussex", and to a lesser extent "The Dykes", they have not numbered among Kipling's more popular poems, and his biographers have tended to regard them as representative of his depressed mood in the wake of the Boer War, which in some respects they are. There is, for example, a strong emphasis on old age, though at the time of their composition Kipling was not yet forty. In "The Song of Diego Valdez", the ageing Spanish Admiral muses wistfully on his lost adventurous youth, while "The Old Men" even appears to countenance self-pity, a mood very rare in Kipling's work:

This is our lot if we live so long and labour unto the end –
That we outlive the impatient years and the much too patient friend:

And because we know we have breath in our mouth and think we have thoughts in
our head,
We shall assume that we are alive, whereas we are really dead.

T. S. Eliot acknowledged that when he wrote "The Hollow Men" he was influenced by Kipling's "The Broken Men", another poem about the lonely and outcast that was first published in *The Five Nations*: it is quite possible he had "The Old Men" also in mind.[1]

The most sriking poem in this context is "The Second Voyage", an immediately appealing yet obscure allegory which portrays young people as so absorbed in their love affairs that they can be of no possible use on a voyage about to be undertaken:

We've sent our little Cupids all ashore –
They were frightened, they were tired, they were cold.

The older generation is left in charge, ageing along with the ship itself:

The sea has shorn our galleries away,
The salt has soiled our gilding past remede;
Our paint is flaked and blistered by the spray,
Our sides are half a fathom furred in weed.
(Foul weather!)

Even "Sussex", a poem of calmness and content, has a link with growing old, written as it was to mark the Kipling family's move from Rottingdean to Burwash in September 1902, and their discovery of a permanent home in Bateman's:

God gave all men all earth to love,
But, since our hearts are small,
Ordained for each one spot should prove
Belovèd over all.

Kipling's choice of one special place to love, publicly announced and celebrated in this poem, was "Sussex by the sea!" It all sounds very much like welcome retirement after long years of wandering and exhausting conflict.

That it was nothing of the sort is apparent from the dedicatory poem, "Before a midnight breaks in storm", which Kipling wrote as the introduction to *The Five Nations*. The mood of the poem is hymnal (with strong echoes of "O God Our Help in Ages Past"); solemn to the point of portentousness (with strong echoes of the prayer-like sections of Tennyson's "In Memoriam"), and obscure. It is a prophecy of terrible violence to come, delivered in a moment of respite while there is still the possibility of preparing for the time when "a midnight breaks in storm" and the "rivers league against the land/ In piratry of flood." False prophets will say that this disaster came from an "unhinting sky". The truth is they have misread the signs, being unable or unwilling to observe the "wavering gusts" that always precede a storm and the seepage of water onto normally dry land that foretells a flood. The images of storm and tempest give way to the clouded visions that fortune-tellers summon up in a crystal ball; then to the "sport-making Gods of old" who can no longer be held responsible for disasters created by mankind itself; and finally to the "wingèd men the Fates may breed/So soon as Fate hath wings." With man's ancient dream of flying now a reality, these "wingèd men" are first and foremost the airmen who will transform the nature of warfare. They may also be modern equivalents of the retributive Harpies of Classical mythology, and, possibly, the Nietzschean *Übermensch* as well.

The complex syntax and archaic language of "Before a midnight breaks in storm" obscure its full meaning, though the message Kipling wished to convey is reasonably clear. Britain is in danger both from an external enemy and from its own weak leaders, the false prophets of the poem. In the past,

Britain had relied on the sea to protect it from invasion, but in an age of "wingèd men" that is no longer sufficient. Nor is it any longer sensible to hope for comfort from ancient superstitions. Responsibility for survival rests entirely on mankind itself. The warnings are there, the storm is definitely on its way, and the only way to avoid being destroyed by it is to act in good time.

Other poems in *The Five Nations* consolidate the message of "Before a midnight breaks in storm" and reinforce Kipling's prophetic stance. "The Bell Buoy", first published some years earlier though appropriately reprinted here, is one of his most successful ventures into anthropomorphism. Set to guard Britain's shores, the bell buoy listens to the sound of church bells ringing on land, compares his role with theirs, and has no doubt which is the more valuable. The refrain to each stanza poses a question on the relative value of the bells' usefulness, and gives the same kind of emphatic answer to all of them:

> Would I barter my place for the Church's grace?
> (*Shoal! 'Ware shoal!*) Not I!

"The Dykes" is closely related to "The Bell Buoy" in that the defence of Britain is its theme, but the mood is one of shame at the crumbling neglect of Britain's defence system: "All that our fathers taught us of old pleases us now no more." That the present generation of Britain's leaders was betraying all that its predecessors had stood for, and, when the test came would betray its own children as well, had become one of Kipling's firmest, and most bitterly expressed beliefs:

> Time and again were we warned of the dykes, time and again we delayed:
> Now, it may fall, we have slain our sons, as our fathers we have betrayed.

In *The Five Nations* Kipling was not only documenting his personal defeat in the Boer War: he was also laying a path for the future based on the lessons South Africa had taught him. He was no longer the prophet of Empire. Nor was he still, in the pre-war sense, England's unofficial Laureate. He had settled in England, for what felt to him the first time in his life, and from now on England would be the focus of his work – its squalid present, glorious past, and its uncertain future. Like the "broken men" about whom he writes so sympathetically, he was in some respects an exile, but at least in his own country. Told repeatedly that his day had passed, that he had become one of the "old men" who should be content to sit quietly and "subsist on the smell" of their youth, he considers the possible truth of such a view, and rejects it: "He who hath not endured to the death, from his birth he hath never endured!" If our "little Cupids" really are too "frightened, tired and cold" to face up to the voyage, then they had better go ashore, for "Foul weather" is definitely on its way. Repeatedly, throughout these poems, advice to stop trying or give up is overthrown by a determination to persevere, often prompted by a spiritual guidance towards some important, as yet unknown, purpose. The speaker in "The Explorer" is told: "There's no sense in going further – it's the edge of cultivation." He accepts the advice, until "one everlasting Whisper" tells him otherwise: "Something hidden. Go and find it."[2] To the imagery of enduringly adventurous old age, new exploration, and stormy voyages, must be added that of architecture, which in Kipling usually carries Masonic implications. In "The Palace", when a self-confessed "King and a Mason" clears the ground to build a palace for himself, he comes across the remains of an earlier building, a "wreck of a palace", which seems to have had no discernible architectural plan or design behind it. He despises the crudity of the earlier palace until the truth is revealed to him:

When I was a King and a Mason – in the open noon of my pride,
They sent me a Word from the Darkness. They whispered and called me aside.
They said – "The end is forbidden". They said – "Thy use is fulfilled,
Thy palace shall stand as that other's – the spoil of a King who shall build".

The lesson learned is that, like these uncovered stones, all man-made structures suffer death and destruction, but if the original work is based on truth, then they also become the crucial foundations for some future architect to build on. This same kind of architectural-masonic imagery was used by Kipling in "The Pro-Consuls", his tribute to Milner published in 1905:

They that dig foundations deep,
Fit for realms to rise upon,
Little honour do they reap
Of their generation.

He and Milner had tried to build a true long-standing palace, and it had been destroyed by people who did not share their vision. Now Kipling would dig the foundations yet again and build anew, for the glory of the work itself and the trust that it would be rebuilt by some "King and Mason" of the future.

What all of this meant, in non-metaphoric language, was that Kipling refused to be pushed aside by the apparent victories of the Boers and the Liberals. He would fight on two fronts, and in entirely different ways. The false prophets of the present generation who were leading Britain to possible disaster would be openly opposed, their pernicious doctrines denounced, and the truth revealed. At the same time, he would appeal to a younger generation, the children, and through them, their parents, not any longer by stirring exhortations to world-wide exploration and dedication to imperial ideals, but by instilling into them an understanding of, and a pride in, their Englishness. They were the foundations of the future, and England's future could only be secure if they understood the past. At no other time in his career is it more apparent that Kipling really was a man with "two separate sides" to his head than in this stretch of time from the close of the Boer War to the outbreak of the First World War, the period that he himself would later categorise as "the years between". From one side of his head came the public poems on political and national themes: from the other, the children's poetry inspired by his move to Sussex.

In the poems on public themes, and more regularly in lectures and letters, Kipling could be not only hard, aggressive and unforgiving, but also wildly offensive, totally incapable of seeing any point of view other than his own, and conspiratorial to the verge of paranoia. To the actions of his opponents, or "enemies" as he regarded them, he did not hesitate to ascribe the meanest possible motives, whether or not he had any evidence to support his accusations. Politicians he disliked were never regarded as pursuing policies in which they genuinely believed, however misguidedly: they were at best cowards, and commonly seen as interested only in lining their own pockets. In correspondence he slipped easily into the casual language of anti-Semitism and racism. He was, to some extent, responding in kind. For years the abuse thrown at him had been as gratuitously offensive as anything he delivered, and, despite the indifference to personal criticism he affected, there can be no doubt that it got through to him. Much can be explained, if not excused, by his obsessive determination to alert his beloved country to terrifying dangers that few people seemed to comprehend or have any interest in. Equally important, however, is the curious fact that in these years, as politicians and influential sectors of the press denounced him as a pathetic has-been, sales of his books simply went up and up. This was a phenomenon that Kipling himself marvelled at and found impossible to explain.[3] At the very least it must have convinced him that he was right to pursue his independent line on how to reverse the state of political decadence into which the country had fallen. After all, there were, obviously, a lot of people who were eager to hear what he had to say, and, unlike many of his turn-of-the-century contemporaries, he had never thought it meretricious to address a large audience or to try to influence it, providing that his own integrity was not compromised in the process.

To what extent Kipling did now sacrifice his long-treasured artistic independence is a matter of interpretation and emphasis. He remained as determined as ever not to accept government posts or honours, and taunts that he was a spokesman for the Conservative Party were bitterly resented.[4] Although he was now willing to describe himself as "a Tory", he was in no sense a reliable or steadfast party man: Conservatives with whom he disagreed were liable to be as fiercely attacked as anyone else. In so far as he can be described in party-political terms, he was now associated with the extreme right of the Edwardian Conservative Party. He was a Unionist (opposed to Irish independence), and a Protectionist (in favour of preferential tariffs throughout the Empire); he was for increased expenditure on the armed forces, and against any movement towards independence for India; he was also becoming a more ardent Monarchist than he had ever been before. Such labels are, however, of limited use: on all of these issues, Kipling would have found allies in the Liberal as well as the Conservative Party, just as a few years earlier he could have acknowledged, if he had wanted to, that not all Liberals were by any means supporters of the Boers. It makes more sense to regard Kipling as anti-Liberal rather than pro-Conservative. He was by instinct a romantic individualist, and he abhorred any restrictions on individual rights, though, as we have already seen, he seems never to have believed that universal suffrage was necessary or particularly desirable. None of this would have been regarded as seriously objectionable in late-Victorian England, but times were rapidly changing, and it was change that Kipling set himself against. The comprehensive programme of social and political reforms initiated in 1906 by the Liberals and their Labour Party allies was simply dismissed by Kipling in its entirety. His response had nothing to do with the desirability of this or that reform: it was the whole liberalising reformist tendency he deplored. When in opposition, the Liberals had undermined the Empire, insulted British soldiers fighting for their country in South Africa, and called for cuts in military expenditure. They were dishonourable; liars; not to be trusted. Now in power, it was inconceivable that anything the Liberals did could be to the good of Britain. In 1907, lecturing in Canada, Kipling told his audience:

> It must be hard for those who do not live there to realise the cross between canker and blight that has settled on England for the last couple of years. The effects of it are felt throughout the Empire, but at headquarters we taste the stuff in the very air, just as one tastes iodoform in the cups and bread-and-butter of a hospital-tea.[5]

When the lecture was published in the *Morning Post* the following year, it was introduced by the poem "A Song of Travel" ("Where's the lamp that Hero lit/Once to call Leander home?") in which Kipling reasserted the continuing romance and wonder of an expanding world. In part, the poem records Kipling's growing tendency to regard Canada as the type of pioneering imperial country, now that South Africa could no longer fill the role: it also demonstrates that the "canker and blight" of Liberal politics had not taken complete hold of his imagination.

During this period of lonely political and artistic revaluation, Kipling enjoyed one unexpected, and welcome, stroke of good fortune. In November 1904, H. A. Gwynne, Kipling's former colleague on the *Friend*, was appointed editor of the *Standard* which had been bought by Arthur Pearson to put the case for tariff reform. Gwynne held this post until 1911 when he became editor of the more prestigious, though equally Protectionist, *Morning Post*. Gwynne was a disciple rather than simply a friend of Kipling's. Disillusionment over South Africa had not lessened the admiration he had expressed four years earlier in his editorial welcoming Kipling to Bloemfontein. In his eyes, Kipling was still the prophet of Empire, with a unique ability to voice the true feelings of ordinary people, and to this view he always remained loyal. Kipling fully understood the nature of Gwynne's discipleship. Immediately Gwynne became editor of the *Standard*, he began receiving from Kipling advice on what policies the paper should follow, what causes it should take up, and which contributors needed to be encouraged.[6] Kipling himself gave a lead. He would still publish poems in *The Times*, and in a variety of other papers and magazines, but gradually he began to give priority to the *Standard* and, even before Gwynne joined it, the *Morning Post*. The public platform Gwynne provided for Kipling was sympathetic and supportive: it also served to place him politically even more firmly within the Conservative Party. Nor was his close association with Gwynne himself entirely beneficial. Although the two men shared very similar political views, there was an element of crankiness about Gwynne that drove him to extreme irrational stances on public issues, and some of his reputation for extremism tended to transfer itself to Kipling, whether deservedly or not. Immediately, none of this mattered to Kipling. What he wanted were loyal allies, and he had found one in Gwynne.

The first of Kipling's major poems published by Gwynne was "The Sons of Martha" which appeared in the *Standard*, 29 April 1907. Based on the Biblical story of Jesus in the home of Mary and Martha (Luke 10:38-42), the poem is a statement of Kipling's personal commitment to a secular world and to individualism. In Luke, Mary sits listening to Jesus, while Martha prepares a meal. When Martha complains that Mary is not helping her, Jesus takes Mary's side, for she "hath chosen the good part, which shall not be taken from her". Kipling portrays the world as divided between the descendants of these two women, with the sons of Martha still waiting on the sons of Mary, but he reverses the emphasis of the Biblical story. For Kipling, the sons of Martha are the workers, dedicated to the task in hand; active; strong; progressive; and working "not as a ladder from earth to Heaven, not as a witness to any creed", but simply from a desire to serve their "own kind in their common need". By contrast, the sons of Mary are languid, sleepy, demanding, dependent on others, and confident that they are the recipients of God's grace. Kipling's preference for active over inactive people was already a familiar theme in his poetry. What was new about "The Sons of Martha" was the inclusive clarity of his philosophical position. These workers are not Imperialists, Tories, or Liberals; they are not distinguished by their wealth or social status; and they are not definable in terms of sociological concepts of class. They are simply the people "in all the ages" who "take the buffet and cushion the shock". This is presented as a "burden" placed upon the sons of Martha because "she was rude to the Lord her Guest", but the emotional force of the poem makes it sound more like a privilege.

It was soon clear, however, that the broad-minded inclusiveness of "The Sons of Martha" did not extend to Liberal politicians, or, as the true nature of Liberal social reforms became clearer, to many of the working-class men who had voted them into power. "The City of Brass" (*Morning Post*, 28 June 1909) was written during the long, acrimonious debate on Lloyd George's proposals to increase income tax and to introduce a new land tax in his "people's budget", though, as the poem makes plain, it was the apparently unstoppable process of reform and the increasingly vocal demands of an organised working-class movement, rather than the budget itself, that provoked Kipling's fury. Now, "the multitude" is denounced along with the Liberal and Labour "panders" who arouse, and surrender to, its "lust". Literally drunk, and also metaphorically drunk on the promised power that democracy will bring, the reeling crowd joyfully assist their leaders to destroy the "walls that their fathers had made them", encourage the perversion of justice, call on "the ruled to rebel", and fling away the "imperial gains of the age". All is done in the name of "the State", but that, Kipling warns, in a bitter reference to the war to come, will not save them, for "an host had prepared their destruction, but still they denied it". There could be no stronger indication of just how far Kipling was out of touch with the reformist spirit of the age than "The City of Brass" which includes, in its damning comprehensive sweep, many of the very people whose spokesman he had previously been. He seems never to have felt any repentance for what many of his readers must have regarded as a betrayal. Indeed, some years later he would proudly instance "The City of Brass" as a justification of his prophetic gifts.[7] But he never wrote another poem in quite the same vein.

The death of Edward VII in May 1910 was marked by Kipling with an elegy "The Dead King" which was published in both the *Morning Post* and *The Times*, and also as a separate booklet, handsomely decorated with black and purple funereal symbols. In poetic terms, it is one of his less inspired compositions, reading today like the assumed type of conventional, eulogistic laureate-poem. Yet, Kipling's praise of the King who had surrendered "dear life for the sake of a land more dear" was widely approved. In the growing industrial, political, constitutional, and diplomatic unrest that affected virtually every part of British society in the years preceding the First World War, Edward had become a hopeful symbol of stability, his earlier worldly image now subdued by that of an ardent diplomat seeking to establish harmony out of chaos. It was commonly held that his life had been shortened by his efforts to bring peace to the country, a point emphasised by Kipling:

> For on him each new day laid command, every tyrannous hour,
> To confront, or confirm, or make smooth some dread issue of power.

On many of those same "dread issues of power" Kipling himself was taking a regular and determined stand, with poems which were intended, and accepted, as contributions to political debate on many of the most controversial topics of the day. He was now openly associated in the public mind with the right wing of the Conservative Party, the "reactionaries", or "Die-Hards" as they were coming to be called. On 29 June 1911 he published in the *Morning Post* a poem called "The Declaration of London" which attacked, and played a part in helping the House of Lords to defeat, a Naval Prize Bill which, if passed, would have restricted Britain's ability in times of war to import food and raw materials. On 20 October of the same year, and in the same newspaper, he took on the militant suffragettes with "The Female of the Species". Originally subtitled "A Study in Natural History", it contained no specific references to contemporary Suffragist activity, but instead illustrated the famous claim that the "female of the species is more deadly than the male" by a series of fiercely-expressed, neatly-quotable, examples drawn from the past:

> When the early Jesuit fathers preached to Hurons and Choctaws,
> They prayed to be delivered from the vengeance of the squaws.
> 'Twas the women, not the warriors, turned those stark enthusiasts
>   pale.
> For the female of the species is more deadly than the male.

The point from "natural history" that Kipling makes in the poem is that the greater deadliness of the female comes from the fact that she "faces Death by torture for each life beneath her breast" and therefore, "may not deal in doubt or pity", but that did not prevent the more local political message from striking home.

The steady drift of the Liberal government towards granting Home Rule to Ireland aroused far deeper anger in Kipling than Suffragist militancy, and he gave his full support unhesitatingly to the movement to save Ulster from absorption into an independent Ireland. It was the type of campaign that Kipling was always able to persuade himself was moral rather than political, and he expressed his views in "Ulster", first published in the *Morning Post*, 9 April 1912, and "The Covenant", which he contributed to the first number of *The Covenanter*, 20 May 1914, a short-lived periodical which was the official mouthpiece of the League of British Covenanters, founded by Sir Alfred Milner to support the cause of Ulster. It was the same events that provoked the most notorious speech of his life, though Kipling's "Indictment of the Government" as it was known, was more a criticism of what he regarded as the widespread corruption of Liberal politicians than simply their Irish policies.[8] Speaking in the open air at Tunbridge Wells on 16 May 1914, he declared that "the bulk of the Cabinet, and certainly the most notorious persons in it, are dependent largely on their official salaries plus what they make in tips."[9] The immediate reference was to the payment of salaries to Members of Parliament which, after many years of debate, had been finally agreed upon in 1911, but Kipling was also alluding to the "Marconi Affair" in which it was rumoured that certain politicians – notably Lloyd George and Sir Rufus Isaacs – had made large sums of money by trading in Marconi shares. A House of Commons committee cleared the two politicians of having acted illegally, but few people were convinced of their innocence. In

October 1913, Isaacs was appointed Lord Chief Justice. Here was the final confirmation for Kipling that the Liberals were more interested in making money for themselves than in serving the country, and he aired his disgust not only at Tunbridge Wells but also in the poem "Gehazi" which was first published in *The Years Between* (1919):

> Well done, well done, Gehazi!
>   Stretch forth thy ready hand,
> Though barely 'scaped from judgment,
>   Take oath to judge the land.

The Biblical allusion is to II Kings, 5:20–27, in which Gehazi, the devious servant of Elisha, is gruesomely punished: "The leprosy . . . of Naaman shall cleave unto thee, and unto thy seed for ever." Kipling wishes the same affliction on Isaacs, and, no doubt, on the rest of the Liberal government as well.

His attention to conflict within Britain, did not, however, blind him to the larger threat from outside. In June 1913, on the occasion of a formal visit to England by the French President, he wrote "France", his tribute to the country "beloved of every soul that loves its fellow-kind!" The old enemies were now allies: instead of fighting each other, they would unite against a common foe:

> We were schooled for dear life's sake, to know each other's blade.
> What can Blood and Iron make more than we have made?

All the time that Kipling was writing these public poems, full of anger, betrayal, bitterness, and fear for Britain's future, he was also writing a series of children's poems of an imaginative delicacy and historical range unmatched by any other English author. These poems, published together with prose stories in *Puck of Pook's Hill* (1906) and *Rewards and Fairies* (1910), or to accompany C. R. L. Fletcher's historical narrative in *A History of England* (1911), were not the first that Kipling had written specifically for children. Their careful blend of entertainment and instruction is foreshadowed in the *Jungle Books* of the mid-1890s, and, their subtle air of intimacy with a youthful audience in *Just So Stories* (1902). The *Just So* poems were intended to be read to very young children. Some of them inculcate simple morals ("The Camel's hump is an ugly lump" and "I keep six honest serving-men"), while "Pussy can sit by the fire and sing" is a classic example of a child being encouraged to observe, and learn from, a common domestic situation. Whether the balance falls in favour of instruction or entertainment, Kipling's main concern is to communicate a pleasure in the rhythms and meanings of words, often revealing a delight in nonsense verse ("When the cabin port-holes are dark and green" and "China-going P. and O.'s") that demonstrates his deep admiration for Lewis Carroll. The later poems, historical and contemporary in setting, were directed at older children, and, as Kipling admitted, their parents as well.[10] The main purpose of the poems (and, of course, the stories) was to instil an understanding of England's past, and through that a sympathetic appreciation of what Englishness represented in the modern world. A number of other poems, written at this time though published elsewhere, are closely related to these concerns, notably "Our Fathers Also", *Traffics and Discoveries* (1904), "The Recall", *Actions and Reactions* (1909), and, some years later, "The Land", *A Diversity of Creatures* (1917) which re-introduces the archetypal countryman Hobden who features in the Puck stories.

"Puck's Song", the opening poem of *Puck of Pook's Hill*, not only establishes an appropriate atmosphere, it also indicates some of the themes Kipling will examine in the book and the historical method he is to employ:

See you the dimpled track that runs
All hollow through the wheat?
O that was where they hauled the guns
That smote King Philip's fleet.

History is a continuous process. The past is not something dead and finished with, but constantly in the present, observable in the paths, brooks, woods, pastures, and ditches of the countryside. These topographical features are reminders of generations of men and women whose activities have moulded the distinctive Englishness of English character – Elizabethan sailors preparing to repulse the Spanish invaders; dark-age settlers; Roman, Viking, and French conquerors. Puck himself epitomises the conviction that the Past is always in the Present. He is conjured up by a performance of Shakespeare's *A Midsummer Night's Dream* on Midsummer's Eve; he represents not only the survival of great art, but also the yet older superstitious world of faerie that Shakespeare could still draw on. The magic Puck employs to bring long-dead people back to life is not really magic at all: it is a metaphor for sight. Look carefully, and all the Past is there to see, everywhere around, and embodied in the two English children Puck befriends. They are the inheritors, and products, of long, complex traditions:

Trackway and Camp and City lost,
Salt Marsh where now is corn –
Old Wars, old Peace, old Arts that cease,
And so was England born.

Not that magic, or at least some spiritual force, can be entirely discounted, for this is not "any common Earth/Water, or wood or air", but England, "Merlin's Isle of Gramarye".

Although it is a prime motive of these poems to awaken and sustain patriotic feelings, there is no "English Flag" or "Et Dona Ferentes" among them; and, with the focus being on preindustrial society, modern manifestations of class-consciousness are also excluded. There are even few poems of spirited exploration or adventure, and those that Kipling did include ("Thorkild's Song" and "Frankie's Trade", for example) seem peripheral. As we are told in "A Charm", it is not the "great nor well-bespoke" who are celebrated here:

> But the mere uncounted folk
> Of whose life and death is none
> Report or lamentation.

So, the Viking invader is portrayed not directly as a bloodthirsty warrior, but through the eyes of his lonely wife in the moving lament "Harp Song of the Dane Women". Kipling frequently adopts an unexpected point of view to reveal the human experiences underlying outwardly glamorous or courageous roles. The focal point of "A Smuggler's Song" is a young girl being given advice on what *not* to notice as the smugglers go about their business, a technique that conveys a more vivid illustration of the important part played by smuggling in many eighteenth-century rural communities than could possibly be achieved by a swashbuckling ballad. Even in "Poor Honest Men", a companion poem to "A Smuggler's Song", which portrays smugglers running goods through a naval blockade during the Napoleonic Wars, there is a distinctly non-heroic edge to the smugglers' activities, with the self-justifying, wheedling tone of their narrrative leaving the reader uncertain of their true motivation.

Distinguished historical figures, imagined and real, are treated in a similarly oblique manner. Sir Richard Dalyngridge, one of the Norman invaders, sings not of his conquests, but of how he has been conquered, by love of England and a Saxon woman. To the accompanying rhythms of a country dance, Queen Elizabeth is portrayed in terms of the reflection of herself that she sees in a looking-glass. It is a study of a suppressed conflict between personal inclination and public duty that provoked from Robert Bridges, himself renowned for his technical knowledge of poetics, an expression of admiration for the concealed brilliance of Kipling's technique.[11] In this respect, "A St Helena Lullaby" is equally impressive. The verse form employed in this poem about Napoleon is closer to that of a traditional ballad than a lullaby, though the relevance of the title is slowly revealed. The poem opens with two questions:

> "How far is St Helena from a little child at play?"
> What makes you want to wander there with all the world between?

To these questions, and the many others in the poem, there can be no convincing answers. All that can be known for certain is that particular events occurred – Austerlitz, the invasion of Russia, Waterloo – which affected the course of world history, but the psychology of Napoleon remains inscrutable. He is a man of destiny: they are definable stages in his life, from the cradle to St Helena.

Running throughout the poems in *Puck of Pook's Hill* and *Rewards and Fairies* is the perennial human need to acknowledge the existence of a higher supernatural power. Puck invokes "Merlin's Isle of Gramarye"; Napoleon is a man of inexplicable Destiny; the Roman Centurion prays to Mithras, "God of the Morning"; the Astrologer places his faith in the stars; Eddi, the Catholic priest ignored by the pagan Saxons, celebrates Christmas with a service for the only two living creatures willing to attend, an ox and an ass. The most substantial poem of Christian faith is "Cold Iron". It is one of a number of Kipling's poems which advances a serious message by means of an apparently inappropriate rhythm. "Cold Iron" can be sung to the tune of the nursery-rhyme "Sing a Song of Sixpence", as the social setting of the opening stanza – the Baron in his "citadel" together with "mistress" and "maid" – indicates. But the poem has nothing to do with blackbirds pecking off noses. It evokes the different symbolic meanings given to iron through the ages, as well as the practical uses to which it has been put, and concludes with an image of the nails that held Christ to the Cross, for "Iron out of Calvary is master of men all".

Kipling's educative impulse is, however, moral and patriotic rather than religious, and his method usually rests on a trust in the child-reader's imagination to interpret the subtle meanings and rhythms of the poems, and to relate them to the prose stories and other poems. In the imagery of one of the most mysterious of the poems, the child is directed to "the way through the woods", but it is left to him or her to discover whether there *is* still a "way" forward, or whether time has obliterated it. Only very occasionally is didacticism allowed to become overt. *Puck* closes with "The Children's Song" which calls on the young readers to "pledge" themselves to their "Motherland . . . head, heart, and hand through the years to be!", but by *Rewards and Fairies*, four years later, this kind of direct nationalistic exhortation had given way to poems teaching lessons of a more general nature. The most remembered of these is "If– ", which, as Kipling observed, "escaped from the book, and for a while ran about the world."[12] Like "The Absent-Minded Beggar", it was copied, parodied, recited, and reproduced in a variety of ways – needlework samplers being a favourite – until its eminently sensible, skilfully articulated maxims became a byword for unacceptable cloying moralism. Less remembered, though a far more successful poem, is "Our Fathers of Old" in which Kipling achieves a seemingly effortless blend of past and present. The "excellent herbs" that "our fathers of old" trusted to cure their ills are celebrated in melodic lists of names ("Almost singing themselves they run") and as though in a mood of unshakeable idealism of the past. But:

Wonderful little, when all is said,
  Wonderful little our fathers knew.
Half their remedies cured you dead –
  Most of their teaching was quite untrue –

Their weird beliefs and crude medicines may have had little real effect on the illnesses that afflicted them, yet "what a wonderful war they waged!" Now that their superstitions have been shown up as nonsense and replaced by the rationality of the modern world, what is there left for our fathers of old to teach us?:

Down from your heaven or up from your mould,
Send us the hearts of our fathers of old!

After *Rewards and Fairies*, Kipling wrote no more stories for children. His own children, Elsie and John, who had been so closely associated with the composition of these works, were now in their teens; and, on a less personal level, the programme he had set himself in the aftermath of the Boer War was now completed. He would almost certainly have written no more children's poems either, had it not been for the friendship he formed with C. R. L. Fletcher.

Fletcher was a Fellow of Magdalen College, Oxford; a respected historian; a Delegate of Oxford University Press; and an enthusiastic supporter of the movement to introduce modern subjects into the university curriculum. His ambitions as an author were, however, political rather than academic. Like Kipling, Fletcher was concerned to justify traditional values in the face of the growing power of the Liberal Party and Liberalism's increasing willingness to accommodate Socialist principles. He was a committed Tory, Anglican, Protectionist, and Imperialist. His political views were so extreme that even his Conservative colleagues at Oxford were wary of him. The task he set himself, and undertook with missionary dedication, was the political education of children through history. This was to be achieved with *An Introductory History of England* which consisted of five substantial volumes, published at irregular intervals between 1904 and 1923. In his preface to the first volume, which carried England's history "from earliest times to the close of the Middle Ages", Fletcher condemned the rote-learning commonly employed in school history classes, and argued that the historian should appeal to children's natural curiosity about the world around them, their idealism, and their love of stories:

> My own view is that English History should be an inheritance of childhood: that its legends and its romance should grow into our thoughts from very early years, and expand themselves with the expansion of our minds; that we should feel History and dream of it rather than have it as a lesson.[13]

Such theories were hardly new, but they were developing at least a new kind of urgency for someone of Fletcher's political convictions. Modern Liberalism and Socialism were regarded as deviations from, rather than developments of, English history. They could flourish only by destroying the past and promising a utopian future. Once again like Kipling, Fletcher saw the Liberals as already embarked on this path of destruction in Ireland, South Africa, and India: as they moved ever closer to the Socialists – who were assumed automatically to be not only anti-capitalism, but anti-empire, anti-army, and anti-navy as well – the total abandonment of the British Empire was certain. Authority for this orgiastic obliteration of tradition was seen as resting solely on specious appeals to "the people" or "democracy". As Fletcher admitted in one of his later books, his faith in democracy as a form of government was no greater than Aristotle's had been, and he preferred to use the word "freedom". Democracy would mean State Control and regulation on behalf of an abstract entity, "the people": it would repress individual endeavour and creativity, and act as the enemy of "freedom", the assumption that all members of society had equal rights under "the Law".[14] Used in this sense, freedom was not regarded as an abstract concept. It was the English way of doing things; what Fletcher liked to call "national character", and, in effect, what Kipling meant by the civilising mission of the white man. It was the product of centuries of struggle against tyranny, and now, at the moment when England should be exporting it proudly to the rest of the world, its very existence was threatened from within by the modern tyranny of the Liberal-Socialist alliance.

It is not known exactly when or how Kipling and Fletcher became acquainted, but it is clear that while Kipling was working on *Puck of Pook's Hill* he came across the first volume of Fletcher's *Introductory History of England*, liked it so much that he read parts of it aloud to his children, and drew on it for background material in *Puck*.[15] Perhaps Kipling simply found Fletcher's book among many others he was using for historical research: perhaps Fletcher sent it to him. Certainly in May 1907 Kipling received a complimentary copy of Fletcher's second volume, and that too arrived at an opportune moment. Kipling was writing the story "Gloriana" which he would later include in *Rewards and Fairies*: by chance, Fletcher's new volume also dealt with Queen Elizabeth I and discussed the circumstances that led to her being known as Gloriana.[16] These small coincidences were nothing compared with the curious fact that both men were busily engaged in using history to chart the development of the English national character and through that to expose the heresies of modern Liberalism. It was this that Kipling would have recognised immediately in the *Introductory History*. Of course, the methods adopted were entirely different. Fletcher's approach to historical narrative had nothing of

Kipling's teasing multi-layered intricacy. His style was clear and straightforward enough to engage the attention of an intelligent child, though frequently disjointed by forced analogies with modern politics:

> For all good government the governed must pay. We Englishmen are very slow to realise this: and peaceable merchants will often grumble at, and misguided men in Parliament get up and denounce, the taxation necessary to build the battleships that defend their hearths and homes.[17]

Kipling would have been only too conscious of the crudity of Fletcher's attempt there to give a contemporary relevance to the decline of the Roman Empire in Britain, but he would also have applauded the sentiments being expressed. As with Gwynne some years earlier, Fletcher was welcomed as a staunch ally in a generally hostile world. He might have lacked subtlety, but he was saying the right things and aiming to influence the right people.

It was probably thinking along these lines that led to the collaboration between the two men on a single-volume history of England for children, though, in spite of their shared political and didactic beliefs, it was not inevitable that they should feel the need to work together. Such a project could have been regarded as duplication of work they were already engaged on. Fletcher was only half-way through his *Introductory History*, and Kipling, who was notoriously unwilling to attempt to repeat a success, had just completed his equivalent books. Yet when, in May 1910, Fletcher put the idea, Kipling's response was swift and enthusiastic. It took the form of a joke-letter from a semi-literate poetical plumber to whom Kipling was supposed to have passed Fletcher's proposal. The plumber is named as Albert Meaking Fletcher, a slip of the pen, as Kipling later acknowledged. In this modern collaboration he would obviously be playing the part of Beaumont:

Honoured Sir,

I have seen your letter to Mr R. Kipling re sittuation oferred one (1) Tory Poet to do Histerecle Poems for yr New Book of Histery and you saying you want a Tory Poet to do Same Sir do not be deseived by Outward appearanses and excuse my bad Pen but I am yr Mann for this Jobb.

The letter goes on to suggest what is needed:

I think it will be best done by Epocks. After you have done a Histerecle Epox in yr Common English then I will do the Epockicle Poetry to fit as per Speceified . . . One Piece Poetry for each Chapter in Book and one extra Peice for the end with a Morrle.

Fletcher is urged to send the separate chapters along as he writes them so that the poetry can be fitted to them, and there is a revealing explanation why the proposal is welcome: "Kipling wants me to do have the Job as he chucked doing a new Histercle book on his Own because he does not know enough for that Jobb."[18]

Beneath the laboured misspelling – which Kipling probably employed simply as a suitable "historical" response, though he may, more specifically, have had in mind the long tradition of artisan poets writing to their patrons – a great deal of valuable information is provided about the relationship between the two men. They are agreed that this is to be "Tory" history, a weapon in their campaign against Liberalism. Their writing roles are to be complementary, with Fletcher's "Common English" providing a simple narrative and Kipling's far greater literary skills adding emotion and memorability: joke though the letter is, this is a rare moment when Kipling refers to his work as "poetry" rather than "verse". The collaboration also represents a union of scholarship and literature. Kipling's admission that he had given up writing just such a history of England on his own because of his lack of scholarship is particularly pertinent. Whatever the quality of his writing for children, Fletcher was a genuine scholar, a type of person (providing, of course, that they had the right political views) that Kipling always admired: in later years, when the *History of England* was largely forgotten, Kipling continued to correspond with Fletcher, mainly about Horace. He was a man who could be relied upon to know about the past, someone who would provide a trustworthy foundation for Kipling's intuitive, impressionistic approach to history. For his part, Fletcher must have known that his *Introductory History* was unlikely to reach the readers he wanted: it was too large, too heavy, too ambitious. It was Fletcher who realised that a short, simply-written one-volume history, combining prose and poetry, might have more effect than his cumbersome five volumes, but it was Kipling who supplied the appropriate phrase for the enterprise. "For babes," he told Fletcher, "one must give peptonized patriotism."[19]

When the contract for the book was being drawn up it was suggested that Kipling should receive a larger royalty than Fletcher. From a business point of view it made good sense: as one of the most famous children's authors in the world, Kipling's name would virtually guarantee high sales. Kipling, however, insisted that he and Fletcher should be regarded as co-authors, with any royalties being divided equally between them.[20] In one sense this is simply another instance of Kipling's generosity on matters of literary business, but it also raises more important questions about the nature of the collaboration and the book it produced. Relations between Kipling and Fletcher were affable, though never close. As we have seen, their political views largely coincided, and there was no disagreement between them about the propagandist purpose the *History of England* was intended to serve. What is less clear is whether Kipling was aware that Fletcher was widely distrusted for his extreme views on the political uses of educational books.

Kipling would almost certainly not have known (until, perhaps, many years later) that Fletcher had repeatedly urged Oxford University Press to publish a school history of England and been turned down.[21] Kipling was Fletcher's trump card. Fearful of losing Kipling and just as fearful of signing up Fletcher, OUP still hesitated and only succumbed when Fletcher threatened to take the book to another publisher. Even then, Charles Cannan and R. W. Chapman, the Secretary and Assistant Secretary of OUP, were so nervous about the agreement that they decided to postpone putting it forward for the necessary approval of the Delegates, one of whom was Fletcher himself. In the words of Peter Sutcliffe: "It had become a conspiracy, a misdemeanour without precedent if it were to carry the Clarendon Press imprint."[22] In later years, when Fletcher wanted to bring the book up to date for a new edition by adding a chapter on the First World War, Kipling tried to dissuade him. He refused to contribute new poems to the edition, and suggested that the title page be changed to indicate that Fletcher was the sole author and that Kipling had simply contributed the verses. Fletcher would not agree to that and the new edition went ahead with the additional chapter and an unchanged title page.[23]

It is clear enough that by 1929 when these exchanges took place Kipling wanted to dissociate himself from the prose section of the book, though the extent of Kipling's contribution to the prose and why he didn't come to distrust Fletcher much earlier remain matters for conjecture. In the years leading to the First World War Kipling's own pronouncements in private letters and public lectures were scarcely less temperate than Fletcher's, though in his imaginative writings such views are subdued or transmuted. He probably did not know how virulently anti-Catholic and anti-Irish Fletcher was, and as Fletcher was keen to secure Kipling's collaboration on the book his approaches would have been diplomatic; perhaps Kipling had heard something of Fletcher's prejudices and ignored them in the greater cause of "peptonized patriotism". As he had read and enjoyed the first volumes of Fletcher's *Introductory History*, he would have known the kind of children's writer he was dealing with. He also read Fletcher's synopsis of the *History of England*; drafts of individual chapters so that he could decide on what poems were needed and where they should go; and a complete draft of the book. At the very least he suggested changes to Fletcher, and almost certainly re-wrote some of the prose. Fletcher insisted that "all the pretty little love-poems in prose to England" were written by Kipling: more cautiously, Kipling himself admitted to another correspondent that in addition to the poems he "helped a little with the text also".[24] That was only to be expected, but it still seems extraordinary that he didn't exercise greater control over the text and cut out some of Fletcher's more outrageous statements or insist on them being modified. There was no sign of him wishing to dissociate himself from Fletcher in 1911 when the book was published. It was received with the now customary critical responses of adulation from some reviewers and disgust from others, and Kipling wrote to Fletcher:

> How badly, how extremely urgently, the Work was needed! And how nice it is to think that anything the Sons of Wantonness produce as a counterblast will only be an imitation.[25]

Given such a gloating and blatantly propagandist attitude, the most extraordinary thing of all about the *History of England* is the discrepancy of tone that is immediately apparent between the prose and the poetry. Two editions of the book were published simultaneously, one for the general market, the other for schools: both carried illustrations by Henry Ford. Eager to boost the school edition, Fletcher also published a *Teacher's Companion to a School History of England* which listed historical sources, indications for further reading, and suggestions on how teachers might use the book in the classroom. Both Fletcher and Kipling were convinced that the reason it didn't flourish as a textbook was because the Liberal government intervened to prevent it being used in State Schools.[26] There were certainly members of the government who would have disapproved of the book, though a more plausible explanation for its failure to be adopted as a textbook lay in the changing nature of historical research and teaching which were already beginning to move away from constitutional and political subjects and giving a more central place to the growth of industrial society, trade unions, and the Labour Party, an emphasis that pertains to the present day. In that context, Fletcher's history was laughably old-fashioned and instantly dated. Kipling's poems, however, were not. Separated from the prose, the best of them were widely admired, frequently anthologised, and learned by heart in schools throughout the country. Very soon few people remembered, or cared about, the poems' controversial first publication.

One of the earliest pieces of advice Kipling gave to Fletcher was that he should pay less attention to Neolithic man and get on to the Romans as soon as possible.[27] Kipling helped him to do this by writing an introductory poem to the *History* called "The River's Tale" in which the Thames tells, in a suitably free-flowing manner, its own early history:

> And life was gay, and the world was new,
> And I was a mile across at Kew!
> But the Roman came with a heavy hand,
> And bridged and roaded and ruled the land,
> And the Roman left and the Danes blew in –
> And that's where your history books begin!

It provided Fletcher with a wonderfully perky lead, and he started his narrative calmly enough, but he was able to behave himself only until he reached the cave-men:

> How clever and hard-working these men must have been! No doubt there were a few sneaks and lazy wretches then, as there are now, who tried to beg from other people instead of fighting for themselves and their wives. But I fancy such fellows had a worse time of it than they have now. A man who wouldn't work very soon died.[28]

Fletcher's colleagues at Oxford University Press had been worried by the thought of what he might write about Ireland, and their fears were justified. All it took was the arrival of St Patrick to set him off:

> St Patrick, you may have heard, had banished the snakes from that island, but had not succeeded in banishing the murderers and thieves, who were worse than many snakes.[29]

Even Fletcher's praise for historical figures he admired was made to sound defamatory rather than elevating:

> Thus you will say I have drawn for you the picture of a monster of cruelty and selfishness? Yes, Henry was just that. But he was also something much more. He was a great patriot, a great Englishman. He taught Englishmen to rely on themselves and their ships.[30]

And, imperialist though he was, there were obviously some colonies Britain could do without:

> The prosperity of the West Indies, once our richest possession, has very largely declined since slavery was abolished in 1833. The population is mainly black, descended from slaves imported in previous centuries, or of mixed black and white race; lazy, vicious and incapable of any serious improvement, or of work except under compulsion.[31]

It is notable that Kipling chose to write poems on none of Fletcher's personal bugbears. There is nothing on the Irish, the Pope, congenitally vicious West Indians, imperial conquest (except when England is the colonised country), or work-shy

English loafers. Even when the text and the poems are closely linked the difference in tone is striking. A good example of this is the concern, shared by both authors, that Britain should maintain a strong navy. Fletcher introduces Kipling's poem on the subject with the statement: "At whatever cost to ourselves, it is our duty to keep our navy so strong that it must be forever impossible for us to be defeated at sea."[32] It sounds like the cue for a rousing patriotic hymn or a ballad of courage and self-sacrifice. What the reader gets is "Big Steamers" ("Oh, where are you going to, all you Big Steamers"), in which a young child asks questions for a steamer to answer. Fletcher's demand for a poem that would boost support for the British Navy is met by Kipling, but not until the sixth stanza and only when the child has developed enough understanding to ask the pertinent question:

> "Then what can I do for you, all you Big Steamers,
> Oh, what can I do for your comfort and good?"
> "Send out your big warships to watch your big waters,
> That no one may stop us from bringing you food."

As in his earlier history poems, and unlike Fletcher, Kipling always has in mind the youthfulness of his readers, and their varying degrees of intelligence and comprehension. The same technique of using a comforting, familiar image (a "Big Steamer") to convey a message of national importance, is applied in "My Father's Chair" to the far more abstruse issue of the Constitution:

> There are four good legs to my Father's Chair –
> Priest and People and Lords and Crown.
> I sits on all of 'em fair and square,
> And that is the reason it don't break down.

Fletcher wants to prepare the reader for a discussion of how Edward I "shaped" various "assemblies into regular parliaments", and this Kipling does by using a commonplace object to represent sturdiness, equality, fair-play, security, and constitutional balance.[33]

The shaping of England and the English national character is, of course, the main theme of the *History*, as it had been of *Puck* and *Rewards and Fairies*, though with Kipling's poems now grounded more firmly in actual events and personalities by Fletcher's narrative. The first third of the book portrays England as weak, divided, and open to colonisation by the Romans, Danes, and the Normans, who finally, in the words of the refrain of the poem on William the Conqueror, "hammer" England "into one!" The internal conflict between Norman and Saxon culminates in the signing of the "Magna Carta", which is celebrated by Kipling with "The Reeds of Runnymede", and followed by the gradual establishment of the parliamentary system evoked in "My Father's Chair". The closing poem of this section of the *History* is "The Dawn Wind" which makes no mention of historical events at all, but, in a highly lyrical vein unusual for Kipling, portrays medieval superstition being blown away by a new spirit of enquiry and discovery. Two of these poems about the early shaping of England – "Dane-Geld" and "The Roman Centurion's Song" – demonstrate Kipling skilfully incorporating a contemporary moral in historical disguise. "Dane-Geld" is a jangling chant in which internal rhymes are used repeatedly to create the memorable lesson that no nation should ever give in to blackmail: "For the end of that game is oppression and shame/And the nation that plays it is lost!" In the *History* it is the Saxons who try unsuccessfully to buy off the Danes, but in 1911 many adult readers of the poem would have grasped the implication that England had been paying too much "Dane-geld" to Germany and sooner or later would have a much larger account to settle.

The contemporary relevance of "The Roman Centurion's Song" is not unrelated to that of "Dane-Geld", though it is communicated with much greater subtlety. Throughout "the years between" Kipling's imagination had been drawn repeatedly to comparisons between the Roman and the British Empires. England had not always been the centre of a vast empire: it too had once been an imperial colony. Like Conrad's Marlow in *Heart of Darkness*, Kipling looked at England and realised that "this also has been one of the dark places of the earth".[34] Nor had England suffered from having imperial light shed on its darkness. The Danes had been largely marauders, but the Romans, and later the Normans, carried civilisation in the wake of military conquest. The Romans especially were settlers, improvers, exporting throughout the world their laws, art, and knowledge. Like the English, they were true "white men". History, however, recorded not only the power and influence of empires, the Roman Empire pre-eminent among them, but also their decline, a point that Kipling had been careful to make in *Puck*:

> Cities and Thrones and Powers,
>   Stand in Time's eye,
> Almost as long as flowers,
>   Which daily die:
> But, as new buds put forth,
>   To glad new men,
> Out of the spent and unconsidered Earth
>   The Cities rise again.[35]

Now, perhaps, it was the turn of the British Empire to make way for another, and in a number of his stories and poems of this period Kipling explored both the declining power of Roman Britain and its positive legacy. The Roman Centurion, like Sir Richard Dalyngridge in *Puck*, has fallen in love with Britain. Ordered back to Rome, he realises that it is Britain he has "served" for forty years, and he seeks permission from his commanding officer to remain, working "at any task you will." He is the type of imperial servant Kipling had admired in India thirty years earlier, but not only that. He also represents the changing pattern of the British Empire in the twentieth century, a world-wide network of colonies and dominions, peopled and served by British settlers who continued to pledge their allegiance to the mother-country, but, generation by generation, were gradually transferring their deeper affections to their own, new, independent countries.

Most of the remaining poems in the *History* are concerned with the expansion of England, at home and overseas, with the development of an imperial power that now, at the moment of writing, was about to face its greatest challenge. As always, Kipling's historical point of view is imaginative and idiosyncratic. "The Dutch in the Medway" is another lively warning that Britain must be prepared for sudden invasion, while the expansionist wars of the eighteenth century are embodied in a celebration of "Brown Bess", the flint-lock rifle, now quaint but once a modern and effective weapon. Fletcher's account of the American War of Independence is framed by two poems. The first is Kipling's clearest expression of his belief that "these worshippers at Freedom's shrine" only became passionate about freedom once England had "put half a world to flight", and the second, with the war lost, is a lament for the dead:

> The snow lies thick on Valley Forge,
>   The ice on the Delaware,
> But the poor dead soldiers of King George
>   They neither know nor care –

Kipling's concern to blend past and present is seen most effectively in "The French Wars". The long centuries of naval battles between England and France are commemorated through a rhythmic listing of the types of ships used by the two countries to wage war on each other, and then abruptly replaced by an up-to-date image of "poor sea-sick passengers" trudging wearily through customs. In this way are old enmities replaced by modern alliances.

As Fletcher moved closer to the present, Kipling's poems became more generally thematic. The achievements of Victorian England are embodied in the person of the Queen herself, though the tribute to her, "The Bells and Queen Victoria", is one of the least successful poems of the whole of the *History*.[36] The Industrial Revolution is represented by "The Secret of the Machines", a vigorous reminder to the young readers that they are living in an age of technological wonders which, for all their power and indications of constant progress, "are nothing more than children of your brain!" In the concluding poem of the book, "The Glory of the Garden", Kipling offered an inclusive, mythic view of England. The central image of England as a garden refers back to Shakespeare, and to the substantial seventeenth-century tradition of country-house poetry. Kipling's opening stanza suggests continuity with that tradition. His garden is "full of stately views": there are "lawns and avenues", "terraces", "statues", even "peacocks". But all of this is merely outward show, a formal representation of a more substantial inner "glory". At the "heart" of this Garden of England there is not a country house at all, but "tool- and potting-sheds", "dungpits", "drains", and "planks". Nor are there any noble residents, only "the gardeners, the men and 'prentice boys". The Sons of Mary have obviously been banished to make way for the Sons of Martha, and rightly so, for gardens such as this are not made "By singing: 'Oh, how beautiful!' and sitting in the shade." They are places of work where "better men than we" begin their careers "grubbing weeds from gravel-paths with broken dinner-knives." However humble their contributions, all workers are welcome to become "partners" in this particular enterprise, though, if the glory of the garden is to be maintained, one further quality is required. As Adam, the first gardener, understood, "half a proper gardener's work is done upon his knees." The pun is neat and conclusive. If the ideal is forgotten, then the Garden of England will go with it. But if it is constantly remembered, and followed, then "*the Glory of the Garden it shall never pass away!*"

[7]
Armageddon

> And they gathered them together into the place which is called in Hebrew Har-Magedon.
>
> Revelation, 16:16

On 4 August 1914, the day that Britain declared war on Germany, Carrie Kipling wrote in her diary: "My cold possesses me." To this Kipling added, "incidentally Armageddon begins."[1] Armageddon – the last great earthly battle to be fought before the Day of Judgement – was the term Kipling had long used in his remarkably accurate predictions of a war to come. He had foretold not only the war itself, but roughly when it would take place, who the principal enemy would be, the important roles that long-range artillery and aeroplanes would play in it, and, most perceptively, that Britain would need to conscript and train a modern army for the huge land battles that would have to be fought on the Continent of Europe. From H. A. Gwynne's articles "Is the Art of War Revolutionised?" which were published in the *Friend* while Kipling was still on the paper's staff, he would even have known the form that the land battles were to take: military stalemate, trench warfare, and the terrible policy of attrition, were no surprise to him. Observing the success of long-range, smokeless rifles in the Boer War, Gwynne prophesied "a state of things which has never been known in the history of war":

> In the future, the curious sight will be seen of regiments or even brigades lying flat on the ground, doing little damage to the enemy and suffering little loss, and yet being as useless to their general as if they were snoring in their barracks at home.[2]

"Yes," Kipling admitted to a close friend on the day that Armageddon began, "I feel like Jonah or whoever it was who went about saying: 'I told you so.'"[3]

Inevitably, he felt aggrieved that so many of his warnings had been ignored and that Britain was not better prepared for the war, but he was not smug and he did not regard the advent of war with enthusiasm. It was Rupert Brooke's youthful romanticism, rather than Kipling's Jonah-like gloom, that welcomed the war and invoked the ancient theme of warriors transfigured by glorious death:

> Blow out, you bugles, over the rich Dead!
> There's none of these so lonely and poor of old,
> But, dying, has made us rarer gifts than gold.[4]

It was also Brooke who "thanked God" for bringing to the young men of Britain "peace" through war, and the opportunity to escape from "a world grown old and cold and weary".[5] In complete contrast, Kipling's opening public statement on the war, "For All We Have and Are", first published in *The Times*, 2 September 1914, was sombre and regretful:

> Our world has passed away,
> In wantonness o'erthrown.
> There is nothing left to-day
> But steel and fire and stone!

The "Hun is at the gate!" and must be resisted: he is a "crazed and driven foe" whom "the nations" must "meet and break and bind". This has to be achieved through war because there is no alternative. The poem was obviously intended to stir patriotic feelings in its readers, but Kipling makes no attempt to do this through appeals to military glory or glamorous resistance. The coming of war means that "the ages' slow-bought gain" has been "shrivelled in a night", and ahead there are only "naked days", "silent fortitude", and "iron sacrifice". He was fully convinced that Germany had been planning the war, cold-bloodedly and hypocritically, for many years, a point he was quick to make in "The Outlaws", the poem he contributed to *King Albert's Book* (1914). Most of the contributors to this handsomely-produced tribute to the King and the people of Belgium concentrated on the gallantry of "little" Belgium's refusal to surrender to the might of the German army, but Kipling stressed the malignant, sadistic nature of the German character:

> Through learned and laborious years
>   They set themselves to find
> Fresh terrors and undreamed-of fears
>   To heap upon mankind.

All the "abominations of old days/ That men believed were dead" were actually being nurtured by Germany until the moment, now arrived, when they could be loosed on mankind. Like many other people at the time, Kipling was eager to believe all the stories of German atrocities being circulated: nothing was too outrageous or bizarre. Britain was confronted with an evil enemy, and must now fight a "holy war", as Kipling was to call it in one of his later poems.

Modern attitudes to war poetry have been influenced so profoundly by the young combatant-poets of the First World

War that Kipling is now rarely thought of as a "war poet" at all, except, occasionally, within a context that places him as a leading representative of the kind of poetic rhetoric which the younger poets were reacting against. In 1914 Kipling was forty-eight years old and he was not, of course, a combatant in the war. Nor, for other reasons, could he be expected to write war poetry like that of Wilfred Owen, Isaac Rosenberg, or Siegfried Sassoon. The poetic tradition he grew up to admire, and to which he had made such a distinctive contribution, was deeply rooted in both English and Classical literature. It did not ignore the hideous suffering of the fighting men, and it was always capable of denouncing unjust wars, but it gave priority to the celebration of the virtues of courage, heroism, self-sacrifice, personal honour, and, above all, the willingness to die for one's country or an equivalent noble cause. There is no lack of these qualities in First World War poetry either, but what goes decisively is the crucial assumption that death in such circumstances is glorious. It was this that Owen, employing a famous line from Horace, dismissed scathingly as, "The old Lie: Dulce et decorum est pro patria mori."[6] Here, Horace is regarded as representative rather than exceptional in claiming that it is "sweet and fitting to die for one's country": the same moral could have been drawn from Homer, Virgil, Chaucer, Shakespeare, Milton, Wordsworth, Scott, Tennyson, and countless other earlier poets. Kipling would always stand by that tradition: in a just war, a "holy" war, it *could* be glorious to die, and sacrifice had to be accepted by everyone. He was never to recover fully from the death of his son in the Battle of Loos, September 1915, though even that could not shake his stern personal conviction that the war was right. "Lots of people are in our position," he told his old school-friend Dunsterville, "and it's something to have bred a man."[7]

Disillusionment with this kind of stoicism, though eventually overwhelming, was slow to develop. At first, it seemed as though little had changed since the Boer War. The British Expeditionary Force that went to France in 1914 was still, in effect, the old regular army. It was poorly equipped, barely mechanised, ill-prepared for the battles it would have to fight, and commanded by Sir John French who had made his name in South Africa. Kitchener was appointed Secretary of War in 1914, and, until his death two years later, provided the dominant public image of British determination through his famous recruiting campaign. Lord Roberts, though too old to hold an official post, died in France while visiting the B.E.F., the army that ever since the Boer War he had argued should be brought up to date, a point that Kipling stressed in his elegy:

> Never again the war-wise face,
> The weighed and urgent word
> That pleaded in the market-place –
> Pleaded and was not heard![8]

The slow, and then sudden, change of attitude to the war was recorded, and dated precisely, by the Welsh poet David Jones. As an infantryman on the Western Front in December 1915, Jones felt himself still in contact with the earlier "attractive amateurishness, and elbow-room for idiosyncrasy that connected one with a less exacting past." It remained just possible to experience "the period of the individual rifle-man, of the 'old-sweat' of the Boer campaign, the 'Bairnsfather' war." All of this was abruptly "terminated" by the Battle of the Somme in June 1916: from now on, the war was more mechanical, technical, and impersonal.[9] Jones doesn't mention Kipling in this context, though he might well have done, for being overthrown, with so much else, was the appropriateness of Tommy Atkins as a literary representative of the British soldier. The term "Tommy" remained in everyday use, and Kipling's ballads were popular with troops and civilians throughout the war and beyond, but it was now clear that they too belonged to a past age of warfare, that time, in David Jones's phrase, when there was still "elbow-room for idiosyncrasy". The old-style regimental songs and barrack-room ballads were being superseded by the products of Tin Pan Alley which, since its first tentative steps in the Boer War, had become a major commercial force in wartime entertainment and propaganda. The songs which were now most widely familiar to soldiers and civilians alike had been written especially for them, the mood carefully calculated to suit particular circumstances, and large popularity achieved not only by means of sheet music and the music hall, but by the gramophone as well. As before, the soldiers responded by enjoying the songs, while, at the same time, composing their own derogatory, debunking, or obscene versions of them. The wartime poetry that was to be so influential was totally involved in the changing nature of the war and with the everyday lives of the soldiers, but it was also highly literary. It was as unrelated to commercial song as it was to Kipling's barrack-room ballads. The cultural fragmentation that now typified literary London was also apparent in the songs and poetry of the trenches.

Kipling seems to have understood instinctively that his role in this war would be very different from that of any other military conflict with which he had been connected. As we have seen, in India and South Africa he had mingled easily with Tommy Atkins and had "tried for to explain" Tommy's "pleasure" and his "pain": in America, when he had expected war with Britain to break out, he made immediate plans to move "closer to the scene of action" so that he could try "to help with a little song or two in the intervals of special correspondence."[10] But in 1914 he did not rush to be with the B.E.F., or present himself as a spokesman for the ordinary soldier, or write barrack-room ballads for the troops. He could certainly have done any of these things. The moment the war started he was approached by the government and urged to help with the writing of official propaganda: this he refused to do. That he was expected by some people to take on an heroic public role is apparent in the false but persistent rumours that during the war he was recruited into the secret service or sent on an undercover diplomatic mission to America. In September 1915, Kipling himself was so puzzled by such rumours that he asked Gwynne to find out where they were coming from.[11] Whatever Kipling chose to do, or not do, in the war, was bound to be complicated by his controversial pre-war reputation. As the man whose prophecies had come true he was accorded a certain amount of grudging admiration, but the politicians who were now taking the country to war were the same politicians he had attacked for a decade as unpatriotic, self-seeking cowards. Their lack of foresight had ensured that Britain was ill-prepared for war, and Kipling had no faith in their ability to follow events through to the necessary victory. At the same time, he was a fervent patriot, determined to do everything in his power to support the struggle against Germany; everything, that is, short of becoming a paid spokesman of the government. As ever, his faith in the British troops was total. Like many other public figures, Kipling offered the government his home for use as a military hospital, visited training camps, spoke at army recruitment campaigns, and continued to argue that the voluntary system of recruitment should be replaced by conscription. But, of course, his main contribution to the war effort would be as a writer, and he was more than ever determined that he should retain his independence to speak the truth as he saw it.

Kipling's virtual exclusion from most studies of First World War poetry is perfectly understandable in terms of the emphasis such studies place on a younger generation of combatant-poets, but quite unreasonable in any wider consideration of poetry written about the war. Kipling's poetry does not challenge, lessen, or in any way diminish that of the combatant-poets. Occasionally his critical tone is similar to theirs, but his point of view is invariably that of the generation that has sent them to war. There is little jollity, no attempt to dramatise their wartime circumstances or feelings, no cheery Cockney accents, no easy emotional appeals on their behalf. All of that is left behind with the barrack-room ballads, or left to other writers and the Tin Pan Alley propaganda machine. In phrases which had long been central to Kipling's philosophy, the troops were the "Sons of Martha", the men who were "doing the work", and anyone who hindered them was the enemy, be it the Kaiser, the Pope, a British politician, or a striking munitions worker. It has often enough been pointed out that in 1914–18 war became total, the business now of civilians as well as troops. If that is correct, there is surely no reason why, in such a war, a civilian shouldn't be as capable as an active serviceman of writing genuine war poetry. In effect, that was what Kipling did. He was an exceptionally well-informed civilian, and a writer with a unique experience of the British army, but a civilian nonetheless, and there can be no doubt that the views he expressed memorably in his poetry were shared by a very large proportion of other British civilians who lived through the painful day-to-day experiences of the war. That he was distanced from the most dangerous centres of the war, and that his poetry could no longer claim to speak for the soldiers at the Front, he would readily have acknowledged.

The volume in which Kipling collected most of his wartime poetry was *The Years Between* (1919). It carried, as previous volumes had done, a line-drawing on the title page to indicate the nature of Kipling's involvement with the poetry. All of the figures in the earlier illustrations had been physically active in one way or another, but the First World War soldier who appears in *The Years Between*, is sad, lonely, and passive. He is portrayed sitting on an up-turned bucket, his elbows resting on his knees. In one hand he is holding a cigarette, and in the other a letter. But he is not reading the letter, or drawing on the cigarette. His head is turned to one side, and he is staring perhaps at something, perhaps at nothing. Whatever his thoughts, they are incapable of being communicated to the reader.

In August 1915 Kipling was asked by the Admiralty to write a series of articles publicising the work of the Royal Navy. The work would be essentially no different from the reports he had already written on his visits to "New Army" training-camps in England and Scotland, and to the Western Front. These had been published initially in the *Daily Telegraph* and then as two pamphlets, *The New Army in Training*, and *France at War* which he had prefaced with his pre-war poem "France". All work of this kind was restricted by wartime censorship regulations, but what was now being asked of him was not government propaganda, and he accepted the Admiralty's invitation. The reason why the navy was felt to need publicity was also a matter of special interest to him. After nearly a year of war, the long-cherished assumption that any conflict between Britain and Germany would be settled by a massive sea-battle was proving to be completely wrong. There had been early naval clashes in distant waters, but the Royal Navy, though denied a spectacular Trafalgar-style victory, had successfully imposed a world-wide naval blockade and forced the German Fleet to remain in harbour.

If anything, British naval policy had so far been too successful. Public opinion in Britain was understandably obsessed with the horrific land battles taking place in France, and questions were beginning to be asked about what the navy was up to. There were more specific criticisms as well. Early in 1915, what might have been a decisive naval operation in the Dardanelles was transformed by a vacillating British government into the disastrous troop landings at Gallipoli. The Royal Navy was also under increasing criticism from neutral countries, America especially, for interfering with peaceful shipping. Britain was concerned that this could strengthen the position of the powerful pro-German lobby in America, jeopardise essential imports, and even bring America into the war against Britain. These fears were suddenly deflected in February 1915 when Germany, adopting a more aggressive policy towards the blockade, announced that the waters around Britain were now regarded as a war zone and that merchant ships entering the zone were at risk. In May the British passenger liner the *Lusitania* was sunk by German U-Boats off the coast of Ireland. More than a thousand lives were lost, many of them American, and the incident immediately developed into a propaganda battle, with Germany insisting that the *Lusitania* was a secret cover for the transportation of military equipment; America pondering whether it could any longer avoid entering the war; and Britain pointing to this attack on helpless civilians and neutral shipping as further evidence of the cowardly unprincipled nature of the Germans. Given less official publicity, though just as intensely felt, was the concern in Britain at the proven power and effectiveness of the U-Boats.

Kipling's brief was not to participate directly in this diplomatic wrangle, but to inform the public about the measures being taken by the Royal Navy to protect the British Isles. In the words used by the *Daily Telegraph* on 17 November 1915 when announcing its forthcoming publication of Kipling's articles, he would describe "the adventurous work of the armed trawlers, patrol boats, mine sweepers and submarines, which ceaselessly maintain our naval grip on the enemy in the North Sea and the home waters." In the mid-1890s when Kipling had written up his experiences on naval manoeuvres as *A Fleet in Being*, his subject had been the powerful new warships of the Channel Fleet. In comparison, the task to hand was less glamorous, though in its own way just as dramatic, and one that suited Kipling's interests and skills to perfection. The men he was to write about were known as "Auxiliaries", a term that Kipling used as a general title for some of his articles, because their main job was to keep the sea-ways open for merchant and naval ships. They were a miscellaneous group, made up of professional sailors who manned the new, experimental submarines; members of the Royal Navy Reserve who were merchant seamen in times of peace; and members of the Royal Naval Volunteer Reserve, mainly amateur sailors and fishermen in civilian life whose knowledge of trawling was transferred from fish to mines in the war. During his research, Kipling visited the Grand Fleet at Scapa Flow, but his main contacts were with the East Coast Patrol based at Harwich and Dover. Altogether he wrote three series of articles, *The Fringes of the Fleet* and *Tales of "The Trade"*, both of which dealt with the Auxiliaries; and *Destroyers at Jutland*, a more distanced and impressionistic account of the long-expected full-scale naval battle between the British and German Fleets that finally took place in the North Sea at the end of May 1916. All of the articles were published in newspapers, as separate pamphlets, and collected together as *Sea Warfare* (1916).

The poems Kipling wrote to accompany the articles reveal, even more forcefully than the articles themselves, his close involvement in the project: as originally published, most of the poems were untitled. One of them, "Be well assured that on our side", was written in Kipling's now familiar semi-official style; determined, solemn, and capped with a catchy refrain appealing to national unity: "The game is more than the player of the game/ And the ship is more than the crew!"[12] Two others ("In Lowestoft a boat was laid" and "Farewell and adieu to you, Greenwich Ladies") were variations on traditional sea songs, consciously adapted to point the continuity of this new kind of warfare with the ancient customs of the British navy.[13] They are communal songs, cheerfully bellicose, and focused on the way that the war has transformed the civilian characters of these volunteer sailors. This was a central theme not only of *Sea Warfare*, but of many of Kipling's other writings, both during and after the war. Each stanza of "In Lowestoft a boat was laid" is a variation on this theme, chanted to the repetitive work-rhythms of a sea-shanty:

> Her mate was skipper of a chapel in Wales.
> And so he fights in topper and tails –

In "The Changelings", a poem not published until many years later, though referring quite specifically to the events of 1915, the mood is calmly retrospective, ironically so given the harshness of "Sea Constables", the story the poem introduced:

> I was a dealer in stocks and shares,
> And you in butters and teas,
> And we both abandoned our own affairs
> And took to the dreadful seas.[14]

A related poem is "The Sons of the Suburbs" which Kipling submitted in December 1916 to *Blighty*, an innocuous comic periodical produced for the troops. According to R. E. Harbord, "the ladies who edited the paper would not print it unless the choruses were modified": this Kipling would not do, and the poem remained unpublished until after his death.[15] Kipling's "sons of the suburbs" are portrayed as quiet, decent young Englishmen, "unaccustomed to strife", but rendered fierce by the war. This point is made in the slightly saucy choruses that the editors of *Blighty* objected to:

> When the clergyman's daughter drinks nothing but water,
> She's certain to finish on gin.

Perhaps these rejected lines influenced the writing of the short story "Mary Postgate" which explores the more deadly transformation of a gentle spinster into a civilian warrior. The inevitability of the process is explained in "The Beginnings", the poem written to accompany "Mary Postgate":

> It was not part of their blood,
> It came to them very late
> With long arrears to make good,
> When the English began to hate.[16]

This, however, is a later mood. In the most successful of the *Sea Warfare* poems Kipling displays a structural control and evocative power reminiscent of the best of his earlier history poems. The courageous "changelings" are now portrayed not as rumbustious sailors or staid businessmen, but totally at one with their work, and their machines. The poem later given the title "Mine Sweepers" is representative:

> Dawn off the Foreland – the young flood making
> Jumbled and short and steep –
> Black in the hollows and bright where it's breaking –
> Awkward water to sweep.
> "Mines reported in the fairway,
> Warn all traffic and detain.
> Sent up *Unity, Claribel, Assyrian, Stormcock*, and *Golden Gain.*"

The first five lines of the stanza set the scene, with the deliberately awkward syntax recreating the swell of the sea that makes the identification of mines in the dawn light so difficult. Once this objective is achieved, the radio message back to base is simple and businesslike, with just a hint of romanticism provided by the listed names of the ships as they move in to deal with the mines. Each of the poem's three stanzas follows the same pattern, though with a shift in time, from dawn, through noon, to dusk. The whole operation, like the poem itself, is completed in a mood of masterly understatement.

The two poems about submarines are similarly objectified. Kipling called them "Tin Fish" and "The Trade". The first title, he explained, came about because many of the naval volunteers had been fishermen and always discussed "their work in terms of fish": the second was widely used by submariners to describe their job, though no one seemed to know its origin.[17] Kipling had written a poem about submarines some years before the war. Called "The Egg-Shell", it portrayed, in a fantastic and slightly gloating manner, the successful torpedoing of a ship from the position of invisibility that was a submarine's greatest strength.[18] The same theme is explored in "Tin Fish", though with more understanding and compassion. Like a fish, the submarine is hunted from above and ensnared from below, plotted and tracked by curious "eyes", the key player in a deadly sport, though ultimately, unlike the fish, it possesses the power to strike back, and, "the mirth of a seaport dies/ When our blow gets home." The same air of secrecy, of fragility and strength, pervades "The Trade". In appropriately plain language, Kipling compares the romantic naming of ships, the tradition he had just used to such good effect in "Mine Sweepers", with the mechanically-sounding letter and number classification given to submarines:

> They bear, in place of classic names,
>   Letters and numbers on their skin.
> They play their grisly blindfold games
>   In little boxes made of tin.

They are truly invisible, peering at the world through "one-eye", leaving "only whiffs of paraffin" on the surface of the sea, and invisible also when it comes to prize-claims or public applause. Invisibility is the essence of their "trade".

By the time that Kipling came to write about the Battle of Jutland in the Autumn of 1916, there was a new air of sadness and loss in his poetry, though set, as always, within a relentlessly stoical mould. He was describing Jutland in retrospect, but while the Battle of the Somme, which was to claim eventually a total of more than a million casualties, was actually taking place. "Have you news of my boy Jack?" the unnamed parent asks in one of the most famous and moving of Kipling's question-and-answer ballads, and there can be no comforting answer, "Except he did not shame his kind/ Not even with that wind blowing, and that tide." In comparison with the bleak message of "My Boy Jack", the determination to look to a brighter future expressed in "Zion" and "The Verdicts", the other poems in *Sea Warfare*, is strained and unconvincing. Closer in mood are two poems, "The Children" and "Rebirth", which were written about this time and published in Kipling's only volume of wartime stories, *A Diversity of Creatures* (1917). Kipling took great care to place them after stories which had been written and first published before the war, so that the poems comment on the tone of the stories, and perhaps on Kipling's own pre-war attitudes in the stories as well. "The Children" is a harrowing cry of pain and guilt by the parents of men who have died in the war which, in its final stanza, places Kipling close to Wilfred Owen in its visualisation of the dead men's flesh "lolled on the wires":

> To be blanched or gay-painted by fumes – to be cindered by fires –
> To be senselessly tossed and retossed in stale mutilation
> From crater to crater.

As in "My Boy Jack", there can be no acceptable response to the one question the parents want answered: "*But who shall return us our children?*"[19] "Rebirth" is more controlled, contemplative, and stoical. Once again restoration of past conditions is considered, but finally dismissed as an impossibility, for "we are what we are", so subdued to the horrors of war that "Death commands/ Hardly observance at our busier hands."[20] Closely related to these poems in which Kipling speaks on behalf of grieving parents, is "En-Dor" which was first published in *The Years Between*. Like many people in their position, Kipling and his wife had been approached by spiritualists claiming to be able to put them in touch with their dead son. His contempt for those who he was convinced were simply making money out of other people's gullibility is made apparent in "En-Dor", but the final impression left by the poem is one of compassionate understanding: "Even so, we have need of faith/ And patience to follow the clue."

Kipling closed *Sea Warfare* with a poem called "The Neutral" which had nothing whatever to do with tin fish, the trade, or Jutland. It was a conscience-stirring appeal to America to enter the war: perhaps Kipling felt that it would have more impact on American readers if they came across it in this particular context. When America did finally declare war on Germany in April 1917, he changed the title of the poem to "The Question", and wrote another poem welcoming the new ally which he called "The Choice". Kipling's ambivalent attitude to America is apparent everywhere in these poems, though this may not have been obvious at the time. In calling the first poem "The Neutral" Kipling was employing, as we shall see, one of the most offensive words he could think of, and it was quickly changed when no longer applicable, but when collected in later editions of his poetry as "The Question", he added the date 1916 and a sardonic explanatory footnote: "Attitude of the United States of America during the first two years, seven months and four days of the Great War." Even "The Choice", which celebrated the reunion of Britain and America, contained a probable rebuke. The speaker of the poem is "The American

Spirit", a reference back to Kipling's "An American" of 1894 in which, as noted earlier, the true American spirit is shown as constantly in conflict with its "avatar", the raucous, anti-British democrat. Kipling was genuinely pleased that the Americans had now joined the Allies, but he may also have been reminding them that in giving so much ground to their anti-British faction, not responding forcefully to the sinking of the *Lusitania*, and re-electing President Wilson who boasted of having kept America out of the war, they had very nearly denied their true spirit and surrendered to the avatar.

"The Neutral" marked Kipling's return to a more abrasive form of public poetry. The fundamental changes of attitude towards the war that David Jones noted as taking place in June 1916, were equally apparent to poets like Sassoon and Owen, and to Kipling. Although there was much hopeful talk of a negotiated settlement, the positions of all of the belligerents were actually hardening. Nobody was truly interested in President Wilson's peace initiative. Germany was already planning the policy of unrestricted warfare on shipping that would force America away from its neutralist stance. In Britain, military conscription had been introduced even before the mass slaughter of the Somme, and in December 1916, Lloyd George, now determined to push the war on to victory, took over from Asquith as Prime Minister. The disillusionment and anger that characterise so much of the war poetry written in 1917 and 1918 developed out of the conviction that the war was being prolonged unnecessarily, that there were no longer any clear national aims or ideals to fight for, and that the main thing now at stake was the vanity of politicians and generals. Kipling was not entirely aloof from these sentiments. He also believed that the war could have been ended earlier, and he blamed, as ferociously as anyone, political incompetence and self-seeking. "How he hates politicians!" Rider Haggard wrote of Kipling after one of their regular wartime meetings, "Worse than I do, even . . ."[21] His poem "Mesopotamia", written in response to the delayed publication of a report on a disgracefully bungled campaign in late 1915, is built on a reiterated contrast between the soldiers who died pointlessly and the army generals and politicians who long escaped censure, and, in the meantime, moved on to higher office. In a satirical mood close to that of Sassoon, Kipling points to the dead soldiers, "the eager and whole-hearted whom we gave," and asks:

> But the men who left them thriftily to die in their own dung,
> Shall they come with years and honour to the grave?

The emphasis of Kipling's poetry was, however, quite different from Sassoon's. The war had lasted longer than it should have done, not because neither side would negotiate a peace settlement, but because Britain had been ill-prepared for it in the first place, and, once committed, had failed to respond with sufficient single-minded determination. Talk of compromise, honourable peace, and negotiations, infuriated Kipling. To his mind, Germany was an evil force in the world, and its leader, the Kaiser, the earthly embodiment of Evil. In taking this line Kipling did not use the word "evil" casually, but with the full force of its theological meaning. No decent or sensible person could even think of negotiating with the Devil, or sitting down at a table with him to talk of peace and compromise. That was nonsensical, a shocking betrayal of the young men who had already given their lives for a just cause. There was only one way to deal with the Devil. He had to be consigned once again to the pit, so that the evil he spread about him could be purged from the world. Anyone who argued otherwise was, knowingly or not, on his side.

This was the kind of thinking, totally unacceptable to Sassoon or Owen, that informed a number of Kipling's poems written towards the close of the war, or shortly after, which were collected in *The Years Between.* "The Song of the Lathes" is described as being a tune hummed by "Mrs L. Embsay, widow" as she works a machine producing shells. Her husband and son have died in France, and now she does the only thing she can to avenge their deaths. Clear-eyed, steadfast, she is a close relative of Mary Postgate and "The Female of the Species", her thoughts and actions at one with the rhythm of the lathes and their deadly refrain: "*Shells for guns in Flanders! Feed the guns!*" Mrs Embsay has the right approach: she is simply getting on with the job at hand. Most of these poems, however, are concerned with people who are either hindering the work at hand or denying its worth. These are "The Hyaenas" whose natural proclivities are transferred to the politicians now carving up Europe and portrayed by Kipling in measured, simple language that just contains his personal fury:

After the burial-parties leave
 And the baffled kites have fled;
The wise hyaenas come out at eve
 To take account of our dead.

How he died and why he died
 Troubles them not a whit.
They snout the bushes and stones aside
 And dig till they come to it.

One such "hyaena" was Pope Benedict XV who several times during the war had tried to initiate peace negotiations and is savaged by Kipling, who believed that any such action was really pro-German, in "A Song at Cock-Crow". Rider Haggard, to whom Kipling read an early draft of the poem, described it as a "really remarkable, and most bitter poem", which it certainly is.[22] As a true descendant of Peter, the Pope busies himself by constantly denying the Lord, but whereas Peter weeps "for his wickedness when the cock crew", the Pope, who has acted out of self-aggrandisement rather than human frailty, can expect no mercy, and his temporal power is reduced by the war, "*(Because of his wickedness) when the cock crew!*"

The Kaiser, the Devil himself, could expect from Kipling even less sympathy than the Pope. "A Death Bed" was based on a report that the deposed Kaiser was dying of throat cancer. The poem interweaves three voices or thought processes – those of the Kaiser, his doctors, and a commentator who makes the crucial judgement that this slow painful death is appropriate for the man who has been responsible for the death of so many other people:

> Some die shouting in gas or fire;
>   Some die silent, by shell and shot.
> Some die desperate, caught on the wire;
>   Some die suddenly. This will not.

"A Death Bed" is Browningesque in its callous flirtation with a subject "on the dangerous edge of things", the voices that never communicate with each other, and the final throwaway line.[23] Also displaying the influence of Browning is "Natural Theology", in which various type-figures blame God for the "afflictions" they have suffered, and, one by one, in the same petulant tone, abandon religious faith. The "conclusion" to the poem expresses Kipling's perennial response to anyone attempting to shift the blame. Man is free, accept and face up to the consequences of your actions: "Only Thyself hath afflicted thee!"

The most remarkable of these poems, uniting all of the concerns just discussed, and finding to express them a perfect vehicle and tone of voice, is "The Holy War". The title is taken from John Bunyan's religious and political allegory of the same name, published in 1682, in which the town of Mansoul is besieged by the evil forces of Diabolus and finally saved by the army led by Emmanuel, the son of King Shaddai. Kipling's poem was first published in the Christmas number of a periodical called *Land and Water*, 6 December 1917. It was given a double-page spread, and ornately illustrated by E. J. Sullivan. In the top left there was a cross above the town of Mansoul, with a drawing of Bunyan announcing "No dealings with Diabolus." On the middle left, a clean-cut St George is preparing to do battle but is hindered by a cringing little man crying "Peace Peace!" The right-hand side depicts Diabolus inspiring a fire-breathing Kaiser. A banner proclaims: "Ich selbst und Gott!" ("I myself and God!"). The illustrations are quite a bit more Gothic than the poem itself, but their blend of old and new is true to the main theme of the poem, that "Two hundred years and thirty/ Ere Armageddon came" one man saw it all "And Bunyan was his name!" Kipling's admiration for Bunyan was long-standing, and there were many, and good, reasons why Kipling should have regarded Bunyan's tempestuous career as in many respects anticipating his own. Bunyan's family background was nonconformist, provincial, and relatively humble. He was assertive, independent, abrasive, self-made; a craftsman, soldier, preacher, moralist, allegorist, a writer of both prose and poetry. He had dedicated his life to the communication of what he believed were fundamental truths about mankind, scorning easy popularity and compromise, enduring long spells of imprisonment and poverty, and, in spite of all attempts to silence him, he had survived to exert a profound influence on the thought and behaviour of generations of readers. Now, Kipling announced, he had been a prophet of the First World War as well.

Kipling introduces the poem by presenting Bunyan's credentials:

A tinker out of Bedford,
A vagrant oft in quod,

A private under Fairfax,
A minister of God –

The judgemental tone of "A Death Bed", the cynicism of "The Hyaenas", the contempt of "A Song at Cock-Crow", are not discarded, but have been replaced by a lighter, more confident note, suitably reminiscent of one of Bunyan's own rousing hymns; direct, simple, controlled. As a working man, outcast, soldier, and minister, Bunyan was fully qualified to comment on a holy war from all angles, and as "holy" wars are always fundamentally the same – struggles between Good and Evil – what he said then, applies now. The "highly-screened positions", the "flame or poison-gas", all "the crimes that we call new":

John Bunyan had 'em typed and filed
In Sixteen Eighty-two.

The colloquial, slangy refrain, embodying Bunyan's and Kipling's true knowledge of what is really going on, is employed to rise above and effortlessly dismiss all objectors to the war. To Bunyan's seventeenth-century type-names (the "Lords of Looseness", "Perseverance-Doubters"), Kipling adds his own: the "brittle intellectuals/ Who crack beneath a strain", "State-kept Stockholmites", "The Pope, the swithering Neutrals", "The Kaiser and his Gott":

Their rôles, their goals, their naked souls –
He knew and drew the lot.

For Kipling, neutrals, pacifists, conscientious objectors, all such interveners, were hindering St George's crusade. If Mansoul/ Britain was to survive, there could be "no dealings with Diabolus".

By the time that Kipling published "Justice", his final public poem of the war, in *The Times* on 24 October 1918, it was clear that the Allies would have to have peace dealings with Diabolus: in fact, they were already under way, being manoeuvred by President Wilson, the despised former "neutral". "Justice" was not written to mark the armistice, which was still three weeks off: it was a contribution to the day of the year, designated "Our Day", when the Joint War Committee of the Red Cross Society and the Order of St John made its annual world-wide appeal for funds to help the sick and wounded. An editorial in *The Times* referred to Kipling's poem solely within this context, though the poem itself took a more conclusive, summarising approach to the war. In the following year, Kipling would use "Justice" as the concluding poem of *The Years Between*. In it, Kipling assumes that the war is all but over, Germany's "hour is past", "Evil Incarnate" has finally been restrained and must now "answer to mankind". But he is reluctant to welcome the final act that will "loose the word/ that bids new worlds to birth". Justice is more important than peace, justice for the sons who have died, and for those who will have to live with the peace terms. Before there can be a just peace, the Germans must "relearn the Law", and conditions in Germany must be such that never again can its "schools" or "priests" or "Kings" build "a people with the hearts of beasts". For Kipling, that point had not yet been reached: Germany, he believed, was essentially unchanged by the war.

If Kipling is remembered at all today as a poet of the First World War, it is not for the poems about the R.N.V.R., submarines, neutrals, pacifists, or holy crusades, but primarily for the important part he played in commemorating the victims of the war. Like many other distinguished writers, he contributed items to the many anthologies compiled for wartime causes, ranging from "The Outlaws" for *King Albert's Book* at the start of the war, through to "A Pilgrim's Way" in August

1918 for *Reveille*, a review of work being carried out to help disabled soldiers, which was edited by John Galsworthy; and, as we have seen, in a number of his poems published during the war, he speaks, representatively, for all parents whose sons have been killed. The unique nature of his association in the public mind with servicemen meant, however, that far more was expected of him, in this respect, than of any other poet or novelist. In spite of the sharp decline of his reputation among the new school of critics and writers, never before had he seemed so obviously the People's Laureate, though his constituency now consisted mainly of men and women from his own, and not necessarily the younger, generation. The commemorative work to which he gave much time in the post-war years epitomises the special kind of status he now held. It was undertaken to honour the dead on behalf of the generation, his own, which was responsible for the war. "For this we shall take expiation," he had admitted at the close of "The Children".

In literary terms, Kipling's most personal act of expiation was the writing of a history of the regiment in which his son had served. *The Irish Guards in the Great War* (2 vols. 1923) was not the type of work for which he was notably suited, but nor was it a task he could possibly avoid: he would have been only too aware of the influential part he had played in obtaining a commission for John Kipling in the Irish Guards, and, more generally, of the many harsh judgements he had passed on the Irish before the war. Any personal emotions Kipling might have experienced when writing the regimental history were scrupulously concealed, and in the old-style ballad "The Irish Guards", composed at the same time, the "wild geese" are portrayed with great gusto as they carry their renowned fighting abilities off to France.[24] The more public side of Kipling's commemorative poetry was connected with the work of the Imperial War Graves Commission which he joined as a committee member when it was founded in 1917 and which he served devotedly until his death nineteen years later.

The Commission's task initially was, in Kipling's own words, "to register, mark, and tend the graves of British soldiers, as well as to answer enquiries from relatives, and, when possible, to send them photographs of the graves," but its scope was quickly expanded to cover all imperial forces, and far more controversial matters.[25] Just as there had never been a war like this one, nor had there previously been such elaborate efforts to commemorate the dead. In addition to the unprecedented difficulties of identifying the mutilated bodies of hundreds of thousands of soldiers, and communicating with their relatives, there were national, religious and political susceptibilities to take into account; disputes on the design and siting of suitable monuments; complaints from politicians about the cost of it all; and at least one objection to Kipling being involved in the Commission's decisions because he was "not a known religious man".[26] Kipling was the Commission's principal literary representative. He wrote pamphlets and articles explaining the work of the Commission to the public, and was looked to for advice on all matters relating to the wording of commemorative inscriptions. It was his suggestion that a quotation from Ecclesiasticus, "Their name liveth for evermore", be adopted as the universal war epitaph. Only after his death did the extent of his involvement in this work become fully appreciated. "Every inscription of a general nature," the Registrar of the Commission acknowledged, "was composed or approved by him."[27] In 1922, when King George V made a "private pilgrimage" to the war graves in France and Belgium, Kipling wrote a prefatory poem "The King's Pilgrimage" for the official record of the event: he also wrote the "farewell speech" which the King delivered at Terlincthun cemetery in Northern France.

The inscriptions that Kipling composed or selected for the Imperial War Graves Commission, and for governments and institutions throughout the world, should not be confused with his series of "Epitaphs", first published in *The Years Between*, and then, slightly expanded and with the more familiar title "Epitaphs of the War", in the *Inclusive Edition* of his poetry. They are a work of the imagination, clearly related to the Commission inscriptions, but, as Kipling confirmed, with "neither personal nor geographical basis".[28] It was built into the very nature of Kipling's public role as a poet that he should be an elegist and memorialist. The deaths of famous people he had known, such as Joubert, Rhodes, Chamberlain, and Theodore Roosevelt, were marked with elegies; as were those of less celebrated personal friends like Wolcott Balestier and Perceval Landon.[29] His intuitive sense of history, and his emotional commitment to history as a living process, often gives an elegiac, or potentially elegiac, tone to his poetry. The close connections he had formed with the army in India and South Africa, and with the Royal Navy at the turn of the century, had long accustomed him to the fragility of life in the Armed Services. "The Crammer's boast, the Squadron's pride/Shot like a rabbit in a ride!", he had observed as far back as 1886.[30] The "Epitaphs" are, therefore, in some important senses, a development of recurrent tendencies in Kipling's poetry. Their newness lies in the tight control and compression that characterise them, and in the comprehensive portrait of the dead they finally offer.[31]

Kipling modelled "The Epitaphs" on *The Greek Anthology*, a collection of epigrams dating from the tenth century, the standard turn-of-the-century edition of which was edited by J. W. Mackail, a relative of Kipling's through marriage to Margaret Burne-Jones. Each of the epitaphs invokes one specific, individual response to death. A few of them are in the third person, but usually it is the dead who comment on their own deaths, their voices that speak directly to the reader. The immediacy of this technique, which could so easily have become over-emotional, is forcefully balanced by the brevity and compression of the poetic form Kipling employs. These dead have thought carefully about their deaths: they compose the inscriptions for their own gravestones. As this is war seen from the individual's point of view, there are no acts of romanticised courage to record, no flag-waving patriotism that would make any sense. Instead, there is a strong emphasis placed on the casual, unexpected and unavoidable nature of death, as in "The Beginner":

> On the first hour of my first day
> In the front trench I fell.
> (Children in boxes at a play
> Stand up to watch it well.)

The young soldier, newly arrived at the Front and eager to see what is going on, peers out of the trench and is shot by a sniper. In the aside, he himself compares the experience to being a child at the theatre, and standing up to see the action on the stage. Everyone in this war must expect the same kind of violent end, as "Bombed in London" makes clear:

> On land and sea I strove with anxious care
> To escape conscription. It was in the air!

Even "The Coward" is subject to no overt criticism. How could it be otherwise, when the lesson he learns for himself is so terrible and so personal?:

> I could not look on Death, which being known,
> Men led me to him, blindfold and alone.

Appropriately for a total war, the epitaphs cover civilians as well as servicemen, grieving parents and dead sons, imperial and British troops, women as well as men, the brave and the feckless; and action on land, at sea, and in the air. The dead are guiltless. Individually, they accept their deaths, as, of course, it is impossible for them not to, but collectively, in "Common Form", they pronounce judgement:

If any question why we died,
Tell them, because our fathers lied.

This bleak recognition of betrayal is also powerfully conveyed in "Gethsemane", not one of the "Epitaphs", but first published with them in *The Years Between*. The Biblical allusion is to Matthew 26:39: "O my Father, if it be possible, let this cup pass away from me." Kipling's soldier, in *his* Gethsemane, Picardy, also begs that this "cup may pass". For neither Christ nor the soldier is there any escape. Christ must die to save the world that will now destroy the soldier with poison gas. All the soldier wants is to participate in the mundane, everyday life that he observes around him: the impossibility of that wish being granted is conveyed by the poem's discordant half-rhymes – was, pass, gas, lass, grass – and the Biblical allusions. When Christ looks around him for comfort, he finds his disciples are sound asleep, unconcerned: the maimed, or dead, soldier can also expect no comfort, perhaps not even from Christ himself.

These poems, in which the servicemen and women voice their own feelings and views, place Kipling much closer to the young combatant-poets of the war than is usually allowed, though a distance between them still remains. Kipling's war poetry is founded on an intense, unavoidable consciousness of dual responsibility: on the one hand, guilt for causing the deaths of so many young people, and on the other, the imperative need to ensure that their deaths have not been pointless. The remainder of Kipling's life was dominated by these two impulses. They are epitomised by two poems from the early 1920s. "London Stone", published to commemorate Armistice Day

1923, is addressed to the parents mourning their dead children. It is a painfully moving lament which finds no hope or comfort for the parents, except that they are united with each other in their grief. "The King's Pilgrimage" is also a tribute, "To them that saved our heritage/And cast their own away," though the symbolic nature of King George's pilgrimage that the poem records allows Kipling to make a more public statement. Is there anything, he asks, that can make the dead "grudge their death"?:

> Save only if they understood
> That, after all was done,
> We they redeemed denied their blood
> And mocked the gains it won.

[8]

Bonfires on the Ice

As it will be in the future, it was at the birth of Man –
There are only four things certain since Social Progress began: –
That the Dog returns to his Vomit and the Sow returns to her Mire,
And the burnt Fool's bandaged finger goes wabbling back to the Fire.

"The Gods of the Copybook Headings"

As with his earlier volumes of poetry, Kipling used the publication of *The Years Between* in April 1919 to record a distinct phase of his career. Here, he gathered together not only the wartime poems, some of which were being published for the first time, but also pre-war polemical works such as "The City of Brass", "The Female of the Species", "The Covenant", and "Ulster". Germany was announced as a central preoccupation by opening the volume with "The Rowers", which had been published originally as long ago as 1902, and closing it with "Justice". For Kipling, there was an obvious unifying pattern in all of this, with *The Years Between* referring back to the bleak aftermath of the Boer War and the determination to make a new start that he had expressed in *The Five Nations*. The programme he set for himself then had been followed through and brought to the only kind of conclusion he was capable of influencing. His devoted admirers understood this, and remained loyal to him, but for most younger readers *The Years*

Between must have seemed a curiously miscellaneous and wilfully old-fashioned collection.[1] It was not simply a matter of Kipling being at odds with post-war trends in both politics and literature: after all, he had been a dissenting force for most of his life, and had thrived on it. More to the point was T. S. Eliot's description of him, in a review of *The Years Between*, as a "neglected celebrity".[2] The paradox is exactly right. Kipling was now more famous than ever. He was still much loved by some, and much hated by others. Sales of his books remained phenomenally high for a writer of his quality. Academic honours, which, unlike political honours, he was willing to accept because they did not threaten to interfere with his independence, were heaped upon him: the universities of Oxford, Cambridge, Paris, Edinburgh, Strasbourg, and St Andrews, queued up to offer him fellowships and doctorates. In 1927 a Society was formed to honour this "most patriotic, virile and imaginative of writers": Kipling would not give it his blessing, but he must have experienced some pride at being the first living English writer since Browning to be treated in this way.[3] And although tributes such as these were in recognition of past achievements, Kipling was by no means finished as a writer. The best of the short stories he wrote during this period were more experimental than ever, and have proved to be the work for which he is most admired today: nor did their originality go as entirely unrecognised as is often supposed.[4] Yet, so little influence did he seem to have on literature of the 1920s and early 1930s that he might not have been alive at all. He was being treated, already, as a dead Classic.

As far as the poetry was concerned, there was some justification for this attitude. *The Years Between* was the last volume of original poetry he published. For the first time in his life, breaking the line that stretched back to *Departmental Ditties*, Kipling's imagination was not centred on one large, absorbing idea to be tested out in a variety of ways and eventually given cohesion in a collection of interrelated poems. There were many new poems to come, and no shortage of newspaper and magazine editors eager to publish them. A Kipling poem was still treated as an event, its publication announced in advance, often accompanied by an editorial comment and illustrations, and given an amount of space that the work of no other contemporary poet could have commanded. But these poems were, more than ever, occasional pieces. The greater part of his poetry was now written to accompany prose works: the largely reprinted sketches and stories in *Land and Sea Tales for Scouts and Guides* (1923), the travel articles *Brazilian Sketches* (1927), and the two major collections of short stories, *Debits and Credits* (1926) and *Limits and Renewals* (1932). Most of this poetry was new, but its impact was deadened by the publication of a mass of anthologies and selections of Kipling's earlier poetry in cheap editions: *Twenty Poems* (1918); *A Kipling Anthology* (1922); *Songs for Youth* (1924); *Thirty Poems* and *A Choice of Songs*, both in 1925.

Nothing was more influential, in fixing Kipling as a poet of the past, than the publication in 1919 of the first comprehensive collected edition of his poetry, an event that should have been the occasion for celebration and serious revaluation of his poetic achievement. There was a genuine need to bring together the hundreds of poems he had published, often in obscure periodicals or barely-remembered circumstances, over the previous forty years. In 1912 Hodder & Stoughton had brought out a one-volume *Collected Verse*, for which Kipling had written an attractive introductory poem "The Fires". What it "collected" were the contents of the four main volumes of Kipling's poetry which had been published up to this point. In 1919 the same publishers undertook to expand the *Collected Verse* and include all of the poems that Kipling wished to see reprinted. The title was changed to *Rudyard Kipling's Verse: Inclusive Edition, 1885–1918*, published first in three volumes, and then, in 1921, in a single-volume edition. Although not truly "inclusive", it was a substantial and adventurous collection, making readily available many poems which were unfamiliar to Kipling's readers. Kipling must have been closely involved in the project, and was, therefore, ultimately responsible for making such a mess of it. The selection and revision were carried out efficiently, but the ordering of the poems was chaotic. It seems likely that the original intention was to print them chronologically, beginning with *Departmental Ditties* and other Indian poems, but for some reason this policy was abruptly changed to one of grouping the poems thematically. Even that was carried out with no apparent editorial consistency. The addition of dates to the titles of poems, often with no indication of what exactly they referred to, made the sudden shifts and turns in the collection all the more disconcerting. Anyone approaching the volume in the hope of enlightenment on Kipling's growth and development as a poet or thinker might reasonably have concluded that the task was pointless: from the *Inclusive Edition* it was hard to discern any development, poetic or intellectual. The serious editorial weaknesses of the *Inclusive Edition* did not, however, prevent it from selling extremely well. Along with many of Kipling's other works at this time, it was probably a popular gift-book, more often presented than read. New editions were published in 1927 and 1933, with, on each occasion, Kipling's latest poems added as appendices, and making the overall structure of the volume appear even more haphazard. In 1940, four years after Kipling's death, some more poems were included, and the title was changed to the *Definitive Edition*. In that form, and unaltered, it has been reprinted ever since.

It is a clear indication of the heterogeneous nature of Kipling's post-war poetry that, throughout the 1920s and early 1930s, the back pages of the *Inclusive Edition* were the only place where his recent poems could have been found collected together. There is a certain appropriateness in this, for apart from the poems which were consciously designed to be united with stories in *Debits and Credits* and *Limits and Renewals*, the poetry tends to divide itself into a large number of small clusters, usually displaying Kipling's continuing involvement in matters with which he had been long concerned, sometimes announcing a sudden new speculative interest, but always revealing the occasional uses to which his poetry was now put. When he turned to issues or approaches which had stirred him in the past, there was often a weariness in the poetry, a sense of it not living up to the standard or the inspiration of his earlier work. The poems, for example, he wrote about his visit to Brazil in 1927, not only lack the verve of those which developed out of his travels to Canada in 1907 and to Egypt in 1913, but are insipid when compared with the even earlier poem in which he recorded his dream of one day visiting Brazil:

> Yes, weekly from Southampton,
> Great steamers, white and gold,
> Go rolling down to Rio,
> (Roll down – roll down to Rio!)
> And I'd like to roll to Rio
> Some day before I'm old![5]

A similar loss of inspiration is apparent in the poems written for *Land and Sea Tales for Scouts and Guides*. The popular assumption that Kipling was intimately involved in the Boy Scout movement is based largely on the adoption by Baden-Powell, the movement's founder, of the *Jungle Books*, which were written long before the Boy Scouts were even thought of. Kipling knew Baden-Powell, admired the work he was doing, and was willing to help him when possible, but his personal connection with the movement was relatively slight.[6] In 1909, at Baden-Powell's request, he had written a lively "Boy Scouts' Patrol Song" for a rally to be held at the Crystal Palace, and it seems possible that the compilation of *Land and Sea Tales* was also prompted by a desire to support Baden-Powell. Although the poetry, unlike most of the prose, was written especially for the volume, it suffers from being either too obviously didactic or too obviously hearty: the poetic skill and moral subtlety that had made the pre-war children's poems so memorable have disappeared. The most enjoyable *Land and Sea Tales* poem is "The Master Cook", a Chaucerian pastiche which accompanies the best story in the collection, "His Gift", and served, perhaps, as a rehearsal for Kipling's far more profound "Gertrude's Prayer", the "modernised" Chaucer of the story "Dayspring Mishandled".[7]

There were strong personal reasons for the spasmodic way in which Kipling's poetry was now published, and for his apparent unwillingness or inability to follow a subject through as he had done earlier in his career. The history of the Irish Guards he had undertaken to write, and his work for the Imperial War Graves Commission, absorbed much of his time, and throughout the period he suffered from virtually permanent ill-health: Carrington records that Kipling was "never free from pain, for more than a few weeks at a time, during the last twenty years of his life."[8] This experience is forcefully present in the short stories he wrote which explore states of mental depression, or, to use his own words from the poem "Doctors", "the shameful nakedness of pain". It is characteristic of Kipling's view of his poetry as a public rather than a private art, that "Doctors" remained unpublished until after his death, and that other poems about illness – "Late Came the God", "Rahere", "The Burden", "The Mother's Son" and "Hymn to Physical Pain" – were all closely linked with stories, thus externalising the personal suffering on which they were often founded.[9] A similar, and in certain respects related, process is observable in his popular poems about dogs. Kipling's interest in animals, and his love of dogs especially, is obvious everywhere in his work. The best of his dog-poems, "The Power of the Dog", was written to accompany the story "Garm – A Hostage", *Actions and Reactions* (1909). Its success comes from Kipling's concentration on the fundamental mystery of the intense, loving, painful relationships formed between human beings and dogs. Why, when "We've sorrow enough in the natural way/When it comes to burying Christian clay . . . Should we give our hearts to a dog to tear?" In the later dog-poems – "Dinah in Heaven", "Four-feet" and "Supplication of the Black Aberdeen" – the emotional involvement is just as strong, though the speculative frame of mind of "The Power of the Dog" is replaced by an overt sentimentality. The dog is now seen entirely in terms of the devotion, loyalty, and companionship it offers, and these qualities are valued mostly for their therapeutic effect on the dog's lonely or sick owner:

> Day after day, the whole day through –
> Wherever my road inclined –
> Four-Feet said, "I am coming with you!"
> And trotted along behind.

When Four-Feet is no longer trotting along behind, the owner returns to a state of total isolation. Significantly, "Four-Feet" and "Dinah in Heaven" were written to frame "The Woman in his Life", one of Kipling's stories of mental breakdown.[10]

That Kipling was not consciously abandoning the more public side of his poetry in the years immediately following the war, is demonstrated most strikingly by the publication of "The Gods of the Copybook Headings" in the *Sunday Pictorial*, 26 October 1919. It was the kind of poem that the *Morning Post* might normally have expected to publish, and Kipling was careful to write to Gwynne to let him know it was appearing elsewhere, though he did not say where or why.[11] He probably felt that a more popular outlet than the *Post* would suit this particular poem. The *Sunday Pictorial* was an early tabloid, full of pictures, snippets of information, and brief news-items. On the same page as "The Gods of the Copybook Headings" there were articles with the catchy titles, "Do the Bishops believe?" and "Is the Flapper to Blame?" The setting was unusual, though not entirely inappropriate. The style of the poem was similar to that used before by Kipling in "The Conundrum of the Workshops" and "In the Neolithic Age". It combined a bouncy, striding rhythm; an apparent jumble of clichés, arcane geological terms, and Biblical allusions; some flashes of surrealistic nonsense; and a clear moral. Against the fundamental, unchanging values of life – the "Copybook Headings" which a child was expected to imbibe while learning to write – Kipling sets the transient, fashionable "Gods of the Market-Place", which can be taken to refer to both trendy attitudes and the public figures associated with them: it was here that the atheistic Bishops and irresponsible flappers, who appeared unexpectedly alongside the poem, came in useful. Drawing on his experiences of various "incarnations", and "peering through reverent fingers", Kipling argues that throughout the ages mankind has always been jostled between wisdom and foolishness. The references to past periods of time appear to reinforce the air of an historical survey, but the geological terms, which are used with apparent authority to support the argument, are fake, and Kipling's concern is not with the past, but with post-war Britain. "When the Cambrian measures were forming" refers to the policies of the Welshman Lloyd George who, in listening to the fashionable talk of "perpetual peace", has "delivered us bound to our foe"; "The first Feminian Sandstones", to the enfranchisement and sexual emancipation of women, which "promised the Fuller Life" and "started by loving our neighbour and ended by loving his wife"; and "the Carboniferous Epoch", to the growing power of trade-unionism, represented here by the miners, which "promised abundance for all/By robbing selected Peter to pay for collective Paul." In the final two stanzas of the poem, the knockabout satire is replaced by a sterner prophetic tone:

> As surely as Water will wet us, as surely as Fire will burn,
> The Gods of the Copybook Headings with terror and slaughter return!

There is no sign of an exhausted imagination in "The Gods of the Copybook Headings". For the moment Kipling was clearly back on form, his moral and political indignation sharply alert and given lastingly memorable expression. Yet this poem also was not followed by others in a similar vein or on a comparable theme, and the prophecy that "terror and slaughter" would return, if Britain continued to heed the Gods of the Market-Place rather than those of the Copybook Headings, was set aside for the next ten years.

Some of the most notable changes in Kipling's writing in the 1920s, the prose as well as the poetry, can be traced to his growing interest in the life and work of universities. It was, viewed from one angle, surprising that someone who was associated so closely with the material world, and who had had many uncomplimentary things to say about those of his fellow-countrymen who preferred to sit at home and read about imperial expansion rather than participate in it, should now become absorbed in the comparatively remote concerns of academic research and scholarship. But although Kipling himself was not university-educated, and had spent much of his life extolling the Sons of Martha above the Sons of Mary, the deep-rooted bookishness in him appealed to scholars like Fletcher, George Saintsbury, Arthur Quiller-Couch, and André Chevrillon, with all of whom he was on friendly corresponding terms. More important than this, and apparent in every phase of his work, was Kipling's fascination with other people's specialist knowledge. "What mystery is there like the mystery of the other man's job," he once wrote, "or what world is so cut off as that which he enters when he goes to it?"[12] Many people with interesting "jobs" have recorded how on meeting Kipling they were questioned exhaustively about their work: initially flattered, they often became annoyed by his probing attention to the minutest technical detail of their working lives. Much of the literary use to which he would put his experiences of the academic world – medical research and the authentication of ancient documents, for example – was of this kind.

Kipling's official connections with universities were centred on his work for the Cecil Rhodes Trust at Oxford, the honorary degrees he was awarded by various institutions, and the Rectorship of St Andrews, which he held for three years from 1922. He wrote three poems based directly on these experiences, the first two of which were inspired by the large number of young men returning to their university studies after serving in the war. "The Scholars", first published in the *Daily Telegraph*, 29 January 1919, is written in the breathless Swinburnian style that Kipling had used many years earlier in his tribute to Wolcott Balestier ("Beyond the path of the outmost sun through utter darkness hurled"), and it suffers from many of the same faults. The contrast between the hard lives the men have led in the war and the gentler existence they are now going to at Cambridge is established effectively, though it is over-elaborated, and weakened ultimately by Kipling's bluff insistence that these men have fully earned their education: "For, by God, if they owe you half a crown, you owe 'em your four years' food!" "The Clerks and the Bells", which Kipling subtitled "Oxford in 1920", was published in *Nash's Magazine*, February 1920, as a double-page spread, and surrounded by ornate drawings pointing the contrast between life in the trenches and life at Oxford. The theme of the poem is exactly the same as that of "The Scholars", but its treatment is completely different. Each stanza of "The Clerks and the Bells" portrays a stage of a regular college day, with the bells notifying the students when it is time to "learn", "eat", "play", "pray", "rest", and then to rise again. The regularity of the students' lives is matched by the tightly-structured poem, with the idyllic scholarly images of the students, constantly undercut by interjections of wartime memories which are, in turn, immediately obliterated by the college bells. The archaic language Kipling employed to describe the students, "the merry clerks of Oxenford", and the general unreality of the medieval Oxford he evokes, may have been intended simply to heighten the contrast between their wartime and civilian existences, but the total effect is disturbingly ambiguous, giving an impression that the students' present is hardly less fragile than their past had been. By 1923 when Kipling contributed "A Rector's Memory" to a book being published to raise money for a student welfare scheme at the University of St Andrews, the Scottish students he met would have had no personal experience of the war, and his poem, while evoking the uncertainty and insecurity of life, is an elegant affectionate tribute to the "passion of Youth" he had encountered in this northern university by "the grey warlock Ocean".

The work of Kipling's that was most obviously "scholarly", the translations and imitations of Horace, was influenced, though not originally inspired, by his academic connections. His interest in Horace's poetry stretched back to his schooldays, and became more of a systematic study just before, and during, the war. Carrington tells us that Kipling carried around with him a copy of Horace's *Odes*, in which "he wrote from time to time, at unknown dates, fifty-five original epigrams in English verse. Some are free translations from Horace; some are critical comments or glosses; and some his own developments of a Horatian theme."[13] When he was collecting together stories for *A Diversity of Creatures* (1917), he wrote a poem in the style of Horace to accompany "Regulus", a hitherto unpublished story about Stalky & Co. Although the poem was really an "imitation", Kipling called it "A Translation" of "Horace, Bk. V. Ode 3." It was the kind of joke he always enjoyed. At the time he was confident that there were only four books of Horace's odes, so readers who possessed this knowledge would realise the poem was really by Kipling, and those who didn't would simply accept it as a translation: it is quite conceivable that he was hoping for some critic or other, who should have known better, to accept it as genuine. The joke, however, suddenly appeared to backfire on him. Shortly after the publication of *A Diversity of Creatures*, he wrote to Fletcher asking him whether or not a fifth book of Horace's odes actually existed.[14] Someone had told him it did, and he was worried that he was the one who was having his leg pulled. Fletcher reassured him, and the joke became not only funny again, but worth extending. Over the next few years, in collaboration with a number of classical scholars, and prompted by Fletcher, Kipling helped to compile enough Horatian imitations to make up a complete fifth book. It was published in 1920 as *Q. Horati Flacci Carminum Librum Quintum.* There was no attempt to fool anybody into believing the work was genuine: the whole project was a harmless, and by no means unprecedented, in-joke. Kipling continued to write Horatian poems, and four of them, no longer masquerading as "translations", were included in *Debits and Credits*.

The problem for the modern reader of Kipling's Horatian poems is not how true in style or form they are to Horace – that, clearly, is a matter for specialists – but whether they are successful as English poems, and for the most part they are not. In many of the epigrams and glosses which Kipling wrote in his own copy of the *Odes*, and which he had no intention of ever publishing, he tended to take the spirit or sense of Horace and give to it a contemporary feel or relevance. They are lively, witty, and show Kipling making good use of his colloquial skills. Horace's advice that "the great lovers of history set limits to their grief" becomes:

Do not always mourn your dead.
Read the Daily Mail instead.[15]

Horace's sharp criticism of an ageing mother who persists in competing sexually with her daughter, is even sharper in Kipling's version:

Old Girl, your day is over.
  It's time to shut up shop.
Your daughter needs a lover –
  You only want one. Stop![16]

In complete contrast, even the best of the "Book Five" poems – "Lollius" and "The Last Ode", for example – are too reverential to their model.[17] The frequently over-complex syntax and metre, and the Horatian names and references which are employed, give an inescapably Latinate feel to the poems: ironically, they often read more like translations than genuine imitations.

When Horace was allowed to influence Kipling's poetry, without the debt being self-consciously acknowledged, the results were more positive. Shortly after the idea for "Book Five" was first suggested, Kipling told Fletcher that he had discovered another poem which Horace had obviously written.[18] He was referring to his own poem, "The Pro-Consuls", published more than a dozen years earlier: it became part of the joke, and was reprinted in *Q. Horati Flacci Carminum Librum Quintum*. And there are other poems which could be similarly placed. Carrington includes "A Recantation" from *The Years Between* in his edition *Kipling's Horace*: the later "Samuel Pepys" and "Untimely" could also be added to the list.[19] But the most distinguished of these poems is "The Craftsman", which Carrington also includes, and the Horatian credentials of which are well established.[20] What sets "The Craftsman" apart, however, and makes its classification as an imitation slightly dubious, is the way in which the influence of Horace is totally absorbed by Kipling and transformed into a highly personal statement about his own art.

The setting of the poem is the Mermaid Tavern in the early seventeenth century. It is late at night, and Shakespeare and Jonson are imagined talking about their work. In the poem, Jonson is the passive recipient of Shakespeare's views which are reported in the third person. Although "The Craftsman" was written around 1918, its main theme had been outlined by Kipling many years earlier. In 1898, in response to an article which claimed that the island in *The Tempest* was "woven out of such stuff as dreams are made on", Kipling wrote a long letter to the *Spectator* suggesting that Shakespeare's inspiration was not dream-like at all: "It seems to me possible that the vision was woven from the most prosaic material – from nothing more promising, in fact, than the chatter of a half-tipsy sailor at a theatre."[21] Kipling was, of course, describing his own method of picking up ideas for poems and stories, recently expressed in "When 'Omer smote 'is bloomin' Lyre": writers have always taken hints from whatever material was close to hand, and then allowed them to be transmuted mysteriously by their imaginations or "daemons", but the initial inspiration comes from the physical world, not the imagination.[22] Some years after "The Craftsman" he wrote a further poem on the same Shakespearian theme, this time even closer to the ideas advanced in the *Spectator* letter. He called it "The Coiner", and it was published in *Limits and Renewals* (1932). The length of time between the *Spectator* letter and the composition of "The Craftsman" suggests that the most fruitful influence Horace may have exerted on Kipling was to focus his mind on the questions of artistry and craftsmanship that, from the war years onward, lie at the heart of some of his finest work.

The story of himself that Shakespeare tells Jonson in "The Craftsman" is made up of a series of personal experiences, out of which he claims to have created his plays. Each stanza, each reminiscence, opens with a heavy stress which enforces Shakespeare's insistence that *this* is how it was done; while, at the same time, the third-person narrative gives an air of impersonality to the account:

> How at Bankside, a boy drowning kittens
> Winced at the business; whereupon his sister –
> Lady Macbeth aged seven – thrust 'em under,
> Sombrely scornful.

Kipling's use of the third-person narrative makes it appear as though Shakespeare is talking about someone other than himself, which, in an important sense, he is. It recalls Browning's similar method in "Caliban upon Setebos", a poem based, very appropriately in this context, on *The Tempest* which is alluded to in the final stanza of "The Craftsman", when Shakespeare leaves the Mermaid Tavern "to hurry after shadows". He is "busied upon shows of no earthly importance, and he knows it!" He is committed, in equal measure to the physical world and to its shadows. That is what it means to be a conscious "craftsman".

It was the stories in *Debits and Credits* and *Limits and Renewals* that benefited most fully from Kipling's own post-war dedication to conscious craftsmanship, though the best of the poems linked to the stories – "A Legend of Truth", "We and They", "The Threshold", "Untimely", "The Expert", "Gipsy Vans", "Gertrude's Prayer" – and "Chartres Windows", a traditional sonnet published separately in 1925, are also impressive testimony to the continuously speculative nature of Kipling's mind in the 1920s.[23] The speculation, however, was not all inward. There was still one burst of public poetry to come.

*

During the last few years of his life, Kipling's poetry began once again to reveal the strong, informing sense of purpose that it had lacked since 1918. He was guided, as so often in the past, by an imperative moral duty to warn the British people of impending danger. The method he employed was also familiar from his earlier campaigns, with individual poems approaching the central concern from a variety of angles and points of view, some very oblique, some direct. The threat to the nation was posed yet again by Germany. For Kipling, of course, this was not a new theme. In 1918 he had warned that a "peace" without "justice" would merely encourage Germany to prepare for another war, and in speeches delivered at the same time, which were dismissed by his critics as warmongering, he was already analysing German ambitions in terms of what everyone would later recognise as Nazi, totalitarian ideology. If we allow a second war to take place, he warned, Germany will be fighting for "racial domination" and the destruction of democracy: moral distinctions would be placed entirely at the service of physical force; women would become "mere instruments for continuing the breed", and Labour "a thing to be worked to death" if it refuses "to submit to the State". From this order of life, he insisted, "there will be no appeal, no possibility of any escape".[24] The evil embodiment of German "Kultur" during the war had been the Kaiser, "Diabolus", and because he had not been cast back into the Pit where he belonged, but was allowed to run free, here he was again, in the shape of Hitler.

It was not only events in Germany that made Kipling feel he was being forced back to the isolated position of ignored prophet that he had held after the Boer War. As Germany was starting to re-establish the economic and political authority it had held then, so Britain was continuing to ignore the lessons it should have learned, once and for all, in those same "years between". The publication of "The Gods of the Copybook Headings" shortly after the war had appeared to indicate that Kipling was about to take up his political poetry where it had been left off in 1914. Instead, he turned, as we have seen, to other, more personal topics, and during the 1920s he wrote almost no poetry on political themes. Controversial public issues with which he had once been closely associated, and on which he would have been quick to pronounce in the *Morning Post* or *The Times*, now passed without comment from him. In November 1921, while a conference was taking place to try to reach a settlement on Home Rule for Ireland, Gwynne reprinted in the *Morning Post* Kipling's pre-war poem "Ulster". He did not consult Kipling about this: perhaps he believed that Kipling's permission for the *Morning Post* to use any of his earlier poems which were relevant to the war effort still applied.[25] Kipling told Gwynne he was an "ass" to have reprinted "Ulster" as though it were a new poem: its appearance, he claimed, prevented him from writing other poems on the current Irish situation.[26] That, however, was almost certainly a convenient excuse: he was unlikely even to want to publish controversial poems about Ireland while he was compiling *The Irish Guards in the Great War*. In January the following year, Haggard recorded that Kipling "takes a most despondent view of the position in Ireland, Egypt and India, and even went so far as to say that it looks as though the Empire were going to fall to pieces."[27] Yet the Laureate of the Empire, the author of "The English Flag" and "The White Man's Burden", seems to have made no attempt to put into poetry his fears that the Empire was on the verge of collapse.

Much the same applies to Kipling's attitudes to domestic politics. From his letters and other sources, it is clear that he retained a keen interest in the political situation. In the immediate post-war years he shared the widely-held view that social disturbance in Britain was being fomented by Bolshevist agitators, that British trades unions had been infiltrated by Soviet agents, and that "the Jews" were somehow or other behind it all. "Kipling who has been lunching here today,"

Haggard wrote in December 1919, "is of opinion that we owe all our Russian troubles, and many others, to the machinations of the Jews."[28] Haggard did not agree with this – he personally preferred to blame the trades unions for "most of our embarrassments and perplexities" – but he suggested they join together to form an anti-Bolshevist society. This they did, though The Liberty League, as it was called, soon folded through lack of support.[29] It is clear that Kipling frequently expressed such views at this time, and, indeed, had done so before the war, but how deeply they were held by him is open to doubt. A comparison with Gwynne is revealing. Gwynne believed totally in what he called the "Jewish Bolshevik" conspiracy. In 1919 he came across some documents, first published many years earlier, called *The Protocols of the Elders of Zion*, which professed to reveal that the Communist movement was controlled by Zionists. A series of articles supporting this theory was published in the *Morning Post*, and as a book *The Cause of World Unrest* (1922), in which Gwynne explained that "there has been for centuries a hidden conspiracy, chiefly Jewish, whose objects have been and are to produce revolution, communism, and anarchy," and through these means to gain a "hegemony of the world by establishing some sort of despotic rule". He also announced that "over 95 per cent of the present Bolshevik Government are Jews," and that Zionists had, for their own purposes, saved Germany from outright defeat in the war.[30] Gwynne tried to enlist Kipling's support by sending him a copy of the *Protocols*. Kipling replied that the documents were clearly fakes, and refused to get involved in Gwynne's crusade.[31]

To Kipling's mind, post-war social upheaval was caused not by Zionists, or even Bolshevists as such, but by the changes in domestic politics which had appalled him some fifteen years earlier. Through their constant willingness to accommodate socialist principles and policies, and their shameless grovelling to public opinion, the Liberals, and Britain along with them, were now paying the price. Kipling noted, sardonically, Lloyd George's final desperate attempts to cling to power; Asquith's elevation to the House of Lords, whose authority he had once helped to undermine; and the Liberal Party itself being superseded by the Labour Party. Labour was not an improvement on the Liberals, but nor was it all that much different. The Liberals were now finished, and Labour politicians and supporters – Ramsay MacDonald, Philip Snowdon, George Lansbury, and Harold Laski – took Lloyd George's place as the target of Kipling's private political jokes and abuse. In this decade of coalition governments, national governments, and short-term Labour and Conservative governments, even Stanley Baldwin, the leader of the Conservative Party and Kipling's cousin, appeared to be a "Socialist at heart".[32] The tendencies that most disturbed Kipling, and felt to him like a particularly ominous re-run of the pre-war period, were the increasing public support being given to pacifist movements, and the reduction, year by year and by governments of whatever political persuasion, of the amount of money being spent on the armed forces. The percentage of the national income spent on defence fell every year from 1922, and by 1933, the year that Hitler became Chancellor of Germany, it was actually lower than it had been in the years immediately preceding the war.[33] Kipling had seen it all before. During the Boer War the Liberal leaders had opposed the war, and when they came to power had reduced defence expenditure. Now the Labour Party, which contained some vociferous pacifists and international disarmers, was in a position to hold power and would follow the earlier example of the Liberals in rendering Britain incapable of fighting the second war with Germany that, Kipling estimated, would probably come in 1936, or perhaps 1937.[34]

In 1929 Kipling published in *The Legion Book* a poem called "The English Way" which seemed totally remote from contemporary political issues. It was written in the form of a border ballad, and its opening lines announced its kinship with two famous examples of the genre – "The Battle of Otterburn" and "Chevy Chase". These were, respectively, the Scottish and English versions of a battle fought in 1388 between the Scots, led by the Earl of Douglas, and the English, led by Sir Henry Percy, Shakespeare's Hotspur. "The English Way" has, however, only indirect connections with the traditional ballads. It opens "after" the battle of Otterburn, and departs from historical events and the earlier ballads in assuming that Percy has been killed in the battle. Percy's shade is addressed by a "witch-wife", who is also a Kipling addition, though the idea for her may have been picked up from a related poem, "Northumberland Betrayed by Douglas".[35] The witch-wife questions Percy about the attitude of his men towards war, and is told that they are enormously brave, yet so modest that, off the battlefield, it would be difficult to recognise them as warriors at all:

> We would not speak of steel or steed,
>   Except to grudge the cost;
> And he that had done the doughtiest deed
>   Would mock himself the most.

Impressed by Percy's account, the witch-wife promises that the same qualities will characterise Englishmen for ever. It will be the "English way" to hide strength and determination beneath an outward display of complaints and indifference. "The English Way" is in effect a reworking, for the special conditions of the late 1920s, of earlier poems, such as "Et Dona Ferentes" and "The Puzzler". Then, as now, Kipling was warning potential enemies that they should not be misled by the English talk of pacifism, disarmament, and never becoming involved in another war: if the country should be threatened again, then the true spirit of England, epitomised by Percy and blessed by the witch-wife, would reassert itelf.

The following year Kipling abandoned allegory in favour of direct attack. He was prompted by Ramsay MacDonald's government informing foreign officials visiting London that they needn't place wreaths at the Cenotaph or on the Tomb of the Unknown Warrior unless they really wanted to. When criticised for this stance, government spokesmen made the situation worse by explaining their desire to prevent the commemoration of the dead from becoming a mere formality, and eventually to bring about the "eradication of memories of the Great War".[36] Kipling's poem "Memories" was published in the *Daily Telegraph* on 3 November 1930. It is a work of bitter satire, reminiscent of Pope's *Dunciad* in that the speakers – in this case "The Socialist Government" – are allowed full freedom to justify their policies, and in doing so condemn themselves. With great pride they outline their plan to "break" the meaning of Armistice Day completely. They will not use "staves or swords", which would smack of the very militarism they abhor, but rely instead on "the power of small corroding words", regularly, slowly, denigrating the dead whose graves so many people still come foolishly to honour:

> Wisely, but yearly, filch some wreath –
>   Lay some proud rite aside –
> And daily tarnish with Our breath
>   The ends for which They died.

In its editorial the *Daily Telegraph* admitted that Kipling's poem was "very hard-hitting", and then attacked Ramsay MacDonald for allowing himself to be dominated by "fanatics of pacifism". Three days later a Conservative periodical, *The Patriot*, reprinted Kipling's "remarkably true and strong words" together with an illustration of a top-hatted figure standing in front of the Cenotaph and reaching out one hand as though to touch the monument. The caption reads "HANDS OFF! – RAMSAY!"[37]

Kipling's imagination was now fully taken up with the double threat to Britain, from the socialist-pacifists within, and from Germany without, but after "Memories", he restricted his public utterances to the external enemy, and he returned to Gwynne and the *Morning Post* where he could be sure to receive loyal support and maximum coverage for his views. His next poem on the subject, "The Storm Cone", was published in the *Post* on 23 May 1932, though without editorial comment or any indication of what the poem was about. Two days earlier, however, Gwynne had taken the opportunity provided by recent suggestions that the Poet Laureateship should be abolished, to draw attention in his editorial to the forthcoming publication of "The Storm Cone". Referring back to some of Kipling's major public poems, and describing him as "the greatest 'voluntary Laureate' of all time", Gwynne announced: "In 'The Storm Cone' which this journal has the privilege of publishing next Monday, the very voice of England is heard." In this manner it was made clear to the *Post*'s readers that Kipling's new poem was to be regarded in the same solemn context as "Recessional" and "For All We Have and Are". Even so, it is surprising that "The Storm Cone", which is another poem strongly influenced by Horace, should have been published without some kind of editorial explanation.[38] The threat to the nation that the poem deals with is powerfully evoked, though vague and generalised:

> This is the midnight – let no star
> Delude us – dawn is very far.
> This is the tempest long foretold –
> Slow to make head but sure to hold.

The hoisted cones warn that a terrible storm is on its way. There is no escape. The Ship of State must ride out the storm, "But, till she fetches open sea/Let no man deem that he is free!"

If the public impact that "The Storm Cone" might have had

was weakened by too vague a presentation in the *Morning Post*, no such complaint could have been made about Kipling's next poem on the subject, "Bonfires on the Ice", or "The Bonfires" as it was later retitled. Kipling began drawing Gwynne's attention to Hitler as early as June 1932, and no doubt the *Morning Post*'s exceptionally thorough coverage of Hitler's rise to power owed something to Kipling's prompting.[39] Gwynne, in turn, publicised Kipling's views on affairs in Germany. On 6 February 1933, a few days after Hitler's election as Chancellor, the *Post*'s main news was of a Nazi Troop Commander killed in riots on the day that Hitler became Chancellor. Prominently on the same page, under the heading "Mr Kipling and Germany", was a letter of Kipling's reprinted from the *Echo de Paris*. In it, he expressed his belief that the future of civilisation rested on good relations between Britain and France, and pointed out that month by month it was becoming clearer that "the German has learnt nothing from the last war." Kipling's view that there was a much greater understanding of the German threat in France than in Britain was already well known, and would be made unambiguously clear in his *Souvenirs of France* which was published in July of this same year. The *Morning Post* letter contained opinions that were neither new nor strikingly expressed, but it served Gwynne's purpose of keeping Kipling's name linked with developments in Germany.

Just how much Gwynne gained from Kipling's insight can be seen from a letter Kipling wrote to him on 13 April 1933. Continental life is once again dominated by "the Hun", Kipling observed: the "Fenrys Wolf" has broken free, and now symbolises the German's ambition to create a new "religion" based on his ancestral "Nordic" folk-tales and "allegory".[40] In Scandinavian mythology, the "Fenrys" or "Fenrir" wolf is a symbol of Evil. The Gods are warned that they must destroy him, but instead they try containment and live in constant fear of him breaking loose. His open jaws, dripping with blood, were said to stretch from earth to heaven, and flames of fire spurted from his eyes and nostrils. At the Götterdämmerung he devours Odin, and is in turn killed by Vidar, Odin's son. Kipling equated Fenrys with Hitler, the embodiment of Nazi ideology.

Kipling's reference to Fenrys in his letter to Gwynne in April 1933, suggests that "Bonfires on the Ice" was at least in his mind, and perhaps already composed. Either way, it was probably his intention to hold the poem back until Armistice Day. As things turned out, that decision was given a more spectacular significance than he could possibly have anticipated. On Saturday, 11 November, the fifteenth anniversary of the armistice, the *Morning Post* published a new piece of prose by Kipling called "The Pleasure Cruise". It was in the form of a Greek Dialogue, modelled on Lucian's *Dialogues of the Dead*, and portrays the shades of dead soldiers returning to England, the land of their birth, to seek reassurance that their ultimate sacrifice has been worthwhile. They find that their loved ones have forgotten them; the country is busily disarming while its potential enemies are rearming; and everywhere people are talking endlessly of war having been abolished. The disillusioned ghost-soldiers take "an extra-strength dose of Lethe" and return to the underworld. It is a sad, bitter piece of work. On the opposite page in the *Post* were two leading articles, both referring to events that were to take place the next day, Sunday. The first editorial drew attention to "The Pleasure Cruise" in which Kipling has dealt with "the sternest of realities"; warned that nations are saved by "the courage and discipline of their manhood and the foresight to provide against dangers while they are still ahead"; and denounced talk of giving up Remembrance Sunday. The second editorial pointed out that while Britain was remembering those who died in the war, Germany would be holding a referendum on whether the German people supported Hitler's policies. There was also an announcement that a new poem by Kipling would be published on Monday.

Monday's headline news was the overwhelming vote of confidence in Hitler given by the German people, and alongside, with almost equal prominence, "Bonfires on the Ice". The poem is made up of a series of clichés, commonplaces, and pompous maxims, which are drawn, the epigraph to the poem suggests, from the utterances of politicians. The communal voice is one of cheerful complacency: "We know . . . We know . . . We know . . ." At this level of communication, everyone knows everything: that one and one make two, that the stick of a fired rocket falls back to earth; that the Fenrys Wolf is on the loose and will have to be confronted. Whether or not they also realise the folly of building bonfires on ice is, however, left open. In his accompanying editorial, Gwynne admitted some difficulty with the poem, but explained its fundamental message: "Bonfires on the Ice, if we interpret the poem aright, are policies built upon falsehood, which cheer and deceive for a time, but in the end fall through the foundations on which they are built."

"Bonfires on the Ice", its presentation carefully stage-managed to obtain maximum attention, was Kipling's final poetic statement on Germany. It was not quite his last poem. In June 1934 he contributed two poems to a gigantic *Pageant of Parliament* that was staged at the Royal Albert Hall, one of which, "Non nobis Domine" was the centrepiece of the pageant's spectacular finale. It is strikingly reminiscent of "Recessional", humbly acknowledging the existence of a controlling spiritual power to whom all credit should go for man's apparent achievements: "Not unto us the praise." To "Non nobis Domine" should be added the ode "Melbourne Shrine of Remembrance", his tribute to the Australians who had died in the war; the more personal "Hymn of Breaking Strain" in which the agonising human consciousness of success or failure is contrasted with the insentient engineering creations which he had so long admired; and "The King and the Sea", written to mark the thirty-fifth anniversary of George V's accession to the throne. In May 1935 he returned to the subject of Germany, in a speech delivered to the Royal Society of St George. He referred to the years of negligence by successive British governments which had allowed Germany to prepare for another war, and drew attention to the large area of Europe that was experiencing "State-controlled murder and torture . . . State-engineered famine, starvation, and slavery." The future continued to look grim, though there was now at least a hint of optimism in what he had to say. Only two months earlier, the National government, led by Ramsay MacDonald, had finally taken the vital decision to follow Germany and re-arm. At last, Kipling observed, steps were being taken to remedy the deficiencies in Britain's armed forces. The worry now was whether there was enough time left to catch up. If there was, the ancient warrior spirit of Britain could be trusted to respond forcefully. If not, then Britain would "join the submerged races of history."[41]

In December 1935, angered that the government, now led by Kipling's cousin Stanley Baldwin, seemed about to impose oil sanctions on Italy over the war in Abyssinia, Kipling sent a poem on the subject to *The Times*, but immediately changed his mind as news of the Hoare–Laval pact became public. Carrington says that Kipling "had some difficulty in suppressing and destroying his poem before publication."[42] What exactly was in the poem, or what form it took, is not known. It was, presumably, the last one he wrote. On 13 January 1936 he was taken suddenly ill, and died five days later. Early in March, German troops reoccupied the Rhineland, breaking the non-aggression treaty which had been signed at Locarno in 1925 and guaranteed by Britain and Italy. The British government was trapped in precisely the kind of crisis that Kipling had long feared. In the words of A. J. P. Taylor: "Baldwin confessed, with tears in his eyes, that Great Britain had no forces with which to sustain her guarantee, and that, in any case, public opinion would not allow it."[43]

In the period immediately following Kipling's death, he was, inevitably, admired more as a prophet than a poet. For years he had condemned both German militarism and British appeasement. To devoted friends and admirers, he possessed the same qualities of lonely commitment to a great unpopular cause, steadfast patriotism, and political foresight, that were now internationally associated with Winston Churchill, a politician greatly distrusted by Kipling.[44] In 1941, his poetry was recruited into the war effort, with the publication of an anthology called *So Shall Ye Reap: Poems for these Days*. There could be no doubt about his patriotism, though the poetry was still regarded with suspicion. It has often been pointed out that when Kipling's ashes were interred in Poets' Corner, Westminster Abbey, on 23 January 1936, the mourners included the Prime Minister, Admirals, Field-Marshals, Ambassadors, High Commissioners, politicians, and official representatives of countries throughout the world, but no British writers of comparable status. The reason for making this point is usually to emphasise how totally isolated from the centre of literature Kipling had become, how the kind of interest so many people had in him was not really "literary" at all. Yet, shortly after his death, the two greatest living poets in the English-speaking world – T. S. Eliot and W. H. Auden – went out of their way to praise Kipling's poetry. That they both did so in the language of guilt and expiation makes their comments all the more remarkable.

The full extent of T. S. Eliot's admiration for Kipling's poetry emerged piecemeal over forty years. In 1919, reviewing *The Years Between*, Eliot found that "the mind" of "most of our discerning critics" is not "sufficiently curious, sufficiently brave, to examine Mr Kipling", and pronounced him to be "very nearly a great writer".[45] Four years later, asked by Ernst Robert Curtius, the German translator of *The Waste Land*, for advice on which writers he should include in a book about modern English literature, Eliot replied with a brief list that placed Kipling third, below James and Conrad, and above Strachey, Joyce, Lewis, and Pound. Curtius was "not amused" by the list.[46] Eliot, however, was not being whimsical. When he compiled *A Choice of Kipling's Verse* in 1941, his advocacy of Kipling now rested on the conviction that "no writer has ever cared more for the craft of words."[47] In 1959, explaining why he had accepted, "like a decree of Destiny", an invitation to address the Kipling Society, he admitted to a deep personal motive: "I have come to have a feeling, almost a superstition, that it is a kind of obligation laid upon me to testify for Rudyard Kipling whenever the opportunity presents itself."[48]

W. H. Auden does not seem to have spent many years pondering how he could right the injustice done to Kipling's reputation as a poet, though it is reasonable to assume that like Eliot, and indeed many other poets of their generations, he could have said that Kipling had "accompanied" him "ever since boyhood".[49] In his review of *A Choice of Kipling's Verse* written in America in 1943, Auden took issue with some of Eliot's critical comments, but on the main aim of the book, and the timing of its publication, he had no qualifications to make: "If today the war makes people discover that Kipling is good, it will be an excellent thing."[50] Auden's more personal tribute to Kipling's poetry had been offered four years earlier in his great elegy on the death of another poet, "In Memory of W. B. Yeats." Auden insists on distinguishing between a poet's political beliefs and his poetry. Of Yeats: "You were silly like us: your gift survived it all." Auden was clearly thinking of himself as well, and of Kipling:

> Time that is intolerant
> Of the brave and innocent,
> And indifferent in a week
> To a beautiful physique,

Worships language and forgives
Everyone by whom it lives;
Pardons cowardice, conceit,
Lays its honours at their feet.

Time that with this strange excuse
Pardoned Kipling and his views.[51]

Here, in 1939, Auden was assuming that Time had already "pardoned" Kipling for "his views", and Yeats for being "silly": the work produced by lives devoted to language could now be relied on to do the rest.

Kipling shared that belief. For him there were no Schools of Art, no literary trends or fashions to be followed, no obviously true or false way of composing a poem. As he made clear in "In the Neolithic Age", all the "nine-and-sixty ways of constructing tribal lays" are "right", at least potentially so. Everything depends on individual vision and complete dedication to the tools of the trade. When the job is done as thoroughly as the capabilities of the artist allows, then "praise Allah and let it go, and 'when thou hast done, repent not.'"[52] This was the aspect of Kipling that Eliot and Auden celebrated in their elegiac tributes. They were, in effect, welcoming him as a fellow craftsman into the community of poets. His place there is secure, even if literary criticism has still to be convinced. Certainly Auden's judgement, made more than half a century ago, that with Kipling carrying a pardon from Time the poetry had been freed to receive the acclaim it deserved was quite a bit premature, but it could yet prove to be correct.

Notes

References to Kipling's prose works are to the Macmillan Uniform Edition, unless otherwise indicated. KP refers to the Kipling Papers, University of Sussex.

[1] "Reading as if for life"

1 *Something of Myself*, pp. 1–3.
2 *Ibid.*, pp. 6–17.
3 "Baa Baa, Black Sheep", *Wee Willie Winkie and Other Stories*, p. 279.
4 *Something of Myself*, p. 20.
5 *Ibid.*, p. 34.
6 *David Copperfield*, chapter 4.
7 *Something of Myself*, p. 20.
8 *Ibid.*, p. 21.
9 *Stalky & Co.*, p. 46.
10 *Ibid.*, pp. 217–8.
11 "An English School", *Land and Sea Tales for Scouts and Guides* (1923), p. 268. First published in the periodical *Youth's Companion*, 19 October 1893.
12 *Something of Myself*, p. 39.
13 "My First Book", *The Idler*, December 1892, p. 478. Collected with other articles in the series as *My First Book*, edited by Jerome K. Jerome (1894).
14 *Ibid.*

15 *Ibid.*, p. 482.
16 "The Propagation of Knowledge", *Debits and Credits*, p. 274.
17 W. B. Yeats, introduction to *The Oxford Book of Modern Verse* (1936), p. ix.
18 *Robert Browning* (1903), p. 171.
19 *Kipling's Reading and its Influence on his Poetry* (Philadelphia 1939), p. 151.
20 Harte's poetry was enormously popular in Britain and available in various editions from the early 1870s onwards. All of the poems mentioned here were included in his *Complete Poetical Works* (1886).
21 "The United Idolators", *Debits and Credits*, p. 91; *Something of Myself*, p. 37; *Early Verse by Rudyard Kipling 1879–1889*, edited by Andrew Rutherford (Oxford 1986), pp. 243–4, 423–8.
22 All of these school poems are contained in *Early Verse by Rudyard Kipling*.
23 "After the Promise", *Early Verse by Rudyard Kipling*, p. 138; "The Finest Story in the World", *Many Inventions*, pp. 133–4; "Dayspring Mishandled", *Limits and Renewals*.
24 "Pro Tem", *Early Verse by Rudyard Kipling*, p. 74.
25 Charles Carrington, *Rudyard Kipling: His Life and Work* (1955), p. 40.
26 *Early Verse by Rudyard Kipling*, p. 162.
27 "My First Book", p. 475.
28 In 1897 Thacker, Spink & Co., published an edition of *Departmental Ditties*, illustrated by Dudley Cleaver, which carried on the title page a line drawing of a galley-slave. They were, presumably, following the example already set by Methuen.
29 Pagett reappeared in a sketch by Kipling, "The Enlightenments of Pagett, M. P.", *Contemporary Review*, September 1890. Interestingly, the arguments used to refute Pagett's Liberal views follow "What the People Said" in claiming that Indians are indifferent to political issues: Kipling's poem is even quoted approvingly by a character in the sketch.
30 The first two stanzas of "The Two-Sided Man" were first published as an epigraph to Chapter 8 of *Kim* (1901); then, in a revised and expanded form in *Songs from Books*.

[2] Poetry and Prose

1 *A Choice of Kipling's Verse* (1941), p. 5.
2 *Stalky & Co.*, p. 216.
3 *Rudyard Kipling*, p. 92. Hilton Brown is equally categorical, though with a different source: "Kipling followed the bold example of Scott and invented his own quotations which he ascribed to imaginary sources." *Rudyard Kipling: A New Appreciation* (1945), p. 193.
4 "Lispeth", *Plain Tales from the Hills*, pp. 6–7.
5 "The Story of the Gadsbys", *Soldiers Three and Other Stories*, p. 170.
6 *The Art of Rudyard Kipling* (1959), pp. 105–6.
7 *Stalky & Co.*, p. 215.
8 *Letters of Travel 1892–1913*, p. 77.
9 Very similar "realist" sentiments are expressed in the opening stanzas of a much later poem, "The Benefactors", first published in its complete form in *The Years Between* (1919):

Ah! What avails the classic bent
And what the cultured word,
Against the undoctored incident
That actually occurred?

And what is Art whereto we press
Through paint and prose and rhyme –
When Nature in her nakedness
Defeats us every time?

These lines are, however, usually quoted out of context. The poem is concerned mainly with the inability of Art to deal satisfactorily with the terrible suffering created by political tyrants.

10 See Roger Lancelyn Green, "Stalky and the Brushwood Boy", *Kipling Journal*, No. 115, October 1955.
11 "The Brushwood Boy", *The Day's Work*, p. 371.
12 *The Irish Guards in the Great War* (2 vols. 1923), I, p. vi.
13 "The Fabulists", first published in *A Diversity of Creatures* (1917), apparently as the second of two closing poems to the story "My Son's Wife". This was probably a printing error. Subsequently,

the poem was placed as the opening poem to "The Vortex", the next story in the collection.

[3] "Soldier, Soldier"

1 "The Blind Bug", *National Observer*, 27 December 1890.

2 *Kipling: The Critical Heritage*, edited by Roger Lancelyn Green (1971), p. 98. First published *Academy*, 28 May 1892.

3 John Macleay, *War Songs and Songs and Ballads of Martial Life* (1900), p. xxvii.

4 Lewis S. Winstock, "Rudyard Kipling and Army Music", *Kipling Journal*, No. 178, June 1971, p. 11.

5 "Love and Liberty: A Cantata", now commonly known as "The Jolly Beggars". It was written in 1785, and first published in its complete form in Glasgow, 1802.

6 "Come and be a soldier", *The Rambling Soldier*, edited by Roy Palmer (Harmondsworth 1977), p. 41. Palmer dates the song c. 1850.

7 "The Maunding Souldier" or "The Fruits of Warre is Beggery", *The Common Muse*, edited by V. de Sola Pinto and A. E. Rodway (Harmondsworth 1965), p. 215.

8 "The Silver Tassie", adapted by Burns in 1788 from a much older song.

9 *Songs and Music of the Redcoats* (1970), p. 67.

10 The opening lines of "Rimini" are used to introduce the story "On the Great Wall", *Puck of Pook's Hill*. The complete song was published in *Songs from Books*.

11 "Tommy", *Barrack-Room Ballads*.

12 *Something of Myself*, pp. 79–82.

13 For related poems, see "The Betrothed", *Departmental Ditties*; "The Vampire", first published 17 April 1897, for the public showing of a painting with the same title by Kipling's cousin, Philip Burne-Jones; and, of course, "The Female of the Species", *The Years Between*.

14 *The Complete Barrack-Room Ballads*, edited by Charles Carrington (1973), p. 169, where the periodical publication of "The Courting of Dinah Shadd" is given erroneously as December 1889.

15 "My Great and Only", *Abaft the Funnel* (New York 1909), p. 267.

The sketch was first published in the *Civil and Military Gazette*, 11 and 13 January 1890.

16 "'Love o' Women'", *Many Inventions* (1893).

17 "Kipling's Magic Art", *Critical Essays on Rudyard Kipling*, edited by Harold Orel (Boston, Mass. 1989), pp. 50–1. First published in the *Proceedings of the British Academy* (1978).

18 "My Great and Only", *Abaft the Funnel*, p. 267.

19 *All in a Garden Fair* (1888), p. 246; *Something of Myself*, pp. 65–6.

20 In a letter to J. B. Booth, dated 15 Febraury 1932; quoted in Booth's *The Days We Knew* (1943), p. 30.

21 Kipling to H. A. Gwynne, 17 September 1903, KP 15/15. Kipling argues that music hall had once touched on every aspect of social life in Britain, but now produces little more than sentimental love songs.

22 When revising his poetry for the *Sussex Edition*, Kipling removed the final "d" from "and" in the first three lines of this stanza, thus slightly emphasising the Cockney accent.

23 *Kipling: The Critical Heritage*, p. 56. First published, *Scots Observer*, 3 May 1890.

24 *Letters from Rudyard Kipling to Guy Paget 1919–1936* (privately printed 1936), p. 73.

25 "Cleared!", *Scots Observer*, 8 March 1890. It was offered first to *The Times*, but turned down, *Something of Myself*, p. 83.

26 For Beerbohm's hostility, and Wilde's comments on *Plain Tales*, see *Kipling: The Critical Heritage*, pp. 20, 104–5.

27 *Ibid.*, p. 103.

28 Quoted, *Early Verse by Rudyard Kipling*, p. 470, where the full poem is also printed.

29 *Ibid.*, p. 472.

30 Kipling's probable influence on Auden seems to have gone unrecognised, but his influence on Brecht has been well documented by James K. Lyon, *Bertolt Brecht and Rudyard Kipling: A Marxist's Imperialist Mentor* (The Hague 1975).

31 *Rudyard Kipling*, p. 193.

32 See, for example, Martin Seymour-Smith, *Rudyard Kipling* (1989), pp. 182–5.

[4] The Seven Seas

1 *Rudyard Kipling*, p. 121.
2 *From Sea to Sea* (2 vols. 1900), I, pp. 219, 193, 314.
3 *Ibid.*, p. 376.
4 *Ibid.*, p. 472.
5 *Ibid.*, II, pp. 55, 58–9.
6 *Ibid.*, p. 130.
7 *Ibid.*, p. 131.
8 Letter to John St Loe Strachey, 2 January 1899, *The Letters of Rudyard Kipling*, edited by Thomas Pinney (2 vols. 1990), II, p. 358. Kipling made the same point some years earlier in a letter to C. E. Norton, *Letters*, II, p. 279. On both occasions Kipling misspells Fergusson's name.
9 *Rudyard Kipling*, p. 124.
10 "Matthew Arnold", *English Illustrated Magazine*, January 1884, p. 241.
11 *From Sea to Sea*, I, p. 478.
12 "Pan in Vermont", first published in the American periodical *Country Life*, December 1902, but written, according to Carrington, seven years earlier, *Rudyard Kipling*, p. 213. In the *Definitive Edition* it is dated 1893.
13 *The Second Jungle Book*, p. 29.
14 Quoted, Carrington, *Rudyard Kipling*, pp. 228–9. The text is slightly different in *Letters*, II, pp. 225–6.
15 *Our Mutual Friend*, chapter 11.
16 Carlyle, "Signs of the Times", *Critical and Miscellaneous Essays* (1838). The phrase is Biblical; Matthew 16:3.
17 "Tommy", *Barrack-Room Ballads*.
18 *Ibid.*
19 "Poseidon's Law", opening poem to the story "The Bonds of Discipline", *Traffics and Discoveries*.
20 *A Fleet in Being* (1898), pp. 7, 40.
21 *Ibid*, p. 35.
22 See David Macaree, "Two Calvinist *Credos*: Robert Burns's 'Holy Willie's Prayer' and Rudyard Kipling's 'McAndrew's Hymn'", *Kipling Journal*, No. 235, September 1985.
23 *A Choice of Kipling's Verse*, p. 14.

24 "To many modern seamen Kipling's verse has no meaning. What steamboatman can appreciate his 'Anchor Song'? . . . Since 1872 I have not heard a Shanty or Song worth the name. Steam spoilt them." W. B. Whall, *Sea Songs and Shanties* (Glasgow 1910), pp. ix, xiii.

25 *The Penguin Book of Hymns*, edited by Ian Bradley (Harmondsworth 1990), pp. 386–8.

26 There are poems written throughout Kipling's life which testify to his religious tolerance. See, for example, "Buddha at Kamakura", *The Five Nations*; "The Rabbi's Song", closing poem to the story "The House Surgeon", *Actions and Reactions*; and "Jobson's Amen", closing poem to the story "In the Presence", *A Diversity of Creatures*.

27 *The Aeneid*, translated by W. F. Jackson Knight (Harmondsworth 1956), p. 52.

28 Maurice Willson Disher, *Victorian Song* (1955), p. 165.

29 *Rudyard Kipling*, pp. 263–4.

30 *Something of Myself*, p. 147.

31 *Letters*, II, p. 303.

32 *Ibid.*, p. 344.

33 *Ibid.*, p. 346.

34 *Ibid.*, p. 350.

[5] A White Man's War

1 Quoted, Renée Durbach, *Kipling's South Africa* (Diep River 1988), p. 12.

2 *Ibid.*, p. 15. These comments are from an interview with Kipling in the *New Zealand Herald*.

3 *Letters.*, II, p. 328.

4 *Ibid.*, pp. 336–7.

5 *Traffics and Discoveries* (1904).

6 *Rudyard Kipling to Rider Haggard: The Record of a Friendship*, edited by Morton Cohen (1965), pp. 35–7. A full report of the meeting is given in *The African Review*, 21 May 1898, pp. 311–2.

7 *Rudyard Kipling to Rider Haggard*, p. 38.

8 *A Fleet in Being*, p. 34.

9 *Rudyard Kipling*, p. 302.

10 Kipling's views on why the war was being fought were set out very clearly in a letter, referring to a meeting of the Imperial South African Association, published in *The Times*, 14 October, 1899, p. 9. "Their demand [i.e. the British government's], I take it, will be for equal rights for all white men from the Cape to the Zambezi; their aim the establishment of a Republic instead of an oligarchy, and their vindication a new and regenerate Transvaal governed under equal laws framed in open council by free men, neither corrupted nor coerced, representing every interest in the land."

11 Albert Chevalier, *Before I Forget* (1901), p. 167.

12 "Bobs" was first published in the *Pall Mall Magazine*, December 1893.

13 Julian Ralph, *War's Brighter Side: The Story of "The Friend" Newspaper* (1901), p. 185.

14 Carrington, *Rudyard Kipling*, p. 306. Also, "Facsimile of a letter written by Mr Rudyard Kipling for a wounded soldier," *Strand*, June 1900, p. 619. The mother of this soldier refused to sell the letter, and donated the fee she received for its reproduction in the *Strand* to a war fund, so this is probably a different incident from the one referred to by Carrington.

15 *War's Brighter Side*, p. 132.

16 *Ibid.*, p. 132.

17 *Ibid.*

18 *Ibid.*, p. 305.

19 *Ibid.*, pp. 311–12.

20 *Ibid.*, p. 18.

21 Durbach, *Kipling's South Africa*, p. 55. Details of this performance, and other matters relating to Kipling's Boer War experiences, are contained in *With Number Three* (Santiago de Chile 1900), a pirated, and extremely interesting, compilation of poems and sketches.

22 Quoted, Carrington, *Rudyard Kipling*, p. 314.

23 Thomas Pakenham, *The Boer War* (Futura edition 1982), p. 570. I am indebted to this excellent book for a good deal of the information about the Boer War contained in the present chapter.

24 On this theme, see also: "Rimmon", *The Five Nations*; "Song of the Old Guard", opening poem to the story "The Army of a Dream", *Traffics and Discoveries*.

25 Roberts wrote to Kipling in December 1901: "If you are in favour of compulsory service for home defence, would it be possible to write some stirring lines to bring home to the public the danger of allowing ourselves to be a second time in the same risky position without any properly trained troops in the country." Quoted, Elizabeth Talbot Rice, "Bobs", *Kipling Journal*, No. 252, December 1989, p. 32.
26 *Rudyard Kipling to Rider Haggard*, p. 46.
27 Introduction to Kipling's *War Stories and Poems* (The World's Classics, Oxford 1990), p. xix.
28 "The Captive", *Traffics and Discoveries*, p. 27.
29 "A People at Home", *Letters of Travel*, p. 134.
30 Donald Read, *Edwardian England 1901–15* (1972), p. 147.
31 *Rudyard Kipling to Rider Haggard*, p. 67.

[6] The Garden of England

1 "The Unfading Genius of Rudyard Kipling", *Kipling Journal*, No. 129, March 1959, p. 9.
2 Like "The Bell Buoy" and several other poems in *The Five Nations*, "The Explorer" was written some years earlier, but given new significance by its placing in this collection. Carrington says that "The Explorer" was begun in January 1895 and completed in June 1897, *Rudyard Kipling*, pp. 213, 264.
3 Kipling, letter to André Chevrillon, 14 January 1919, KP 14/37. Kipling is referring specifically to the post-Boer War period.
4 When, in 1913, Kipling was described by a Canadian politician as the "hired versifier and Poet Laureate of the Unionist Party", he asked Gwynne to watch for the phrase being picked up by "Rad. papers" in Britain so that he could "jump on 'em for libel." Carrington, *Rudyard Kipling*, p. 404.
5 "The Road to Quebec", *Letters of Travel*, p. 119.
6 KP 15/15.
7 Kipling to Gwynne, 16 August 1911, KP 15/15.
8 This was far from being simply a personal quirk of Kipling's: there was a widespread public conviction that politicians in newly-democratic Britain were corrupt, as G. R. Searle records in *Corruption in British Politics 1895–1930* (Oxford 1987).

9 The text of the speech is given in *The Readers' Guide to Rudyard Kipling's Work*, edited by R. E. Harbord (8 vols., privately printed, Canterbury, Kent, 1961–72), VII, p. 3329.
10 "The tales [in *Rewards and Fairies*] had to be read by children, before people realised they were meant for grown-ups." *Something of Myself*, p. 190.
11 Robert Bridges, "Wordsworth and Kipling", *Collected Essays* (10 vols. 1933), Essay No. 13, pp. 33–4; first published, *Times Literary Supplement*, 29 February 1912.
12 *Something of Myself*, p. 191.
13 *An Introductory History of England*, volume 1 (1904), p. v.
14 *The Great War 1914–18: A Brief Sketch* (1920), p. xii.
15 Kipling to Fletcher, 21 April 1907, KP 15/4.
16 *Ibid.*, 24 May 1907.
17 *An Introductory History of England*, I, p. 24.
18 Kipling to Fletcher, 16 May 1910, KP 15/4.
19 *Ibid.*, 18 May 1910.
20 *Ibid.*, 21 July 1910.
21 Peter Sutcliffe, *The Oxford University Press: An Informal History* (1978), p. 158.
22 *Ibid.*
23 Kipling to Fletcher, 19 June 1926; 31 May 1929; 6 June 1929, KP 15/4.
24 Quoted, Sutcliffe, *The Oxford University Press*, p. 162; Kipling, letter to André Chevrillon, 11 October 1919, KP 14/37.
25 Kipling to Fletcher, dated 1911, KP 15/4.
26 Fletcher, *The Great War*, p. 1; Kipling, letter to André Chevrillon, 11 October 1919, KP 14/37.
27 Kipling to Fletcher, 10 April 1915, KP 15/4.
28 C.R.L. Fletcher and Rudyard Kipling, *A History of England* (1911), pp. 11–12.
29 *Ibid.*, pp. 68–9.
30 *Ibid.*, p. 121.
31 *Ibid.*, p. 240. For the "corrected impression" of 1930, the final words of this passage were changed to "lazy, it must be owned, and perhaps incapable of serious improvement, but physically fine and strong and good-tempered."
32 *Ibid.*, p. 235. In 1930, the "Air Fleet" was included here with the Navy.

33 *A History of England*, p. 94.
34 *Heart of Darkness* (Penguin Classics, Harmondsworth 1985), p. 29.
35 Opening poem to the story "A Centurion of the Thirtieth", *Puck of Pook's Hill.*
36 Originally, the title of this poem was "The Bells and the Queen," but it was changed, along with the titles of several other poems in the *History*, for the *Definitive Edition.* I have used the later, more familiar titles.

[7] Armageddon

1 Quoted, Lord Birkenhead, *Rudyard Kipling* (1978), p. 258.
2 Ralph, *War's Brighter Side*, pp. 149–50.
3 Quoted, Birkenhead, *Rudyard Kipling*, p. 258.
4 "The Dead", *The Poetical Works of Rupert Brooke*, edited by Geoffrey Keynes (1960), p. 21.
5 "Peace", *Ibid.*, p. 19.
6 "Dulce et Decorum Est", *The Poems of Wilfred Owen*, edited by Jon Stallworthy (1985), p. 117.
7 Quoted, Carrington, *Rudyard Kipling*, p. 438.
8 "Lord Roberts", first published *Daily Telegraph*, 19 November 1914.
9 David Jones, *In Parenthesis* (1937), p. ix.
10 "To T.A.", *Barrack-Room Ballads*; *Letters*, II, p. 225.
11 Kipling to Gwynne, 15 September 1914, KP 15/15.
12 "Be well assured", given the title "A Song in Storm" when reprinted in *The Years Between.*
13 "In Lowestoft. . ." was later called "The Lowestoft Boat"; "Farewell and adieu . . ." remained untitled, but with the "Greenwich ladies" of the first line changed to "Harwich Ladies". Both poems were collected in the *Inclusive Edition* (1919). Kipling probably felt they were too light in tone for *The Years Between.*
14 "The Changelings" (first line "Or ever the battered liners sank"), *Debits and Credits*, p. 23.
15 *Readers' guide, Verse I* (1969), p. 1916, where the complete poem is reprinted. When "The Sons of the Suburbs" was finally published in 1936, Brecht cut it out of the *New York Times* and pasted it into

his copy of Kipling's *Inclusive Edition*, Lyon, *Bertolt Brecht and Rudyard Kipling*, pp. 102–4.

16 *A Diversity of Creatures*, p. 442.

17 *Sea Warfare* (1916), pp. 18, 97.

18 "The Egg-Shell", first published in part with the story "Their Lawful Occasions", *Traffics and Discoveries* (1904), and expanded for *Songs from Books*.

19 "The Children", closing poem to the story "The Honours of War", *A Diversity of Creatures*.

20 "Rebirth", closing poem to the story "The Edge of the Evening", *A Diversity of Creatures*.

21 *Rudyard Kipling to Rider Haggard*, p. 101.

22 *Ibid.*, p. 100.

23 "The dangerous edge of things", Browning, "Bishop Blougram's Apology", line 395.

24 "The Irish Guards", *The Times*, 18 March 1918, and *The Years Between*. The poem was written to raise money for the Irish Guards' War Fund.

25 *The Graves of the Fallen* (1919), n.p.

26 Philip Longworth, *The Unending Vigil: A History of the Commonwealth War Graves Commission 1917–1967* (1967), p. 48. The objection to Kipling was made by Lord Hugh Cecil.

27 Quoted, Colonel C. H. Milburn, "Epitaphs by Rudyard Kipling", *Kipling Journal*, No. 39, September 1936, p. 93.

28 *Ibid.*, p. 86.

29 "A Song in the Desert (P.L. Ob. Jan. 1927)", first published in the *Inclusive Edition* (1927).

30 "Arithmetic on the Frontier", *Departmental Ditties*.

31 Kipling did, however, compose epitaphs, strikingly similar to those relating to the First World War, much earlier. Milburn, "Epitaphs by Rudyard Kipling", p. 88, instances the lines on the war-correspondent G. W. Steevens who died at Ladysmith, 15 January 1900:

> Through war and pestilence, red siege and fire,
> Silent and self-contained, he drew his breath,
> Too brave for show of courage – his desire
> Truth as he saw it, even to the death.

Published in the *Friend* , 24 March 1900, and Ralph, *War's Brighter Side*, p. 155. This, and other similar poems, are included in volume 35 of the *Sussex Edition.*

[8] Bonfires on the Ice

1 For a discussion of the critical reception of Kipling's later poetry, see the essay by Maurice Hungiville, "Epithets and Epitaphs: Rudyard Kipling's Reputation as a Poet", in *Critical Essays on Rudyard Kipling.*

2 "Kipling Redivivus", *Kipling: The Critical Heritage*, p. 322. First published, *Athenaeum*, 9 May 1919.

3 *Kipling Journal*, No. 1, March 1927, p. 5.

4 The two most substantial books on Kipling in the years shortly after his death – Edward Shanks, *Rudyard Kipling: A Study in Literature and Political Ideas* (1940), and Hilton Brown, *Rudyard Kipling: A New Appreciation* (1945) – both emphasised the experimental nature of Kipling's later stories. Shanks, however, was far more appreciative than Brown of Kipling's poetry.

5 "I've never sailed the Amazon", closing poem to the story "The Beginning of the Armadilloes", *Just So Stories* (1902).

6 See Hugh Brogan, *Mowgli's Sons: Kipling and Baden-Powell's Scouts* (1987).

7 "Dayspring Mishandled", *Limits and Renewals* (1932).

8 *Rudyard Kipling*, p. 474.

9 "Doctors", dated 1923 by Kipling, but first published in the *Definitive Edition.* "Late Came the God" and "Rahere" with the story "The Wish House"; "The Burden" with "The Gardener", *Debits and Credits.* "The Mother's Son", with "Fairy-kist", and "Hymn to Physical Pain" with "The Tender Achilles", *Limits and Renewals.*

10 "The Woman in his Life", *Limits and Renewals.* "Supplication of the Black Aberdeen" was not linked to a story: it was first published in the *Strand*, January 1928.

11 Kipling to Gwynne, 25 October 1919, KP 15/15.

12 *Sea Warfare*, p. 205.

13 *Kipling's Horace*, edited by Charles Carrington (1978), p. vii.

14 Kipling to Fletcher, 24 April 1917, KP 15/4.

15 *Kipling's Horace*, p. 55.

16 *Ibid.*, p. 63.
17 "Lollius", written for *Q. Horati Flacci Carminum Librum Quintum*; "The Last Ode", closing poem to the story "The Eye of Allah", *Debits and Credits*.
18 Kipling to Fletcher, 12 January 1918, KP 15/4.
19 "Samuel Pepys", first published *The Times*, 23 February 1933; "Untimely", opening poem to the story "The Eye of Allah", *Debits and Credits*.
20 See Arnaldo and Susan Treggiari, "The Craftsman", *Kipling Journal*, No. 196, December 1975. The poem was first published in *The Years Between*.
21 *Spectator*, 2 July 1898, p. 15.
22 "When 'Omer smote . . .", first published in *The Seven Seas* (1896).
23 "Gipsy Vans", with the story "A Madonna of the Trenches"; "Untimely", with "The Eye of Allah", *Debits and Credits*; "A Legend of Truth" and "We and They", with "A Friend of the Family"; "The Threshold", with "Unprofessional"; "The Expert", with "Beauty Spots"; "Gertrude's Prayer", with "Dayspring Mishandled", *Limits and Renewals*. "Chartres Windows", first published in the *Daily Telegraph*, 15 April 1925.
24 Harbord, *Readers' Guide*, VII, pp. 3345–49.
25 Kipling to Gwynne, 13 August 1914, KP 15/15.
26 *Ibid.*, letter dated November 1921.
27 *Rudyard Kipling to Rider Haggard*, pp. 117–8.
28 *Ibid.*, p. 110. In 1929, after visiting Palestine, Kipling wrote a poem which traces the hostility between Jews and Arabs from Genesis to modern Zionism. The poem, "In ancient days and deserts wild", is untitled, though it is sometimes called "The Truth". It portrays, in a mildly satirical manner, the twentieth-century Jew brooding "steadfast on Jerusalem". Kipling seems never to have tried to publish the poem. It is discussed by Carrington, *Rudyard Kipling*, p. 498, and is printed in full by Birkenhead, *Rudyard Kipling*, pp. 354–6.
29 *Rudyard Kipling to Rider Haggard*, pp. 110–12.
30 *The Cause of World Unrest* (1922), pp. 9, 10–11, 15.
31 Kipling to Gwynne, 25 October 1919, KP 15/15.
32 *Ibid.*, 26 August 1931.
33 A. J. P. Taylor, *English History 1914–1945* (The Oxford History of England, Oxford 1965), p. 375.

34 Kipling to Gwynne, 10 January 1934, KP 15/15.
35 The three ballads are placed together in *The Oxford Book of Ballads*, edited by Arthur Quiller-Couch (1920), pp. 651–83. Kipling was very familiar with Quiller-Couch's Oxford anthologies. See F. G. Atkinson, "Kipling and 'Q'", *Kipling Journal*, No. 231, September 1984, pp. 18–24.
36 Kipling uses this phrase, which he attributes to a "Socialist Government Organ", as an epigraph to "Memories".
37 *The Patriot*, No. 456, 6 November 1930, pp. 444–5.
38 See Horace, *Odes*, I, 14, and Susan Treggiari, "Kipling's Classics", *Kipling Journal*, No. 181, March 1972, p. 10.
39 Kipling to Gwynne, 11 June 1932, KP 15/15.
40 *Ibid.*, 13 April 1933.
41 Speech reported in *The Times*, 7 May 1935, p. 9.
42 *Rudyard Kipling*, p. 503.
43 *English History 1914–1945*, p. 386.
44 Carrington, *Rudyard Kipling*, p. 387.
45 *Kipling: The Critical Heritage*, pp. 322–6.
46 Peter Godman, "T. S. Eliot and E. R. Curtius: A European Dialogue", *Liber*, No. 1, p. 5, *Times Literary Supplement*, 6 October 1989.
47 *A Choice of Kipling's Verse*, p. 14.
48 "The Unfading Genius of Rudyard Kipling", p. 9.
49 *Ibid.*
50 "The Poet of the Encirclement", *Forewords and Afterwords*, edited by Edward Mendelson (1973), p. 352. First published *New Republic* 24 October 1943.
51 *The English Auden: Poems, Essays and Dramatic Writings 1927–1939*, edited by Edward Mendelson (Faber paperback 1986), pp. 241–2.
52 *Something of Myself*, p. 208. Kipling is talking specifically at this point about the stories, though also, more generally, about his working methods. On the same page, he quotes some lines of poetry, which are unattributed but presumably by Kipling himself, on the inspirational function of a "Personal Daemon" in an artist's work:

> This is the doom of the Makers – their Daemon lives in their pen.
> If he be absent or sleeping, they are even as other men.
> But if he be utterly present, and they swerve not from his behest,
> The word that he gives shall continue, whether in earnest or jest.

Taking up Auden's attitude to language in the Yeats elegy, it is worth noting Kipling's insistence that the "Daemon lives in the pen" of the Maker, or Artist, and not outside in this or that political or social system. Whether the "views" expressed by the pen come from the Daemon or the Artist is unclear. Presumably Kipling would argue that if the Daemon is "utterly present" and the Artist swerves "not from his behest", then what the pen writes is inspired and therefore true. It is characteristic of Kipling, as we have seen, that at this moment in the autobiography he should turn from prose to poetry to make this kind of fundamental statement about his art.

Kipling's Poetry
A Select Bibliographical Note

Unless otherwise indicated, the place of publication is London

1 Editions

Rudyard Kipling's Verse: Definitive Edition, first published in 1940 and frequently reprinted, has to be accepted as the standard edition, though for reasons discussed earlier (pp. 216–7), it is in many respects unsatisfactory. The four volumes devoted to the poetry in *The Sussex Edition of the Complete Works in Prose and Verse of Rudyard Kipling* (35 volumes 1937–39) are organised more sensibly than the *Definitive Edition*, and they also contain additional items and further textual revisions: unfortunately the *Sussex* was a limited edition, and is usually available only in major libraries. The sole modern scholarly edition of Kipling's poetry is Andrew Rutherford's *Early Verse by Rudyard Kipling 1879–1889* (Oxford 1986) which reprints, with full annotation, all of the juvenilia and Indian poetry not included in the *Definitive Edition*. There are no similar editions of Kipling's major volumes of poetry. In *The Complete Barrack-Room Ballads* (1973), Charles Carrington adopts a sufficiently broad definition of "barrack-room ballad" to include "The Absent-Minded Beggar" and "Epitaphs of the War": the annotation relating to military matters is particularly useful, though publication details are sometimes unreliable. *Kipling's Horace* (1978), also edited by Charles Carrington, is a valuable bilingual collection of Kipling's poetic responses to Horace. The most influential selection of Kipling's poetry is T. S. Eliot's *A Choice of Kipling's Verse* (1941): Eliot's introductory essay is justly renowned, but he followed the *Definitive Edition* in the ordering and presentation of poems, and in doing so duplicated many of that edition's faults. *Rudyard Kipling: Selected Poems* edited by Peter Keating

(Penguin Selected English Poets, 1993), is a representative collection of the poems, annotated and arranged chronologically.

Several recent thematic collections of works by Kipling contain material relevant to a study of his poetry. *Kipling's India: Uncollected Sketches 1884–88* (1986), edited by Thomas Pinney, includes articles by Kipling on Indian and Anglo-Indian poetry; in *Kipling's Japan: Collected Writings* (1988), Hugh Cortazzi and George Webb offer detailed discussions of a number of poems, notably "Buddha at Kamakura" and "The Rhyme of the Three Sealers"; *Kipling's Lost World*, edited by Harry Ricketts, and published by Tabb House, Padstow, Cornwall, in 1989, collects stories and poems on literary themes; Andrew Rutherford's edition of Kipling's *War Stories and Poems* (The World's Classics, Oxford 1990), includes Indian, Boer War, and First World War poems; and, a different kind of work, notable for its unusually enthusiastic approach to Kipling's poetry, is Marghanita Laski's radio script, *Kipling's English History* (BBC Books 1974).

2 Reference

Because of the complicated publishing history of many of Kipling's poems, and the virtual absence of critical studies of the poetry, reference books are of particular importance. The standard bibliography is *Rudyard Kipling: A Bibliographical Catalogue* by James McG. Stewart, edited by A. W. Yeats (Toronto 1959). R. E. Harbord's *The Readers' Guide to Rudyard Kipling* (8 volumes, privately printed, Canterbury, Kent), is an extraordinary, eccentric, and indispensable compilation of notes on, and facts about, all of Kipling's works, only one volume of which, *Verse I* (1969) deals with the poetry. This lists the poems in chronological order, and gives details of their first publication. Harbord intended to publish an accompanying volume of annotation, or what he himself described as his "lovely batch of notes on the poems", but never managed to achieve this. Because Harbord was planning to cover all of Kipling's poetry together, his detailed discussions of the prose works do not usually include similar annotation for the poems which were written to accompany the prose. Much of the kind of information Harbord would have offered is available, for the earlier poems at least, in Ralph Durand's *A Handbook to the Poetry of Kipling* (1914). Covering a similar period, though with less specific reference to the poetry, is A. W. Young's *A Rudyard Kipling*

Dictionary (1911), which has been up-dated by J. H. McGivering (1967). Lloyd Chandler's *A Summary of the Work of Rudyard Kipling* (New York 1930), remains valuable for details of the original publication of individual poems. Norman Page, *The Kipling Companion* (1984) is concerned mainly with the prose, and gives very little space to the poetry.

3 Biography and Letters

Rudyard Kipling: His Life and Work (1955) by Charles Carrington was the biography finally authorised by Kipling's surviving daughter, Elsie Bambridge, after several possible biographers had been turned down. It is the most influential book in Kipling Studies, with the arguable exception of Harbord's *Guide.* Its main weakness, which it shares with other biographies of Kipling, is its relatively meagre treatment of the last twenty or so years of Kipling's life. Lord Birkenhead's *Rudyard Kipling* was one of the biographies rejected by Mrs Bambridge, and did not appear in print until 1978. It contains extensive quotation from otherwise unpublished letters, but apart from this adds little of substance to Carrington's biography. Nor does Angus Wilson's *The Strange Ride of Rudyard Kipling* (1977), though, unlike Birkenhead, Wilson is always interesting on Kipling's writings, and often perceptive on individual poems. Among a number of handsomely illustrated general biographical studies of Kipling are: Martin Fido, *Rudyard Kipling* (New York 1974); Kingsley Amis, *Rudyard Kipling and His World* (1975); *Rudyard Kipling: The Man, His Work and His World* (1972), a collection of essays edited by John Gross which includes Robert Conquest's "A Note on Kipling's Verse"; and Marghanita Laski, *From Palm to Pine: Rudyard Kipling Abroad and at Home* (1987).

The Letters of Rudyard Kipling are currently being edited by Thomas Pinney. Two of a projected four volumes, covering the years 1872–99, were published in 1990. Also of considerable interest are: *Rudyard Kipling to Rider Haggard: The Record of a Friendship*, edited by Morton Cohen (1965), and *"O Beloved Kids": Rudyard Kipling's Letters to his Children* edited by Elliot L. Gilbert (1983).

4 Criticism

Kipling: The Critical Heritage, edited by Roger Lancelyn Green (1971), is a useful survey of critical responses to Kipling's work from 1886 to

1936. Ann M. Weygandt, *Kipling's Reading and its Influence on his Poetry* (Philadelphia 1939) remains the essential introduction to this subject. Most general books on Kipling do, of course, include some discussion of the poetry, though it is usually given far less attention than the prose. Probably the best introductions to the poetry are contained in two books by Bonamy Dobrée: *Rudyard Kipling* (Writers and their Work, 1951) and *Rudyard Kipling: Realist and Fabulist* (1967). André Chevrillon's essay on Kipling in *Three Studies in English Literature* (1923) has a special interest because Kipling admired Chevrillon's work and corresponded with him: after Kipling's death, Chevrillon expanded the essay and published it as *Rudyard Kipling* (Paris 1937).

Among other books, published since Kipling's death, which contain some discussion of the poetry, are: Sir George MacMunn, *Rudyard Kipling: Craftsman* (1937); Edward Shanks, *Rudyard Kipling: A Study in Literature and Political Ideas* (1940); Hilton Brown, *Rudyard Kipling: A New Appreciation* (1945); Roger Lancelyn Green, *Kipling and the Children* (1965); Louis Cornell, *Kipling in India* (1966); P. J. Keating, *The Working Classes in Victorian Fiction* (1971); James K. Lyon, *Bertolt Brecht and Rudyard Kipling: A Marxist's Imperialist Mentor* (The Hague 1975); Shamsul Islam, *Kipling's Law: A Study of his Philosophy of Life* (1975); J. S. Bratton, *The Victorian Popular Ballad* (1975); M. Van Wyk Smith, *Drummer Hodge: The Poetry of the Anglo-Boer War* (Oxford 1978); Renée Durbach, *Kipling's South Africa* (Diep River 1988); Martin Seymour-Smith, *Rudyard Kipling* (1989); *Critical Essays on Rudyard Kipling*, edited by Harold Orel (Boston, Mass. 1989), which reprints Andrew Rutherford's "Some Aspects of Kipling's Verse", J. S. Bratton's "Kipling's Magic Art", and Maurice Hungiville's "Epithets and Epitaphs: Rudyard Kipling's Reputation as a Poet"; and Ann Parry, *The Poetry of Rudyard Kipling: Rousing the Nation* (Buckingham 1992).

The *Kipling Journal*, founded in 1927 and still going strong, is an invaluable source of information about all aspects of Kipling's life and work, the poetry included.

Index

Index

Index

Index

Index

Index

Index

Index